Tianfu Culture and the Modern Pursuit of Chengdu

天府文化与成都的现代化追求

谭 平　冯和一　周翔宇　唐　婷　著
彭蕴希　谭俊峰　姚　键　译
陈　静　苗倬鼐　策划

四川大学出版社
Sichuan University Press

项目策划：舒 星 敬铃凌
责任编辑：敬铃凌
责任校对：余 芳 刘 畅 周 洁
封面设计：墨创文化
责任印制：王 炜

图书在版编目（CIP）数据

天府文化与成都的现代化追求 = Tianfu Culture and the Modern Pursuit of Chengdu：英文 / 谭平等著；彭蕴希，谭俊峰，姚键译. — 成都：四川大学出版社，2020.12
ISBN 978-7-5690-4106-4

Ⅰ. ①天… Ⅱ. ①谭… ②彭… ③谭… ④姚… Ⅲ. ①文化史－成都－英文 Ⅳ. ①K297.11

中国版本图书馆 CIP 数据核字（2020）第 261569 号

书　名	天府文化与成都的现代化追求
	Tianfu Culture and the Modern Pursuit of Chengdu
著　者	谭 平　冯和一　周翔宇　唐 婷
译　者	彭蕴希　谭俊峰　姚 键
出　版	四川大学出版社
地　址	成都市一环路南一段 24 号（610065）
发　行	四川大学出版社
书　号	ISBN 978-7-5690-4106-4
印前制作	墨创文化
印　刷	成都市金雅迪彩色印刷有限公司
成品尺寸	170mm×230mm
印　张	17.5
字　数	439 千字
版　次	2021 年 1 月第 1 版
印　次	2021 年 1 月第 1 次印刷
定　价	138.00 元

◆ 版权所有 ◆ 侵权必究

◆ 读者邮购本书，请与本社发行科联系。
　电话：(028)85408408/(028)85401670/
　(028)86408023　邮政编码：610065
◆ 本社图书如有印装质量问题，请寄回出版社调换。
◆ 网址：http://press.scu.edu.cn

四川大学出版社
微信公众号

Preface:
A Sketch of Chengdu

Chengdu is the capital of Sichuan Province and one of the major cultural, economic, and political centers in West China. It has a long history. During the Three Kingdoms period (220–280 CE), it was the capital of the state of Shu. During the Tang Dynasty, Chengdu was one of the most prosperous cities in China. Much later, a transition occurred from the late Ming governance to that of the early Qing (roughly the 1620s to 1680s), during which Sichuan experienced more than half a century of war that devastated the economy in the region and damaged the cities. Yet in the early Qing, the economy and culture were gradually restored.

Thanks to its geographically isolated position, Chengdu was little affected by the Opium Wars (1839–1842 and 1856–1860), apart from missionary activities, and it also suffered little during the Taiping Uprising (1851–1864). In 1877, Chengdu became the site of the Sichuan Arsenal (*Sichuan Jiqi Ju*), established as part of the self-strengthening movement. The arsenal was the first modern factory in Sichuan. After nearby Chongqing was opened as a trade port in 1890, Chengdu became less isolated and began to experience the cultural contact and conflict apparent in cities closer to the coast. In 1895, a large-scale anti-Christian movement broke out in Chengdu, and some churches were burned down. A few years later, a group of local intellectuals participated in the reform movement by organizing the Society of Sichuan Learning (*Shuxue Hui*) and publishing the *Journal of Sichuan Learning (Shuxue Bao)*. Many new schools were also established at this time.

Tianfu Culture and the Modern Pursuit of Chengdu

In the first half of the twentieth century, Chengdu was one of the largest cities in inland China, with a population of around 340,000 at the turn of the century, increasing to around 440,000 by the 1930s. By 1945, due to wartime migration, its population had reached 740,000, falling to 650,000 in 1949. As the capital of Sichuan Province, Chengdu experienced almost all of the political, economic, social, and cultural transformations that occurred from the late-Qing reform period to the Communist victory in 1949. In the 1900–1910 period, Chengdu, under the influence of the new policies and self-government movement, became a center and model of industrial, commercial, educational, and social reforms in the Upper Yangzi region. Local elites, supported by state power, enthusiastically participated in reforms that built their social reputation and expanded their influence over ordinary people.

The Sichuan Police Force was set up in 1902, symbolizing the establishment of an early form of urban administration. In 1910, the City Council of Chengdu and Huayang (*Chenghua Cheng Yishihui*) was formed as part of the self-government movement; the council's members were elected. Both the police and the council became the early foundation of the Chengdu municipal government, but the former played a much more important role. In 1911, many residents joined the railroad-protection movement, contributing to the climate of protest that led to the revolution in October of that year. In late November 1911, Sichuan declared independence and organized the Great Han Military Government (*Dahan Sichuan Jun Zhengfu*).

Post revolution, Chengdu suffered from the chaos general to the warlord era. In 1917, two wars erupted in the city—the first between the Yunnan and Sichuan armies in May, and the second between the Guizhou and Sichuan armies in July. Thousands of people were killed, and thousands of houses were destroyed, leading to a mass of refugees. Despite social disorder, under the influence of Westernization, new publications and new forms of entertainment such as modern drama emerged in Chengdu during the May Fourth and New Culture movements. The city's most famous writer of this period was Ba Jin (1904–2005), whose autobiographical novel *Jia (The Family)*, written in 1932, deals with intergenerational family conflict and its impact on political and social change during the 1920s.

Preface:
A Sketch of Chengdu

By 1926, Sichuan's military leaders were able to expel first the Yunnan Army and then the Guizhou Army from the province. After warlord Yang Sen (1884-1977) became governor in 1924, he launched large-scale urban reconstruction in Chengdu by opening new commercial districts and widening the main streets, changing the urban landscape. In 1928, the Chengdu municipal government was established. During this period, the central government barely controlled Chengdu and instead the city was in the hands of five warlords who shared power under the System of Defense Districts (Fangqu Zhi). The Nationalist government finally extended its power into Sichuan between 1935 and 1937.

The War of Resistance Against Japanese Aggression (1931-1945) brought Sichuan and Chengdu to central stage in national politics. The Nationalist government's move to Chongqing led to the relocation to Chengdu of many offices of the central government, as well as those of other provincial governments. Many social and cultural organizations, schools, and factories from eastern China also arrived in Chengdu. In addition, a huge number of refugees flooded the city, bringing with them many new cultural elements. All this had a profound impact on Chengdu, and changed the relationship between Sichuan and the central government. After the war, Chengdu became a stage of political struggle between the Guomindang and Communists, mirroring the situation in the country as a whole. Runaway inflation and food shortages led to food riots. On December 27, 1949, nearly three months after the establishment of the People's Republic of China, Chengdu achieved its peaceful liberation.

During the early socialist period, Chengdu gradually developed into an industrial city producing electronics, machinery, metal goods, chemicals, and textiles, among other products. Facilities were also gradually improved, with attention paid to street widening, residential construction, sewerage, and bridges. After 1964, the central government launched *Sanxian Jianshe* (the Third-line Construction) defense plan for preparation against future wars, which stimulated a new wave of industrial development in Chengdu.

China's reform and opening-up stimulated rapid development in Chengdu. From 1993 to 1998, the landscape, environment, and living conditions in the city were greatly improved by the

Tianfu Culture and the Modern Pursuit of Chengdu

dredging of the Funan River, which circles the city, and the construction of parks along its banks. Chengdu also benefited from the central government's ambitious Great Western Development strategy (*Xibu Dakaifa*), launched in 2000 and directed at balancing coastal development by attention to the hinterland.

Today's Chengdu is a large metropolitan area, holding over sixteen million people, of whom nearly eight million live in Chengdu city. Chengdu is rivaled by Chongqing, which in 1997 ceased to be part of Sichuan Province when it became a provincial-level municipality. In response to Chongqing's growing economic power, Chengdu has shown its momentum by building up the economy of western Sichuan. With more than three thousand software companies, Chengdu has become one of the ten largest bases for software production in the nation. In 2019, Chengdu's gross domestic product was RMB 1.7 trillion *yuan*, and the export and import total was RMB 582 billion *yuan*.

Chengdu is an important scientific, educational, and cultural center in western China, hosting many universities and research institutions. Tourism has also become a major economic driving force. In 2019, Chengdu attracted more than 280 million visitors. Among its tourist attractions is the Jinsha Museum, the most advanced modern museum in China, which opened in 2007. The museum holds the country's most important archeological discoveries related to the prehistoric civilization of the Upper Yangzi region. Other attractions include the Du Fu Thatched Cottage Park and the Temple of Marquis Wu. Chengdu is best known, however, for its leisurely lifestyle, encapsulated in its teahouses and their clients, which do much to sum up the richness of the city's history and culture. Furthermore, Chengdu's strong cultural offer includes two UNESCO World Heritage sites, 150 museums, and over 2,000 bars and nightclubs. Chengdu is also known as the bookstore capital of China, with over 3,400 stores. Its bookstores have become important in promoting culture and engaging citizens, by providing space for various cultural activities.

Chengdu's vision, outlined in the City's "Plan for Building Western Cultural Creativity Centre (2017–2022) ", is to continue developing itself as an important creative and cultural hub

Preface:
A Sketch of Chengdu

in China. Under the Plan, by 2022, the city will be home to 100 globally influential innovative designers, and build 200 professional museums and 1,000 bookstores. In addition, it will set up a RMB 10 billion *yuan* culture and creative investment fund to promote its cultural and creative sectors, specifically focusing on film, media, advertising and fashion industries. Meanwhile, as with all ancient cities, one of Chengdu's key challenges is to preserve its history, preventing cultural assets from being lost or misappropriated through modernization and commercialization. The city is exploring ways to raise public awareness of declining traditions and the value of Chengdu's cultural heritage.

Wang Di
Remarkable Professor and Head of History Department,
University of Macau

Contents

Chapter One
The Origin and Presentation of Tianfu Culture

The Romantic Ba-Shu Civilization 003

Sources of the Tianfu Culture 026

The Unique Charms of Tianfu Culture..052

Chapter Two
Chengdu from the Perspective of Tianfu Culture

Origin of Civilization 108

Chengdu's Grand Pattern in Han and Tang Dynasties......................113

Chengdu's New Look in the Song, Yuan, Ming and Qing Dynasties ...120

Revolutions in Chengdu and Its Peaceful Liberation 129

Famous Scholars and Sages in Chengdu 133

Chapter Three
Many Firsts in the World or in China in the History of Chengdu

Many Firsts in the World in the History of Chengdu 148

Many Firsts in China in the History of Chengdu 152

Chapter Four
Chengdu in the Literary Works of the Past Dynasties

Chengdu in "*Fu*" of the Han and Wei Dynasties 164

Chengdu in the Sui and Tang Poetry 168

Chengdu in the Poetry of the Song Dynasty 174

Chengdu in the Yuan and Ming Literary Works 180

Chengdu in the Poetry of the Qing Dynasty 183

Chengdu in Modern and Contemporary Literature and *Quyi* 190

Chapter Five
Historical and Cultural Relics of Chengdu

Historic City Sites of Chengdu 196

The Splendid Sanxingdui Site 201

The Shi'erqiao Cultural Sites 204

Buddhist and Taoist Cultural Relics 207

Varied Ancient Bridges and Ancient Towns 213

Chapter Six

Chengdu in the Map of World Civilization

Chengdu and the Silk Road ………………………………………………………220

The Spread of Buddhism in Chengdu ……………………………………………223

The Three Kingdoms Culture and Chengdu ……………………………………230

Chapter Seven

Tianfu Chengdu Towards a New Era

Modernization of the City ………………………………………………………236

The Regional Central City ………………………………………………………247

A Central City in the National Strategy …………………………………………251

A World Famous Cultural City …………………………………………………257

Copyright Notice for Photos ……………………………………………………266

Chapter One
The Origin and Presentation of Tianfu Culture

Located in the core and most prosperous region of Sichuan Province the world-renovated Land of Abundance, Chengdu covers an area of 14,334 square kilometers and boasts a beautiful natural environment and profound cultural context. In spite of more than 4,000 years of ups and downs such as the collision and fusion of multiple civilizations and numerous natural disasters and man-made calamities, this city has risen like a phoenix from the ashes with her tenacious vitality and creativity. Her humanistic character possesses not only the generality of Chinese civilization, but also the outstanding individuality nourished by the local nature and culture and sharpened by her unique historical circumstances (Fig. 1).

Tianfu Culture and the Modern Pursuit of Chengdu

In April 2017, Chengdu set the goal of "deepening reform and opening-up, focusing on innovation-driven development, striving for constructing a national central city that fully embodies the new development philosophy" with the heritage of the Ba-Shu civilization, development of Tianfu Culture, and construction of a "World Cultural City" as its cultural mission. The new concept of "Tianfu Culture" mainly refers to the city's cultural values – "Innovation and Creation, Fashion and Elegance, Optimism and Tolerance, Kindness and Public Welfare," which are derived from the cultural and historical accumulation of more than 2,300 years, greatly enriched by the striking achievements thanks to the reform and opening-up policy, and leading Chengdu to optimize and highlight the cultural pursuit. As for over 160 million Chengdu residents, "Tianfu Culture" is not only a description of cultural individuality, but also a guide to cultural behaviors and an important measure to construct Chengdu into a World Cultural City as well. For this reason, the first question this book is going to answer is what the soil for giving the birth of Tianfu Culture is (Sources of Living Water or Civilization) and what Tianfu culture means.

Fig. 1 Chengdu with a sight of faraway snow mountain

Chapter One
The Origin and Presentation of Tianfu Culture

The Romantic Ba-Shu Civilization

The Ba-Shu culture is long-standing and well established. According to the demonstration by archaeologists, the Ba-Shu culture has the history of more than 5,000 years, and together with Central Plain Culture, Qi-Lu Culture, Jing-Chu Culture and Wu-Yue Culture constitutes the main regional culture system of ancient China, making a unique contribution to the formation and development of Chinese culture. Thus, some specialists regard the land of Ba-Shu not only as one of the cradles of Chinese people, but also one of the birthplaces of world civilization. With respect to the relationship of the Ba-Shu culture and Chinese civilization, Li Xueqing, a professor from Tsinghua University, an archaeologist and the chief scientist of the Project for Chronology of Xia, Shang and Zhou dynasties, indicated, "It can be asserted that, if there wasn't the in-depth study of the Ba-Shu culture, the complete image of the origin and development of Chinese civilization cannot be formed. In consideration of the characteristic of the Ba-Shu culture, and its relationship with cultures of central plains, the west and the south of ancient China, lots of problems regarding Chinese civilization probably could only be solved by means of research in the Ba-Shu culture."

1. Geographic Features of the Ba-Shu Land

The Ba-Shu cultural region is a territorial community located in Southwest China, with the Sichuan Basin as the center and combining the culture-related, custom-resembled surrounding

Tianfu Culture and the Modern Pursuit of Chengdu

areas. Its central domain, lying in the central inland area of the upper reaches of Yangtze River, is divided by the line of Longmen Mountain-Daliang Mountain into two parts, with the Sichuan Basin in the east, and the Western Sichuan Plateau and mountain regions in the west. With numerous rivers, diverse landforms and abundant animal and plant resources, it is a treasure land of the most stable agricultural civilization in Western China. Its geometric features and cultural context have decided that the cultural origin of this area (now equivalent to the area of Sichuan and Chongqing) was not only influenced by the outside civilizations, but more importantly, shaped by its own resources and conditions.

The leading authorities in Chinese historiography in the 20th century, such as Xu Zhongshu (1898-1991), Gu Jiegang (1893-1980) and others, all agreed to the above-stated judgment. From 1995 to 2003, eight archaeological sites of historic cities were discovered successively in the Chengdu Plain, including Baodun Site in Xinjin County, Ancient City Site in Pidu District, Yufucun Site in Wenjiang District, Mangcheng Site in Dujiangyan City, Shuanghe and Zizhu Sites in Chongzhou City, Yandian and Gaoshan Ancient City Sites in Dayi County. These scattering ancient city sites equivalent to political centers in the ancient time reveal that it was very hard to establish fixed political centers due to frequent flooding in the Chengdu Plain before the flood-control project by Li Bing. From another point of view, this phenomenon could reflect the consciousness of hardship of residents in the ancient Shu. Historians and archaeologists think that these sites represent the *chiefdom stage* in development seen from the anthropology. The ancient sites in the Chengdu Plain are the oldest, largest and most-densely-distributed ancient site groups in Southwestern China. These discoveries are profoundly exciting in the academic field. The international archaeological field also showed great concern on the excavation and research of the sites and joined in these processes. In this case, the Chinese-American and Chinese-Japanese archaeological research teams were formed successively. From 2005 to 2007, the International Archaeological Research Team for Chengdu Plain Ancient Sites were formed by Chengdu Municipal Cultural Relics and Archaeology Research Institute, the Department of Archaeology of Beijing University, Department of Anthropology of Taiwan

Chapter One
The Origin and Presentation of Tianfu Culture

University, Department of Art History and Archaeology of Washington University in St. Louis, and Department of Anthropology of Harvard University. At first, this team made a thorough survey of the ancient city site in Pidu District as well as its surrounding areas. The research report suggested that the archaeological evidence of social complexity of the Chengdu Plain demonstrated a social-complexity development process that distinguishes from but may not be totally irrelevant with other regions of China. This would contribute to the comprehension of the social complexity processes of different regions of China and even the East Asian areas on the scale of different spaces, different social structures and different times.

Duan Yu (1953-), a researcher of Sichuan Academy of Social Sciences, indicated that the Sichuan Basin is an independent geographical unit with its elevation gradually dropping from the peripheral mountain to the central part of the basin, and the rivers also presenting an asymmetric centripetal structure. It was this centripetal structure, combined with the superior natural conditions of the basin, that made it easy to attract the groups engaged in highland agriculture in the peripheral mountainous areas to develop and settle down in the lowlands, and attract various ancient cultures to move to the Chengdu Plain in the central part of the basin along the centripetal geographical structure formed by the descending river and mountain valleys, thus providing a natural basis for the blending of ancient cultures and enabling the Chengdu Plain to develop a developed ancient Shu civilization. Besides, as the Minjiang River, Jialing River, Tuojiang River and Yangtze River flowed throughout the basin and radiated in all directions, they have spread the ancient Shu civilization into other areas. This kind of centripetal and radiating power of the Ba-Shu culture has a strong humanistic shaping function, which, to a large extent, comes from its own unique geographical conditions. For thousands of years since the pre-Qin period, the same basic patterns have been maintained, and the Land of Abundance has not only been able to regain its economic prosperity, but also can continue its unique context and maintain its basic and consistent humanistic characters through vicissitudes after vicissitudes (including the extinction of almost all the aborigines caused by two violent wars lasting from the late Song Dynasty to early Yuan Dynasty, and from the late Ming Dynasty to

Tianfu Culture and the Modern Pursuit of Chengdu

early Qing Dynasty, respectively).

As far as the relationship between natural geography and human geography is concerned, the Ba-Shu region, with an altitude drop of more than 5,000 meters, boasts almost all kinds of geological and geographical landscapes except the sea and desert, the rare biodiversity and abundant animal and plant species. In terms of its magic and magnificent beauty, there are many well-known old sayings; for example, "the Jianmen Pass is the most dangerous in the world; Kuimen Mountain, the most majestic; Qingcheng Mountain, the most secluded; Mount Emei, the most beautiful." In addition, there is also a striking and years-carved primitive ecology, including snowy plains and glaciers holy as virgins, plateau sceneries where it seems that people could almost capture stars, pick the moon, chase the wind and touch the clouds, and the warm, simple and bold ethnic customs. Sichuan has 56 ethnic groups with a population of 4.6 million ethnic minorities, making it the second largest Tibetan area, the only Qiang people's settlement area and the largest Yi people's settlement area in the country. Religious culture is rich in landscapes, rituals and classics. Sculptures, music, paintings and various intangible cultural heritages on religious themes make people forget to return home. In particular, the corridor of Tibetan, Qiang and Yi culture is colorful and enjoys the worldwide fame.

In history, one of the four outstanding poets of the early Tang Dynasty, Wang Bo (c. 650–676), wrote "Thirty Poems on a Journey into Shu" praising the uniqueness of the Ba-Shu mountains and waters, and lamenting "an excellent visit to the Heaven and a unique view of the universe." Du Fu (712–770), the "Poem Saint" of the Tang Dynasty, took refuge in Chengdu after the "An-Shi Rebellion," but was treated well by the officials and people there. He wrote, "Traveling in the changeable scenery of mountains and rivers, I suddenly found I was on the other side of the sky." Obviously, the novelty of the Ba-Shu landscape dazzled and refreshed him. He also marveled at Chengdu's "reputation as a metropolis, where people are singing, dancing and playing instruments." It was a music city full of vitality. "Poetic Genius" Li Bai (701–762, from Jiangyou County of Sichuan) praised the Three Gorges in his poem: "Leaving at dawn the White King crowned with rainbow cloud, I have sailed a thousand miles through Three Gorges in a day. With

Chapter One
The Origin and Presentation of Tianfu Culture

monkeys' sad adieus the riverbanks are loud, my boat has left ten thought mountains far away." It can be seen how the beautiful scenery along the way made him relaxed and happy. Again, he praised Chengdu in the following lines: "Chengdu seems like the beauty of Heaven, with a picturesque scene of thousands of households. The grasses, trees, clouds and mountains are as beautiful as brocade, and even leaving Chang'an too inferior to bear comparison." Lu You, a great poet of the Song Dynasty and a former official in Chengdu (1125–1210, a native of present-day Zhejiang), was deeply attached to Chengdu in his later years. In his poem "Memory of Chengdu," Lu You wrote, "Being bold and unconstrained even in fifties, I still dream of that prosperous Chengdu. On a peach-dotted horse I am riding, with a wine pot at waist and the black rein in hand. Saying goodbye with friends at the cockfighting site of the upper city, I often hit pheasants in the western suburbs. Strongmen's sleeves were woven with green eagles, and beautiful women's robes painted with golden phoenix..." Chengdu's beautiful scenery, wine, flowers, tea, and its vibrant and colorful city life are vivid and sparkling in his lines. Selected as the opening speech in *Romance of the Three Kingdoms*, "The Immortals at the Riverside" written by the great writer Yang Shen (1488–1559, from Xindu County of Chengdu) of the Ming Dynasty even left behind a famous saying of the eternal beauty of nature and humanity: "Wave on wave the long river eastward rolls away; Gone are all heroes with its spray on spray. Success or failure, right or wrong, all turn out vain; Only green mountains still remain to see the setting sun's departing ray. The white-haired fishermen sail on the stream with ease, accustomed to the autumn moon and vernal breeze. A pot of wine in hand, they talk as they please. How many things before and after all melt into gossip and laughter!" This poem was written in Sichuan. It is very apt that Professor Xie Yuanlu (1949–) of Sichuan Normal University, a scholar of the Ba-Shu culture, once used the term "China's Back Garden" to describe Chengdu's status and characteristics in China's natural and human geography.

2. Evolution of the Ba-Shu Region and Its Cultural Characteristics

According to the earliest inscriptions on bones or tortoise shells in China, the word "Ba"

Tianfu Culture and the Modern Pursuit of Chengdu

originally meant a snake. The ancient Ba residents worshipped giant snakes and used them as their totems. "Shu" is a silkworm. In Chinese folklore, Huangdi or the Yellow Emperor (the common ancestor of all ethnic groups in ancient China, who lived about 4,800 years ago) sent his first wife Lei Zu to the Shu region to teach the Shu people how to plant mulberry trees and raise silkworms. Therefore, the word "Shu" should also come from the totem worship of silkworm, and this demonstrates that Shu is the birthplace of human silk civilization at the same time. Generally speaking, the ancient Ba people came from barbaric ethnic groups and ancient Shu people from Qiang minority. The activities of the Ba people were centered in area of today's Chongqing, reaching the east of Sichuan in the west, the west of Hubei in the east, the south of Shaanxi in the north, and the south of middle Guizhou and western Hunan areas. The Ba Kingdom appeared in China's political stage from the beginning of the Xia Dynasty. According to *Spring and Autumn Annals*, When Dayu (who lived around 2100 BC) "met governors and kings at Kuaiji, they went there with treasures for peace, and among them were the Ba and Shu envoys." It can be seen from this event that in the period (Dayu came from the western Qiang area or today's Wenchuan and Beichuan in Sichuan), the Ba and Shu ethnic groups all joined the political alliance of the Xia Dynasty only in the name of governors of emirates instead of the king of states.

The Shu ethnic group rose from the valleys in the upper reaches of Minjiang River and gradually migrated to the Chengdu Plain. In addition to the Shushan clan, there were three kings of the Shu Kingdom in the Xia and Shang dynasties, including Cancong, Baiguan and Yufu (dates of birth and death unknown). Their ethnic groups and areas of activity were different, but they are commonly known as the "Shu." The Shu Kingdom created the brilliant Sanxingdui Culture and Jinsha Culture in the Shang and Zhou dynasties (16th century to 8th century BC). Regarding the background of these two cultures, Researcher Huang Jianhua (1949–) of Sichuan Provincial Cultural Relics and Archaeology Research Institute believes, "the ancient Shu Kingdom in the Shang and Zhou dynasties had no threat from foreign enemies but a good alliance among the tribes, and with the highly unified theocracy and

Chapter One
The Origin and Presentation of Tianfu Culture

kingship, it maintained a good political order of the common king, enjoyed its social and national prosperity, and formed the brilliant bronze culture and ancient Shu civilization. The bronze statues unearthed at Sanxingdui Site and a large number of precious cultural relics unearthed at Jinsha Site are the best explanations of the civilization form and social situation of the ancient Shu Kingdom in this period." The Ba and Shu communities had various contacts through war, trade and diplomacy in the Xia, Shang and Zhou dynasties. After the Qin State conquered the Ba and Shu kingdoms, the two kingdoms were downgraded into prefectures. In a unified country, the Ba and Shu cultures and their psychology were gradually converged. In history, the Ba and Shu regions were separated and united in terms of the administrative relations for many times, but their ups and downs were roughly the same. Because of the deep convergence and integration of the two ethnic groups and cultures and with roughly the same overall values and lifestyle, they became an important branch of Chinese regional culture.

The characteristics of the Ba-Shu culture could be felt from the following typical people and things:

The Ba Snake Swallowing an Elephant is the folklore from the book *Shan Hai Jing* (*Legends of Mountains and Seas*), which was compiled by an unknown author from the Warring States Period to the Qin and Han dynasties. It says, "The Ba snake swallowed an elephant and excreted the latter's bones after three years of digestion. If a man takes the bone, he will be invulnerable by any heart and abdominal diseases." As the snake is the totem of the Ba people, such a story is a metaphor for the great imagination. Even Qu Yuan admired in his *Chu Ci: Tian Wen* (*Elegies of the South: Asking Heaven*), "What a big snake that can swallow an elephant!"

The Story of Ba Manzi: Ba Manzi, born in Zhongzhou in the ancient Ba Kingdom (now Zhongxian County, Chongqing City), was a general of the country in the middle of the Warring States Period. In the 4th century BC, the Quren District (now in Wanzhou, Chongqing) in the Ba Kingdom suffered from civil strife and the monarch was unable to curb the rebellion. Manzi was very anxious, so he invited the Chu troops to quell the civil strife at the price of promising to reward the Chu State with three cities. When it came true, the Chu emissary came to claim the

Tianfu Culture and the Modern Pursuit of Chengdu

three cities. Manzi believed that the Kingdom could not be divided. As a minister, he could not cede the territory privately, but he had to fulfill his promise. Manzi told the Chu emissary, "Please go to report on the fulfillment of your task with my head to your king because the cities cannot be given to you." Then he committed suicide in front of the Chu emissary. The King of Chu State was greatly moved. He not only stopped demanding the cities, but also buried Ba Manzi's head in accordance with their rites. Ba Manzi's loyalty and faith by saving the cities with his head has become a heroic story that has been passed down through the ages in the Ba-Shu land.

The Ba Widow Qing: A famous female entrepreneur in the Qin Dynasty and honored by Qin Shihuang (259-210 BC, the first emperor of Qin). Qing was born in Badi (now in Changshou, Chongqing). Sima Qian, the father of Chinese historiography (from 145-?) recorded in *Shi Ji* (*Records of the Historian*) that there was a widow named Qing in Badi. After her ancestors found the cinnabar mine, they made profits from it for several generations and became very rich. Qing, just a widow, held on to the possessions of her family and defended her compatriots from being violated with her strong financial resources. Qin Shihuang, who was the first to realize the unification of China, summoned her to the palace and built a platform for her to be honored and remembered, for he held her in high esteem because of her virginity, her influence in Badi, and her contributions to the country.

The War against Mongolia in Diaoyu Castle: Diaoyu Castle is located on Diaoyu Mountain five kilometers east of Hechuan District, Chongqing City. As the Jialing River, Qujiang River and Fujiang River converge at the foot of the mountain, it is surrounded by water in the south, north and west, thus having a very dangerous terrain. In 1239, Peng Daya (?-1245), who had visited Mongolia before and knew more about it, became one of the highest military commanders in Sichuan. He ordered Gan Runchu to build Diaoyu Castle for the first time. Later, Yu Jie (1199-1253), the then temporary military commander of Sichuan and magistrate of Chongqing, adopted the suggestions of the Bozhou brothers Ran Jin and Ran Pu, and rebuilt the Diaoyu Castle in 1243, stationing troops and accumulating grain, serving as a barrier to protect Chongqing. In 1258, Mongolian Great Khan Mengge (1209-1259) ordered Kublai Khan

Chapter One
The Origin and Presentation of Tianfu Culture

(1215-1294, the founding emperor of the Yuan Dynasty) to attack Ezhou, Tsatar to attack the areas south and north of the Huai River, Wulianghatai to attack Yunnan, and he himself led the troops to attack Sichuan. In February 1259, Mengge led a large army to Diaoyu Castle and sent people to persuade his enemy into surrendering. Wang Jian (1198-1264), the magistrate of Hechuan in the Song Dynasty firmly refused his offer and killed the emissary. However, Mengge's attack on the Diaoyu Castle met tenacious resistance from Wang Jian and his lieutenant Zhang Jue (?-1280). In the battle, the general of Mongolian army Wang Dechen was killed; Mengge was wounded by artillery on the castle, and then died in Wenquan Temple. As a result, the Mongolian army had to retreat. Since then, the Mongolian army failed to attack many times. The arduous and epic resistance lasted until 1279, when the Southern Song Dynasty was completely destroyed. After repeated persuasion and promise not to kill those who would surrender, Wang Li, the commander in chief, led the army and the people to lay down their arms, thus officially ending the 36-year history of resistance to Mongolia. The long-term containment of Genghis Khan's descendants' powerful force and attention in the Diaoyu Castle War has greatly reduced their barbaric conquest in various parts of the world and saved the conquered countries in Europe and Asia to a great extent. Therefore, Europeans also call this Castle "the eastern Mecca City" with full respect.

Gold Leaf of Holy Sunbirds (Fig. 2): It was unearthed at the Shang-Zhou ruins in Jinsha Village, Supo Township, west of Chengdu City. Archaeologists believe that this site is the capital city of the ancient Shu Kingdom, the ancient civilization center in the upper reaches of the Yangtze River from 12th to 7th centuries BC. This exquisite pattern, with an outer diameter of 12.5 cm, an inner diameter of 5.29 cm and a thickness of 0.02 cm is very similar to the modern paper-cutting process, on which four birds are flying around the sun. This concise, smooth, delicate and dynamic pattern is an outstanding representative piece of work of ancestors who worshiped the sun and yearned for freedom. It has become a symbol of Chinese heritage. The pattern almost covers the three relationships between the sun and birds in Chinese mythology.

Tianfu Culture and the Modern Pursuit of Chengdu

Fig. 2 Gold Leaf of Holy Sunbirds

The Bronze Mask with Extruding Eyes (Fig. 3): The mask was unearthed at the Sanxingdui Site of Guanghan in the Chengdu Plain (the site's cultural relics almost cover the history of 3000−1000 BC). It is a rare and shocking mysterious bronze object with a width of 1.38 meters and a height of 0.645 meters. Its eyes are cast into two torchlight-like rods, and its two huge ears spread out to both sides like banana leaves. Its shape is solemn, magnificent and full of mystery and tension. It should be interpreted that the ancestors hoped that they had clairvoyance and pleasant ears for further understanding of the universe and life and seeking new wisdom.

Chapter One
The Origin and Presentation of Tianfu Culture

Fig. 3 The Bronze Mask with Extruding Eyes

<u>Leshan Giant Buddha</u> (Fig. 4): Leshan Giant Buddha, also known as Lingyun Giant Buddha, is located close to the confluence of the Dadu River, Qingyijiang River and Minjiang River and on the side of Lingyun Temple on the east bank of the Minjiang River in the south of Leshan City, Sichuan Province. It is a 71 meters-high sitting statue of Maitreya, and the largest cliff-carving statue in China. Leshan Giant Buddha was excavated in the first year (713 AD) of Kaiyuan's Reign in the Tang Dynasty and completed in the 19th year (803 AD) of Zhenyuan's Reign, lasting for about 90 years. The most funds came from voluntary donations by officials and people. This statue not only reflects the ancestors' beliefs in Buddhism, but also is the crystallization of the great efforts to control floods and pray for peace and the superb application of the engineering skills of ancient craftsmen.

Tianfu Culture and the Modern Pursuit of Chengdu

Fig. 4 Leshan Giant Buddha

Jiaozi (Fig. 5): Jiaozi is the world's earliest paper currency, issued in Chengdu in the early Northern Song Dynasty (1023), 600–700 years earlier than the European paper currency. The original Jiaozi was a deposit certificate. In the early years of the Northern Song Dynasty, there appeared "Jiaozi shops" in Chengdu that operated cash custody business for merchants who were unable to carry large sums of iron money (the main currency in circulation in Sichuan as stipulated by the imperial court). The depositor delivered the cash to the shop owner, who filled in the deposit amount on the kozogami paper roll, and returned it to the depositor with a certain storage fee. This kind of paper coupon is called Jiaozi. With the increase of its circulation and the improvement of its credit standing, Jiaozi gradually possessed the characteristics of credit currency and became a real paper currency through the efforts of Jiaozi shop owners to unify the denomination and format and issue it as a new circulation method in the market. During the

Chapter One
The Origin and Presentation of Tianfu Culture

years of Jingde's Reign (1004-1007) of Song Zhenzong, Zhang Yong (946-1015), the prefect of Yizhou granted the exclusive right of Jiaozi business to 16 wealthy businessmen by means of rectifying Jiaozi's shops and banning illegal traders. So far, the imperial court officially approved the issue of "Jiaozi." In the first year (1023) of Tiansheng's Reign of Song Renzong, the court approved the establishment of Yizhou (the alias of Chengdu at that time) Jiaozi Service, with a reserve fund of 0.36 million *guans* (a *guan* was equivalent to 1,000 money units at that time). The first issue of "Official Jiaozi" was 1.26 million *guans* in value, with a reserve rate of 28%, which indicted the official birth of the bank note guaranteed by national credit in China. As a reliable credit is the key support for human financial undertakings, the Chinese people have always attached great importance to the value of honesty. *Yan Yuan* of *The Analects of Confucius* reads, "Zi Gong asked about government. The Master said, 'Enough food, enough weapons and the confidence of the people.' Zi Gong said, 'Suppose you had no alternative but to give up one of these three, which one would be let go of first?' The Master said, 'Weapons.' Zi Gong said, 'What if you had to give up one of the remaining two which one would it be?' The Master said, 'Food. From ancient times, death has come to all men, but a people without confidence in its rulers will not stand.'" Obviously, in Confucius's mind, the value of credit is incomparable in political life. Jiaozi was born in Chengdu, and this event at least proves that Chengdu's industry and commerce in the Song Dynasty had high prosperity and reliable credit, and Jiaozi itself is a great

Fig. 5 *Jiaozi*

Tianfu Culture and the Modern Pursuit of Chengdu

innovation and creation in the history of human finance.

Sichuan Red: It was the world's best printed and dyed textile product created by Chengdu's skillful craftsmen in the Song Dynasty, the only unfading colorful dyed fabric (Shu Jin, the famous brocade made in the Shu Kingdom) with red as the main tone at that time. When Wen Yanbo (1006–1097), a famous politician in the Northern Song Dynasty, was the prefecture chief of Shu, he fell in love with such beautiful goods. A few years later, when he returned to the capital, he bought one and gave it as a gift to Zhang Guifei (Guifei means the highest-ranking imperial concubine), whom Song Renzong (1010–1063, the emperor at that time) loved so much. It was very conspicuous when Zhang Guifei attended various royal parties in high profile and in well-dressed clothes presented by Wen Yanbo. It soon caused a political storm when the inspector Tang Jie (1010–1069) wrote to the emperor, requesting to impeach Wen Yanbo for bribing the royal family. Having heard of different arguments from the ministers, the emperor demoted both Tang Jie and Wen Yanbo from central to local place. However, as everyone knew Wen Yanbo was an honest and upright official, the emperor decided to transfer him back to the court since he also missed Wen Yanbo. Unexpectedly, Wen Yanbo proposed to transfer Tang Jie back to the court at the same time as the condition of his returning. Of course, the emperor was happy with the result. Such a story actually triggered by a little Shu brocade product presented by a well-known official as a gift to the imperial concubine whom the emperor doted on really shows the preciousness and attraction of the Shu brocade. A variety of colorful designs with red as the keynote reflect Chengdu people's extreme pursuit of elegant and fashionable clothing in the Song Dynasty.

Tambouring and Singing Figurine (Fig. 6): This pottery figurine was unearthed in 1957 from a cliff tomb of the Eastern Han Dynasty in Tianhui Mountain, Chengdu. It is 56 cm high and is made of argillaceous grey pottery. The original color painting on the figurine has fallen off. This figurine is sitting on the ground with his right leg raised, a round flat drum under his left arm and a drumstick in his right hand. He is laughing heartily with the mouth open as if he were going to the highlights of the talking and singing performance. The humorous expressions on his faces are portrayed so vividly and expressively as to make people today deeply moved. Now this

**Chapter One
The Origin and Presentation
of Tianfu Culture**

figurine is collected in the National Museum of China. "Talking and Singing Performance" is the main feature of Chinese folk art. The discovery of this figurine proves that as early as in the Eastern Han Dynasty, Chengdu's talking and singing art had matured and spread widely among the people, and there should be widely-known folk artists of idol level. It can be seen that the city's rich and colorful cultural activities and the optimistic life of ordinary people are of long standing.

Yin Changling: Yin Changling (1868−1942), whose ancestral home was in Pixian County, became a resident of Huayang County after his forefathers came to Chengdu for business. He was one of the "Five Elders and Seven Sages" in Chengdu during the Republic of China (1912−1949). He was one member of

Fig. 6 Tambouring and Singing Figurine

the Imperial Academy and the magistrate of Xi'an in the late Qing Dynasty. In 1923, he was elected to preside over the affairs of Cihuitang, one of the Chengdu government-run charities. With 20 years' thrift and hard work, he succeeded in transforming a failing institution into a production and service-oriented charity organization with dozens of units including factories (such as the famous Peigen Match Factory), primary schools and nurseries and orphanages, holding altogether 249 houses, 24 single-family courts, 8,348 *mu* (equivalent to approximately 5.565 million square meters in unit) of land and millions of *yuan* in cash and saving thousands of suffering people. That is why it is called the index of the embryonic form of modern social welfare cause in China. As he did not get any profit for himself and left no money to his family, they could not even afford the funeral when he died in 1942. The national government issued a commendation for his deeds, and had his life story displayed in the National Museum of History. He is recognized as the most successful and respected philanthropist in the Republic of China and the "best philanthropist" in China at that time.

<u>Lu Zuofu</u>: Lu Zuofu (1893-1952), born in Hechuan, Chongqing, a famous patriotic industrialist, educator, social activist and pioneer of rural social work. Born from a poor family, he had to drop out of school then became educated through self-learning. Minsheng Company founded in 1925 was one of the largest and most influential private enterprise groups in contemporary and modern China. In the early years of the founding of the People's Republic of China, Mao Zedong (1893-1976) once told Huang Yanpei (1878-1965) that in the modern history of China, there are four people we must never forget - Zhang Zhidong engaged in heavy industry, Zhang Jian engaged in textile industry, Lu Zuofu engaged in transportation industry, and Fan Xudong engaged in chemical industry. Lu Zuofu crossed over the three major fields of "saving the nation by revolution, by education and by industry," and made achievements in each of these aspects. His greatest contribution in his life was made after the outbreak of the War of Resistance against Japanese Aggression when the National Government appointed him as the director of the Land and Water Transportation Management Committee of the Military Commission, taking specific command in Wuhan, Yichang and other places. In the autumn of 1938, Wuhan was lost. A large number of people were ready to be evacuated to Chongqing and nearly 100,000 tons of factories' equipment and materials to Sichuan were concentrated at Yichang and constantly bombarded by Japanese planes. Regardless of all kinds of difficulties and risks and the indiscriminate bombing of Japanese planes, Lu Zuofu concentrated all the vessels and most of the business personnel of Minsheng Company and successfully transported all the personnel and materials to Sichuan within 40 days by rushing segmented transportation day and night before the fall of Yichang. As a result, China could maintain the most precious and important factories and materials for the War of Resistance against Japanese Aggression and the defeat of Japanese fascists. He is a well-deserved national hero. It is worth mentioning that

Chapter One
The Origin and Presentation of Tianfu Culture

in 1924, Lu Zuofu came to Chengdu specially to set up a popular education center for the people and served as a curator. In Shaocheng Park, he built various cultural and entertainment venues such as exhibition halls, museums, libraries, sports grounds, music playing rooms, amusement parks and zoos, bringing together all kinds of engineering and technical talents and literary and artistic experts from Chengdu and giving full play to their talents. Yet this hadn't lasted for long due to the warlord politics later. However, later generations admire him for his love of his native place.

Each of the above-mentioned objects and figures is outstanding in one field or aspect in Chinese or human history. However, they are only a small part of the achievements of the Ba-Shu culture.

Eastern Sichuan is rich in mountains while Western Sichuan boasts abundant water resources; so there are descriptions of Mountainous Ba and Waterish Shu in geography. The Ba culture is of more mountain features, hot, straightforward, masculine and strong, while the Shu culture is characterized with more water charms, romantic, gentle, delicate and tough. As the old saying goes, "More generals are made from the Ba people while more prime ministers produced from the Shu people." This is a brief description of the differences in the types of talents nurtured in this humanistic soil. Also, most of Sichuan's famous literary figures come from Western Sichuan, and this fact shows that the Ba and Shu people indeed have their unique endowments of cultural characters. However, in history, especially in the development process of modernization and globalization, the Ba and Shu people can share weal and woe with their own country, seek common ground while reserving differences in various aspects, realize the integration and fusion of economy and culture, and carry forward the commonness of Ba-Shu civilization characterized with romance, enthusiasm, inclusiveness, combination of firmness and flexibility, emphasis on business and culture, and daring to be the first, and will pass it on from generation to generation.

3. Excellent Genes of the Ba-Shu Culture

(1) Emphasis on Physical and Mental Freedom

A history of human civilization tells us that it is human nature to pursue freedom of body and mind. Ethnic groups and individuals who value and have more freedom can not only release and show stronger innovative and creative ability, but also have higher happiness index. Because the Ba-Shu land has boasted beautiful and mysterious mountains and rivers, abundant products, industrious and intelligent people, and rich and colorful lifestyles since ancient times, is generally far away from the political center of China, and has been deeply influenced by Taoist thoughts and Taoism (in Chinese culture, compared with Confucianism's emphasis on collectivism and adherence to ethical codes, Taoism, which calls for settling for a regular break and letting nature take its course, emphasizes individualism and liberalism), the Ba-Shu humanistic spirit is characterized by attaching importance to physical and mental freedom, which has been played to the full in the romantic, broad-minded and indifferent characters of ancient and modern Sichuan literary and artistic stars and scholars, causing and being caused by the birth and spread of a large number of myths and legends in the sense of the earliest master editions in China.

Judging from the continuation and expression of cultural genes, one of the important manifestations of the Ba-Shu culture's emphasis on physical and mental freedom is that the earliest Chengdu emerged from free trade, as Professor Xu Zhongshu put and discussed it in the 1980s. As a leading authority in Chinese paleography circle, Xu Zhongshu pointed out, "'Du' (one of the characters that form the word of 'Chengdu' in Chinese) was a free city without city defense construction on the ancient border." The seven free cities named "Du" recorded in Chang Qu's *Chronicles of Huayang* are the most precious materials for exploring the history of the ancient Shu. In consideration of the widespreading of exquisite lacquerware of Chengdu during the pre-Qin period, he believed, "Chengdu grew up gradually from a ting (a gross-roots administrative unit in ancient China) to a free city." The second important embodiment is that

Chapter One
The Origin and Presentation of Tianfu Culture

the officials and people here have not stuck to dogma, though they have complied with the general trend since ancient times and participated in the construction of China's core civilization. They have extremely rich imagination, speculative power, and numerous objects concerned to discuss, and have maintained their own personality in values, outlook on life, aesthetics, lifestyles and other aspects. Since ancient times, the Ba-Shu scholar-bureaucrats have shown a free and easy attitude towards life (such as leisure politics to be discussed later in this chapter), and ordinary people in urban and rural areas are living a life of distinct regional characteristics; for instance, they are fond of gaudiness of heavy colors, spicy and delicious food, etc.

The well-balanced quality of Chengdu's leisure culture and lifestyle from ancient to modern times is also closely related to it. The third important embodiment is that since ancient times, studies of *Book of Changes* in the Shu region has been especially developed, and the relative historic records about the "three kinds of people of extraordinary talents" have emerged without cease. Liu Xianxin (1896−1932), an outstanding genius in modern Chengdu, wrote in *San Yi Lu*, "There are three kinds of renowned people of extraordinary talents: hermits, magicians and immortals. Immortals are also hermits, and hermits must know astrology. In ancient times, the so-called immortals were no more than magicians. It was hard to tell from one another because they were often confused. They are all so-called people of extraordinary talents in the world. In China, the Shu region was most popular for such kinds of people because its secluded land blocked by deep mountains made it easy for people to contemplate." These three kinds of people, with obvious causal relationship with the geographical environment of Sichuan and appearing in the doctrines of Confucianism, Taoism and local myths, are a scenery line full of legends in traditional Chinese folk and society bringing people rich imagination and enlightening literature and art. As the people extremely free in mind and body and allowed by both the government and the people in the traditional society to remain at arm's length, either hidden or visible, they have endowed Tianfu Sichuan with unique romantic and carefree personalities and amorous feelings for more than 2,000 years.

Tianfu Culture and the Modern Pursuit of Chengdu

(2) Openness

The Ba-Shu civilization in its infancy was an open and inclusive system. The early narration of the Ba-Shu region is interwoven with history and myth. On one hand, the ancient Shu and her people were ready to accept the influence of external people and things. For instance, Lei Zu, the first wife of the Yellow Emperor (living in about 28th and 27th centuries BC, dates of birth and death unknown), and his son Changyi established the economic and blood ties with the Shu people through sericulture and marriage, respectively; Emperor Wang Du Yu, who replaced the Yufu Dynasty, came from Yunnan; Bieling, who replaced Du Yu and established the Kaiming Dynasty, came from the Jingchu area, Hubei. On the other hand, the Ba-Shu region was also actively influencing the outside world. For example, the Ba-Shu region had already been a member of the Central Plains Political League in the Yu's Reign of the Xia Dynasty, had many collisions with the Shang Dynasty, and later took part in the just war to destroy King Zhouwang of the Shang Dynasty and to establish the Zhou Dynasty.

Scholars generally believe that the ivory unearthed from the Sanxingdui Site is from the areas of Indus civilization, and the currency for trade and exchange between the two sides is seashells from the Indian Ocean. According to *Records of the Historian: Biography of Xinanyi*, when Bo Wanghou (diplomat) Zhang Qian (164–114 BC) returned from his mission to Daxia (ancient Afghanistan) in the first year of the Yuanshou's Reign of Emperor Hanwu (122 BC), he said that when he lived in Daxia and saw the Shu clothing and bamboo sticks made in Qionglai, he sent someone to ask where these came from. That person answered, "From Juandu in the southeast, thousands of miles away, you may reach there to do business with people from the Shu Kingdom." Juandu meant the ancient India in Chinese. This is the earliest historical record that Chinese goods appeared abroad through international trade. For more than 2,000 years, Chengdu has often been an international city, where China and its civilization have repeatedly collided and merged with the civilizations of the South and West Asia by taking economy, trade and exchanges of Buddhist studies and Buddhism as the main ties.

In October 1995, members of the Sino-Japanese research team discovered a piece of

Chapter One
The Origin and Presentation of Tianfu Culture

Shu brocade in an ancient tomb at Niya Site in Minfeng County, Hetian Prefecture, Xinjiang, which was named "Five Stars out of the East for China" and regarded as one of the greatest discoveries in Chinese archaeology in the 20th century. This cultural relic is a Shu brocade arm guard of the Han Dynasty, 18.5 cm long and 12.5 cm wide, in a rectangular shape with rounded corners, edged with white silk, decorated with three white silk ribbons of about 21 cm long and 1.5 cm wide on each of the long sides and woven with eight Chinese characters "Five Stars out of the East for China." It strongly shows that Shu brocade is a precious commodity on the Silk Road, and Chengdu is also an important force that cannot be ignored in the mutual learning between Chinese and foreign civilizations realized on the Northern Silk Road. This national treasure, now collected in Xinjiang Museum, is also permeated with the craftsman's strong feelings of home and country. Apart from the Southern and Northern Silk Roads, there are other cultural landscapes that could best show that the Ba-Shu ancestors were not satisfied to live in the basin only, but took the initiative to move to the outside world, such as various plank roads represented by Baoxie Road, Jinniu Road, Micang Road, winding across the great rivers and waves, among the mountains and cliffs, and the extremely difficult and dangerous ancient Tea-Horse Roads as well.

(3) Integrity

Firstly, the so-called integrity refers to the fact that the Ba-Shu culture has gradually started to merge into the unified regime of the Central Plain and national axis culture since its birth. In the historical process of realizing the broadest cultural identity of the Chinese nation, it has been a regional culture with the most centripetal force, bearing capacity and creativity. Secondly, since the Qin Dynasty, either the officials or the people here have yearned for, maintained and supported the national unity with a particularly strong feeling and consciousness. For the separatist forces and regimes formed and rising here, unless they were regarded as of legitimism, might unify China within a certain period of time. In fact, this situation only existed during the rule of Liu Bei (161−223) and Zhuge Liang (181−234) in the Three Kingdoms, or

Tianfu Culture and the Modern Pursuit of Chengdu

could really play the role of protecting the people and their homes, the Shu people would never bear their development without opposition or recalcitrance to the end, mainly because the Shu people living in this rare paradise on earth have the deepest understanding of the benefits of national unity and the deep-rooted memories and rational understanding of the disasters brought to the region after the country was torn apart by war (like the two great man-made disasters the Chengdu Plain suffered in the late Song and early Yuan dynasties, the late Ming and early Qing dynasties, in which almost all the aborigines were wiped out, and these events are very rare in the history of cities of the same level in China). This has also accelerated and consolidated the regional culture's support to and integration of the national axis culture in the mainstream values and lifestyles.

In history, there were countless top-notch figures in the Ba-Shu region who went straight ahead regardless of fame and wealth, and devoted themselves to the country, such as Su Shi (1037–1101) and Yang Shen (1488–1559). Talented as they were, they were down on their lucks. However, no matter how many hardships they encountered in their lives, their concern for the rise and fall of the country and the common interests of the whole people would not change. The great pressure of their life disasters could be dispelled under the joint action of Confucianism, Buddhism and Taoism, so that their personality would never sink, and their literary creation could continue to produce well-known eternal masterpieces. In addition to frequently dominating the peak of Chinese literature and art, the Ba-Shu culture has also made outstanding achievements in the first-class local education, and the construction and inheritance of Confucian classics and historiography. With profound ideological and cultural accumulation, sages, martyrs, celebrities and masters have appeared one after another, who love their country, dare to bear all kinds of hardships and difficulties, innovate, create all kinds of wealth, and leave behind many famous articles, deeds and great achievements.

(4) Advancement

The Ba-Shu region, which covers almost the whole fertile land on the upper reaches of the Yangtze River, is one of the earliest areas where human beings existed, and one of the most important sources of Chinese civilization as well. In the pre-Qin period, compared with other parts of China, the Ba-Shu region, centered on the Chengdu Plain, was a land of geomantic treasures, giving birth to Sanxingdui and Jinsha civilizations. Since the Qin and Han dynasties, a prominent spiritual characteristic of the Ba-Shu culture in history has been of sufficient self-confidence. Compared with other regions in the deep inland of China, people here have a distinct personality in thought, are full of imagination and critical spirit, dare to query any authorities and accepted theories, and are even fond of "ridiculing" powerful people. Therefore, enlightening theories and comments often originate here, and great masters endowed with great talent and learning emerge one after another, bringing a new vitality to China's spiritual home. As long as possible, the officials and people here dare to be the first in the world to achieve their virtues, do great deeds and deliver their ideas. They dare to try, create and innovate anything in work and life. As a result, compared with the world's and China's number ones created by China's inland areas in the history, Sichuan ranks first (see the later chapters).

Tianfu Culture and the Modern Pursuit of Chengdu

Sources of the Tianfu Culture

Tianfu Culture is both the flower and the fruit of the Ba-Shu civilization, the enrichment and wonderful presentation of the Ba-Shu civilization, and the main representative when the Ba-Shu culture collides, exchanges and merges with other regional cultures in China and other civilizations in the world. The mission and function of this representative sometimes work as a bridge, sometimes a guide, sometimes both.

In China, the recognized "Tianfu" originally refers to the Guanzhong Plain in Shanxi Province and its surrounding areas, once the best prosperous and rich place suitable for ancient farming civilization in the Yellow River Valley, and the capital location of eleven dynasties. However, in the course of the successive demise of the Eastern and Western Han dynasties, the Guanzhong region was devastated in war chaos. In addition to the gradual destruction of the ecological environment caused by human activities, especially the major changes in the global climate during the Eastern Han Dynasty, the resources and conditions supporting the sustainable and stable prosperity of the Guanzhong Plain gradually withered. At the latest, from the late Eastern Han Dynasty onwards, the special term of "Land of Abundance" began to refer to the Ba-Shu region centered on the Chengdu Plain. The Ba-Shu people and ancient people of Chengdu in past dynasties were all proud of such a beautiful name of their hometown.

Throughout history, Chengdu has the following eight unique or leading natural and human resources (including tradition) in China and even in the world, so it can converge the Ba-

Chapter One
The Origin and Presentation
of Tianfu Culture

Shu civilization and to a certain extent the essence of the entire Chinese civilization, and has become the stable center or core of the "Land of Abundance" and the representative of the "Tianfu Culture."

1. Unique Water Conservancy

Throughout the history of the world, the Chengdu people created and owned Dujiangyan Irrigation System, a great water conservancy project built 2,300 years ago, which has played an uninterrupted role in making a vast plain free from floods and droughts and people from hunger (Fig. 7). This is unique to all mankind, and Dujiangyan Irrigation System has thus become the mother weir of the Land of Abundance. The Chengdu Plain used to be a marshland all the year round and was not suitable for human habitation. According to *Records of Shu*, Volume III of *Chronicles of Huayang*, after Li Bing led the people to complete the construction of Dujiangyan Irrigation System, the Chengdu Plain "lies thousands of miles in fertile fields with rich natural resources. In case of drought, water will be diverted to irrigate crops; in case of rain, the water

Fig. 7 Overlook of Dujiangyan Irrigation System

Tianfu Culture and the Modern Pursuit of Chengdu

gate will be blocked. Therefore, it is said that floods and droughts are under the human control, people are free from hunger, and there are harvests year after year. It is so called Tianfu or the Land of Abundance."

Peng Bangben (1955–), a famous scholar of the Ba-Shu culture and professor of Sichuan University discussed the proposition in Dujiangyan Irrigation System: the "Great Pioneering Work and Eternal Monument of Human's Water Civilization" from five aspects. He wrote that apart from inheriting the flood control experience of Dayu, the Du Yu Dynasty and the Kaiming Dynasty in ancient Shu region, the scientific and exquisite survey and design, the economic and efficient mode of ecological engineering of water diversion without a dam, the inexpensive and endless local construction materials and simple engineering technologies, the annual maintenance system that rewards the diligent and adapts to local conditions and the water conservancy concept of following nature and integrating nature with man are the secret for Dujiangyan Irrigation System to continuously benefit future generations and become a world-famous cultural heritage. He also believes that this project "has broken several world records in the history of dam-free water conservancy project construction: the longest duration, the largest irrigation area, the highest comprehensive benefit and the best ecological environment protection, thus winning the crown of world cultural heritage." In fact, it was only after the completion of this project that the Chengdu Plain began to go neck to neck with the Guanzhong Plain in economy and livability and finally surpassed it in the late Eastern Han Dynasty. Thanks to this project (coupled with the supporting projects of future generations, continuously expanding water resources while reducing water disasters), the Chengdu Plain became the most secure granary in the era of agricultural civilization, and an area rich in various products. No other cities or regions in China could match Chengdu in this respect. Till today, this project still guarantees irrigation of tens of millions of *mu* of fertile soil all the year round. At the same time, Dujiangyan's water comes from Minjiang River almost without industrial pollution, thus ensuring the natural and clean water for living and production in the Chengdu Plain and its surrounding urban agglomerations. Also, few large cities can enjoy such an advantage. In

Chapter One
The Origin and Presentation
of Tianfu Culture

addition, Dujiangyan Irrigation District has also won the title of UN World Natural Heritage because it is a famous habitat of giant pandas (Fig. 8).

Fig. 8 Pandas

2. Mild Weather

Chengdu, located in the transition zone from the Northwestern Sichuan Plateau to Sichuan Basin at 104.1° of the eastern longitude and 30.6° of the northern latitude, is featured with distinctive climate resources. First, the eastern and western areas have different climates. Due to the disparity in altitude between the east and the west, the east is warm and the west is cool. In the west, the temperature at the foot or on the top of the mountain can differ by several degrees at the same time, and climate types may vary with the increase of height from warm temperate zone, temperate zone, cold temperate zone, sub-cold zone, to cold zone, etc. This change has created very favorable conditions for the development of agriculture in Chengdu, especially its diversified economy. Second, it enjoys four distinct seasons with a wet and cold winter, earlier spring, and longer frost-free period. Since the average temperature is 1 – 2° C higher than that in the middle and lower reaches of the Yangtze River at the same latitude, its spring comes half a month earlier. Third, there is less rain in winter and spring, but more in summer and autumn; the overall rainfall is abundant, with an average annual rainfall of 900 – 1,300 mm and small annual variation. Fourth, the condition of basically well-balanced light, heat and water is very conducive to biological reproduction. Fifth, the wind speed is small, with the wind speed of 1 – 1.5 m/s in vast plains and hilly areas. Sunny days are few, with the sunshine rate of 24%–32%, the annual average sunshine hours of 1,042–1,412, and the total annual average solar radiation amount of 83.0–94.9 km/cm^2.

In a word, few other parts of China can match with Chengdu in a stable, season-distinctive and mild climate of neither severe cold in winter nor extreme heat in summer, suitable for production and livability, and remaining almost unchanged since ancient times. Chengdu almost has no extreme climatic phenomena that would damage human production and life, and few natural disasters. Looking at the whole history of Chinese civilization, few cities have been so lucky as Chengdu in terms of the stable support provided by climatic conditions.

3. Abundant Products of All Kinds

Chengdu has a variety of land types, a large ratio of plain area and a high wasteland reclamation index. Located in a humid subtropical region of fertile soil, convenient irrigation, and with 94.2% of usable area, Chengdu enjoys complex topography, extremely diversified natural environments and abundant biological resources due to its high altitude drop. According to preliminary statistics, there are more than 3,000 species, 764 genera, 200 families and 11 classes of animal and plant resources alone, which can survive, be grown, cultivated or domesticated here. For example, Chengdu is indisputably known as the world's "Home of

Chapter One
The Origin and Presentation of Tianfu Culture

Panda" – the best base for wild survival and artificial breeding of the giant panda. Chengdu is also rich in mineral resources of various types, with relatively concentrated distributions and more symbiotic minerals. Obviously, these resources are all favors from nature. In the Chengdu Plain and its surrounding areas in a close tie and mutual exchange with each other, all the material resources and products for basic life of ancient and modern people can be more efficiently and quickly produced and gathered because of the above-mentioned three advantages, especially the industry, wisdom and hard work of the local officials and people of past dynasties, as well as species and products imported through foreign economic and cultural exchanges represented by the three Silk Roads.

In most of the peaceful years in Chinese history, the prices of daily necessities here were much lower than those in other densely populated areas. For example, according to the *Records of Food and Goods* in Volume 24 of *Han Shu (The History of the Han Dynasty)*, "At the beginning of the Han Dynasty, there were many problems left behind from the Qin Dynasty. The princes rebelled; the hungry people didn't have a livelihood; rice per *dan* (60 kg) cost 5,000 copper coins; the population was reduced to half. Then Emperor Gaozu ordered the people to sell their children to the land of the Shu-Han Regime, where they could eat. After the situation calmed down, the people had no houses to live in, and the king could not find four horses of the same color to pull his cart. The civil and military officials did not even have horse-drawn carriages, so they could only take ox carts." Obviously, the Chengdu Plain at that time was the easiest place to make a living. This author has studied the grain prices in the main grain-producing areas of China in the three reigns of Kangxi, Yongzheng and Qianlong in the Qing Dynasty. For at least 150 years, the grain prices in Chengdu were the lowest. Until the late Qing Dynasty, Chengdu was better than other places of China for its rich products and prosperous commerce. The most typical records (published in Volume 9 of *Yu Bao*) in the 24th year of the Guangxu's Reign (1898) by a French traveler Victor H. Mair, after traveling in Chengdu read, because of the delay in the construction of municipal facilities, the streets and lanes in Chengdu at that time were of poor hygiene and "narrow," but there were many shops and local specialties,

Tianfu Culture and the Modern Pursuit of Chengdu

such as bronze wares, knives, toothpicks, earpicks, straw hats and other items, as well as goods from other neighboring provinces, such as Tibetan sheep skin, medicines and so on. Mair highly praised it by saying, "This is really an unexpected grand view," "presenting the new atmosphere of China" and even "Guangdong, Shanghai, Chongqing and Beijing cannot match with Chengdu." Although these words are somewhat flattering, there is no doubt that Chengdu was rich in products either produced by or distributed to it through commercial trade at that time.

Abundant products and low prices of major daily necessities have enabled the people here to live harmoniously and calmly since ancient times, so they have more chances to engage in various innovative undertakings and the construction of spiritual civilization at their leisure. Chengdu has been an elegant and fashionable city since ancient times. Countless historical materials tell us that as long as there is political stability and social peace, this would be a city of music, a city of gastronomy and a city of fortunes.

4. Various Environments

The ancient and modern Chengdu Plain and the jurisdiction of Chengdu as the capital have an elevation drop of nearly 5,000 meters. Here, almost all the beautiful geographical and geological landscapes except the sea and desert are available, and various relaxing and beautiful natural landscapes constitute the basic environment for people to live and travel in. Since ancient times, Chengdu has been a "pastoral city" with a harmonious blend of nature and humanity, city and country, and of different customs and unique fashions. It not only provides its people with living conditions of a high happiness index that stimulate various aesthetic feelings and romantic imagination but also provides literary and artistic masters of past dynasties with a source of creation and endless inspiration that have been turned into numerous first-class literary and artistic works in China and the world. In addition to the miraculous masterpieces of art and imagination represented by the Gold Leaf of Holy Sunbirds, the Bronze Mask with Extruding Eyes, and the Sacred Tree unearthed from Sanxingdui and Jinsha Site respectively, and the fairyland-like depiction of "Luan birds are free to sing while Phoenix free to dance here;

Chapter One
The Origin and Presentation of Tianfu Culture

the trees of Lingshou blossom and bear fruits on time, and dense grass and trees grow" in *Hai Nei Jing* of *Shan Hai Jing (Legends of Mountains and Seas)*, Zuo Si (c. 250–305), a literary giant in the Western Jin Dynasty, praised Chengdu as one of China's three richest and most romantic cities in "San Du Fu", and "A Quatrain" by Du Fu in the Tang Dynasty reads, "Two golden orioles sing amid the willows green, /a row of white egrets fly into the blue sky. /From my window the snow-crowned western hills are seen, /beyond the door the east-bound ships at anchor lie." And in his "Rejoicing in Rain on a Spring Night", he wrote, "A good rain knows its appointed time, right in spring it brings things to life. It enters the night unseen with the wind, and moistens things finely, without a sound. Over wilderness paths, the clouds are all black, a boat on the river, its fire alone bright. At daybreak look where it's wet and red – the flowers will be heavy in Brocade City." Zhang Ji (c. 766–830) of the Tang Dynasty wrote in "Song of Chengdu," "In west Jinjiang River hangs mysterious mist and water green, the litchi on the hillside is mature in the rain. There are many restaurants near Wanli Bridge in the south. To which do people like to lodge?" Liu Yuxi (772–842) wrote in "Lang Tao Sha (Ripples Sifting Sand)," "Banks of Jinjiang River are full of flowers. Spring wind blows the waves that scoured gravels out. The girl cut off a piece of brocade mandarin duck-patterned, threw it into the midstream to match the sunset" Lu You (1125–1210) of the Song Dynasty wrote in "Travel to Chengdu, " "Patting the jade pot and playing on the zither, traveled in Chengdu a self-conceited scholar. Countless crabapple plants seen in Chengdu everywhere, to its prosperity and beauty none can compare." In their realistic writings, there are countless such praises, not only natural scenery and delicious food, but also the glory of the sages who built merit here.

Chengdu's beautiful landscapes and rich humanities have stimulated the artistic inspiration of countless sages and attracted numerous artists to come here to show their aspirations. Therefore, Chengdu has become an indispensable and important part in the history of Chinese painting. In *Records of the Historian: Biography of Li Si*, it says, "(If not) decorated with the golden tin from the south of the Yangtze River and the red and green pigments from the west of Shu, " what would the palace look like? This shows that at least in the Qin Dynasty, Chengdu

Tianfu Culture and the Modern Pursuit of Chengdu

already enjoyed a good reputation for its painting pigments. A large number of Han Dynasty brick reliefs were unearthed in Chengdu area, depicting all aspects of the economy, politics, culture and education, art, and street life at that time. They were vivid and full of life flavor and had unique aesthetic values of humanity and arts. Chengdu's Buddhist Daci Temple was the country's leading art palace during the Tang and Song dynasties. Li Zhichun (dates of birth and death unknown), an official of the Song Dynasty, said in his *Records of Paintings in Daci Temple*, "Chengdu collects more Tang paintings than those of other cities in China, but Daci Temple holds the most in Chengdu..."

Li Zhichun lived in the Shenzong's Reign of the Northern Song Dynasty, and created *Records of Paintings in Daci Temple* when he was Prefect of Chengdu. The numbers of paintings are relatively exact, which were calculated one by one by his religious officials and the monks of the temple as he ordered. It has high accuracy. Another example is the flower-and-bird painting school of Western Shu in the Five Dynasties and represented by Huang Quan (c. 903–965) and Huang Jucai (933–993) from Chengdu. It went neck to neck with painting schools in the regions south of the Yangtze River. And in the Song Dynasty, they brought the style of Western Shu's court painting into the capital's court painting academy and ruled the court flower-and-bird painting style of the Northern Song Dynasty for about a century. As a matter of fact, without the beautiful nature and humanity, and singing and dancing birds in Chengdu area, there would have been no such great two major flower-and-bird painting schools and their lingering charm that have influenced people today.

In history, Chengdu is not only full of excellent painters and paintings, but also a highland for criticism and appreciation of Chinese paintings. Huang Xiufu, a native of Chengdu in the Northern Song Dynasty, compiled the painting history book *Record of Yizhou Famous Paintings*, which embodies the aesthetic fashion that has a great influence on later generations and has always been highly valued. In the academic history, *Additional Records of Paintings* by Deng Chun, a Shuangliu native of the Southern Song Dynasty, set a precedent for compiling painting history by comprehensively using predecessor's poems, notes and other materials. The book's

**Chapter One
The Origin and Presentation
of Tianfu Culture**

appreciation and promotion of literati paintings have far-reaching influence on the painting theory of later generations. Furthermore, Yang Shen, a versatile scholar and literary giant of the Ming Dynasty, also wrote *Appreciation of Paintings*, in which he put it, "Far and remote the Shu State is, there are more painters than those of other regions." Some items in the book are insightful, such as the discussion of the influence of regional culture on painting art: "Painting arts in the regions south of the Yangtze River are too resplendent and unrestrained, but lack of the backbone of Shu people." In short, Chengdu has made irreplaceable contributions to the painting practice and theory in Chinese history. And the development of this urban and rural visual art originates from the beauty of its rich and three-dimensional natural environment, and they both bring out the best in each other.

When it comes to the natural beauty of Chengdu (Fig. 9) and its connections with ancient and modern histories, one can also take as an example the famous painting *Beautiful*

Fig. 9 Overlook of Emei Mountain

Tianfu Culture and the Modern Pursuit of Chengdu

Landscapes of Sichuan by Li Gonglin (1049–1106), a painter of the Northern Song Dynasty, which was once collected in the imperial palace of the Qing Dynasty and most appreciated by Emperor Qianlong (1711–1799) of the Qing Dynasty as one of his "Four Beauties" and is now collected in the Freer Gallery of Art in Washington, United States. Li Gonglin, antiquarian and erudite, good at poetry, skillful at authenticating antiques, especially famous for his paintings, and fine at painting almost everything such as historic figures, stories of Buddhism and Taoism, horses, landscapes, and flowers and birds, was regarded as the first painter in the Song Dynasty. The picture scroll, 32.2 cm high and 746.5 cm wide, depicts the famous mountains, rivers and city features of the then four prefectures of Sichuan (now Sichuan and Chongqing) in the Song Dynasty. It starts from Wenshan and Minshan Mountains, the birthplace of the traditional Yangtze River, along with Maozhou, Shiquan, Yongkanjun (now Dujiangyan City), Qingcheng Mountain (Fig.10-1, Fig.10-2), Chengdu City, Shuangliu, Xinjin, Pengshan, Long'an, Meizhou and Qingshen, then strides across Jiazhou, Xuzhou, Luzhou, Yuzhou and Fuzhou, and

Fig. 10-1 Qingcheng Mountain, the holy mountain for Taoism

Chapter One
The Origin and Presentation of Tianfu Culture

Fig. 10-2 Qingcheng Mountain, the holy mountain for Taoism

Yun'an, Kuizhou and Wushan. In addition to the picture itself, it also has detailed annotations on the geographical names of the Song Dynasty. Among them, the marked place names are most concentrated in Chengdu area under the jurisdiction of Sichuan Prefecture and Kuizhou, of Kuizhou Prefecture. The perfect combination of the beautiful landscapes and the first painter in the Song Dynasty has made this masterpiece of painting history that vividly reproduces the extraordinary beauty.

On September 2nd, 2017, the China Youth Network reported it with a title of "Start Chengdu Tianfu Greenway Construction to Reproduce *Beautiful Landscapes of Sichuan*" that this art treasure of painting by Li Gonglin of the Northern Song Dynasty and regarded as one of the four beauties of Emperor Qianlong of the Qing Dynasty, depicts the extremely beautiful scenic spots, houses, yards and restaurants along the sides of Jinjiang River. Such wonderful scenery that only exists in writing, painting and poetry will reappear in Chengdu in the near future. At the same time, the construction of Jincheng Greenway, one of the "three rings" of the regional greenway system of "one axis, two mountains, three rings and seven belts," has started, with a total length of about 200 kilometers, integrating ecological protection, pastoral life and cultural innovation into one, and creating the new version of *Beautiful Landscapes of Sichuan*. The diverse beauty of the natural environment and its expression has always been the powerful source of creativity for Chengdu people to optimize their living environment and lifestyle and to speak for China's beauty and wealth in many circumstances.

In addition, one of the outstanding landscapes is the unique Lin Pan (the rural living environment formed by the organic integration of the farmhouses and surrounding trees, bamboos, rivers and cultivated lands in the Chengdu Plain and its hilly area), through which Chengdu people have personalized and refined their living environment. The famous scholar Tan Jihe (1940–) said in an interview with reporters on the theme of "Tianfu Culture," "For example, Chengdu's dwelling culture during the farming period was the Lin Pan culture – 'Thatched huts surrounded with bridges, flowing waters and bamboos,' which was unique in the world. Now in the period of industrial civilization, everyone lives in the city and does not need farming, but can the characteristics of Lin Pan be preserved and transplanted to the city? The streets should be designed with more green trees and the urban areas equipped with more parks so that the city can be built into an ecologically beautiful one. This is also a cultural reservation." This author deeply agrees with his judgment and proposition. Lin Pan, as a typical symbol of the lifestyle of ancient Tianfu people, is a harmonious unity between nature and man, representing our ancestors' feelings of approaching nature and pursuing personalized and elegant lifestyle.

5. Balanced Spread of the Three Religions

Chinese culture is extensive and profound, taking Confucianism, Buddhism and Taoism as its core ideas. Comparatively speaking, Confucianism mainly focuses on the relationship between people, provides the core values of the destiny community of the Chinese people,

Chapter One
The Origin and Presentation of Tianfu Culture

including benevolence, righteousness, propriety, wisdom, loyalty, filial piety, integrity and shame, advocates the philosophy of "the golden mean," which emphasizes balance, consideration, coordination and tolerance, and advocates a positive and rational attitude towards life. It is the main body of Chinese traditional culture and has the most significant and comprehensive influence on Chinese history and world history. Buddhism and Taoism are an important supplement to Chinese culture. Buddhism mainly tells the relationship between people and their hearts. It is a foreign but Sinicized ideological system and has a great influence on Chinese philosophy, aesthetics, literature and art, and even the lifestyles of Chinese people. Taoism is mainly concerned about the relationship between man and nature (including man's body and various desires arising from it), emphasizing that individuals should restrain their desires and get satisfied with the status quo for a safe and happy life and the maintenance of their personality and holding that "Human beings are a manifestation of the earth; the earth, a manifestation of the physical universe; the physical universe, a manifestation of Infinity; Infinity, the potential of all things." (Chapter 25, Lao Zi's *Tao Te Ching*) As a reflection of understanding the world, avoiding disasters and coping with and resolving contradictions, it is full of wisdom, especially its thought of following nature and living in harmony with nature is of special modern significance.

Lao Zi, the founder of Taoism, left Luoyang and lived in seclusion in Chengdu. According to Scholar Yang Xiong (53 BC-18 AD) of the Han Dynasty and other documents, after Lao Zi wrote *Tao Te Ching* for Yin Xi, he said at parting, "Go advocating the doctrine, and find me at Qingyang Fair of Chengdu 1,000 days later." Three years later, when Lao Zi and Yin Xi met as promised, Lao Zi appeared as an immortal sitting on the lotus throne, and Yin Xi conducted incisive explanation of the Taoist doctrines. Since then, the Qingyang Palace had become a holy place for immortals to gather at and Lao Zi to propagate his doctrines in. In the Tang Dynasty, the scale of Qingyang Palace was quite large. Taoism, born in the Chengdu Plain, has made important contributions to Chinese civilization. Chengdu naturally has an irreplaceable core position in the spread of Taoism and Taoist thoughts and cultures (Fig. 11).

Tianfu Culture and the Modern Pursuit of Chengdu

Fig. 11 Shangqing Palace in Qingcheng Mountain

Chengdu has always been an indispensable and important part in the history of the existence, development and dissemination of Buddhism and Buddhist studies in China. In some periods, some fields and the eyes of some eminent monks, Chengdu represented the highest level. For example, the first Buddhist sutra collection *Kaibao Tripitaka* ordered to be printed by Emperor (Song Taizu) was carved and printed in Chengdu. It took 13 years and amounted to 130,000 cut blocks, including 5,048 volumes in 480 books well carved with exquisite calligraphy. It is the best version of the Song Dynasty and well-known at home and abroad. As far as Chinese Zen Buddhism is concerned, at least five of the ten Zen sects listed by the eminent monk Zong Mi (780-841) of the Tang Dynasty in *On Theories of Zen Sects* are related to and many famous figures were also produced in Sichuan, and this phenomenon shows the important position of Sichuan and esp. Chengdu. In the Song Dynasty, Buddhism and Buddhist studies in

Chapter One
The Origin and Presentation
of Tianfu Culture

Chengdu Prefecture developed unprecedentedly. In Song Shenzong's Reign, there were only over 200,000 monks and nuns in the whole country, but there were "over 10,000" in Chengdu Prefecture. Su Shi could not help admiring, "In Southwest China, Chengdu is really a metropolis, where Buddhism prevails." (Fig.12-1 to Fig.12-3)

In this book, the so-called balanced spread of the three religions in Chengdu first refers to the close connection between the three religions and Shu Studies. Professor Tan Jihe pointed out, "The cultural source of Shu Studies is the academic source of Chinese literature." "The Ba-Shu culture has made contributions as an open source to Taoism and Confucianism. Daoism originated from the magic doctrine of immortal life of ancient Shu, and the five ancient Shu kings all achieved the immortality. The worship of birds in Sanxingdui and Jinsha Site proves that the worship of birds, marked by 'the belief of immortal life,' was widespread 3,000 years ago.

Fig. 12-1 Emei Mountain, the holy mountain for Buddhist

Fig. 12-2 Emei Mountain, the holy mountain for Buddhist   Fig. 12-3 Emei Mountain, the holy mountain for Buddhist

Taoism founded by Zhang Ling directly inherited the magic doctrine of immortal life of ancient Shu, which became the core of Taoist classics. The romantic cultural imagination characterized by immortals has been passed down in Shu studies. Dayu, born in the western Qiang area, was the first person of primitive Confucianism, and Confucianism was created by Shu people ... The Theory of 'Five Elements' – the source of Confucianism, was derived from Dayu's control of water ... In terms of the doctrine of Zen Buddhism, the Ba-Shu Zen School founded by Zhi Shen, Wu Xiang and Mazu Daoyi, both different from and compatible with the southern and northern Zen schools, put forward the academic concept of 'the principle is to let nature take its own course,' thus laying a basic foundation for the secularization of Buddhism as part of ordinary life. Therefore, the source of Shu studies can be summarized with the three characteristics: 'The doctrine of immortal life came from the Shu region,' 'Confucianism originated from the Shu

Chapter One
The Origin and Presentation of Tianfu Culture

region' and 'Taoism was founded in the Shu region.'" Professor Shu Dagang (1959–) of Sichuan University concluded when discussing the heyday of ancient Ba-Shu Studies in the period of the Southern and Northern Song dynasties, "At that time, men of talent came out in succession with great achievements in Shu Studies, such as literature, history, medicine, mathematics, politics, family culture and other aspects, indicating the characteristics of peaceful coexistence of the three religions as well as other doctrines."

In addition, Chengdu has not only been the center of research, development and dissemination of the three religions in Southwest China, with numerous erudite scholars, eminent monks, and immortals, who had their own audiences and advantages, but also seen the peaceful coexistence of the three religions and their followers, giving full play to the vitality of the spiritual home of Chinese culture that is open, inclusive, rational and complementary. On the way to integrate Confucianism, Buddhism and Taoism to benefit the learning and the mentality of ordinary people, Chengdu scholar-officials have never stopped their pace. For example, Zhang Shangying (1043–1121, from Xinjin County), Prime Minister of the Northern Song Dynasty, definitely advocated that the three religions were indispensable to one another. In history, many of the Ba-Shu scholars have always kept the traditions of being content with poverty to pursue the perfection, well read, incorporating things of diverse nature, broad-minded and self-confident. For example, in the Qing Dynasty, Liu Yuan (1768–1855) in Shuangliu, Chengdu, created the legendary folk academic school, "Huai Xuan School," whose academic attainments were interesting to famous scholars in the 20th century, such as Zhang Shunhui (1911–1992), Nan Huaijin (1918–2012), Xiao Tianshi (1909–1986), Wu Tianchi (1913–2004), and Li Xueqin (1933–2019). Liu Yuan's book *Pandect of Huai Xuan School* is a masterpiece of huge volumes, based on the spirit of the Confucian canons and integrating Taoism and Confucianism. Nan Huaijin said, "Liu Yuan (or Zhitang) was born in Shuangliu in Western Shu between the reigns of Qianlong and Jiaqing. At the beginning, he was a learned scholar and looked down upon any fame, but finally followed Taoism. Legend has it that he learned the true essence from Lao Zi and became immortal. He is famous for his profound studies and works about Confucianism,

Tianfu Culture and the Modern Pursuit of Chengdu

Buddhism and Taoism, and Huai Xuan School is called as 'Liu's School,' with many branches in the north and south of the Yangtze River, especially in Fujian and Zhejiang." This shows that it had great influence on scholar-officials and the people, and manifested the Ba-Shu culture's enough confidence in the coexistence and integration of the three religions.

Third, the patterns and traditions of balanced spread of the three religions mutually compatible with one another have made Chengdu a successful bridge for the communication and integration of Han Buddhism, Tibetan Buddhism and its followers, Han culture and Tibetan, Qiang and Yi cultures and endowed Chengdu with unique generosity and vitality. Up to now, Chengdu has played a decisive role in the political geography, economic geography and national unity in the western part of the country.

6. The Renovated Silk Road

There were many silk roads in China's history, but mainly three in terms of importance and continuity. They refer to the Land Silk Road from Chang'an and Luoyang to Europe and North Africa through the Hexi Corridor, North-South Road at Mt. Tianshan of Xinjiang and Central Asia, the Maritime Silk Road composed of three major routes, and the Southern Silk Road formed in the pre-Qin period, taking Chengdu as the start point and the main commodity supplier, connecting Myanmar, India, Central Asia and Western Asia through the southwest ethnic minority areas (now southern Sichuan, Yunnan and Guizhou), reaching the Mediterranean region of Europe, which has established and developed economic and cultural ties with Southeast Asia. Of the three silk roads, the first two were the witness of commodities and caravans from Chengdu, and the third one was established with Chengdu as the leading role.

In 2013, one of the six major archaeological discoveries in China was the excavation of the Han Tomb in Laoguanshan, Tianhui Town, Chengdu, from which the "Three Treasures" of the loom models, medical slips and a human medical model were unearthed. Among them, the Shu Brocade Jacquard Model (the restored one displayed in Cheng Museum now), as the physical prototype of vertical loom unearthed for the first time in China, has filled in the blank

**Chapter One
The Origin and Presentation
of Tianfu Culture**

of the world textile history. According to Wang Junping, an expert of Shu brocade, relevant authorities and experts at home and abroad have agreed that this "wooden loom" is the earliest and most advanced brocade loom discovered in the world's archaeological history. "Since there are four sets of such unearthed from the same tomb, it is strongly proved that the so-called 'City of Brocade' and 'Capital of Brocade' of Chengdu are true to their names." Archaeologist and curator of Chengdu Museum Wang Yi said, "The discovery of jacquard looms of the Han Dynasty 2,000 years ago has made up for the regret of lacking of such a kind of historical materials in the textile history of China and even the world, and also confirmed that Chengdu was the starting point of the Southern Silk Road in history."

Professor He Yimin (1953–) of Sichuan University has a very incisive analysis of Chengdu in ancient economic geography as follows:

> Although Chengdu is located in the inland of China and at the bottom of the basin, Chengdu has a special location advantage, that is, it is located at the junction of the three major economic and cultural zones of the ancient Yangtze river economic zone, the Southern and the Northern Silk Roads, ... this advantage, unavailable in any major city in ancient China, has made Chengdu the hub of ancient China's opening up to the outside world... Because of the special geographical location, Chengdu has had a long history of communicating with the outside in many aspects. The ancient Shu culture represented by Sanxingdui Culture and Jinsha Culture was closely related to the Central Plains Culture and the Western Asian Culture. Bronze wares, jade wares and gold wares unearthed from these sites all reveal the information of multi-cultural integration. During the Han and Tang dynasties, with the country's prosperity, opening up to the outside world and great development at home, Chengdu's economic and cultural ties with the Northern and the Southern Silk Road and the Yangtze River Basin were continuously strengthened, and it became a national central city. In the Han dynasty, Chengdu was "listed as one of the five standby capital cities"; while in the Tang Dynasty, Chengdu was considered as "the

Tianfu Culture and the Modern Pursuit of Chengdu

most prosperous city only next to Yangzhou".... In the Han and Tang dynasties, Chengdu developed into a world-famous metropolis for many reasons; of course, one of the important reasons that cannot be ignored is that Chengdu benefited from the interaction of the accessibility of the Northern Silk Road, the sustainable development of the Southern Silk Road, and the economic prosperity of the Yangtze River Basin. It is Chengdu's unique geographical location that promoted Chengdu's three rises in the pre-Qin, Han and Tang dynasties.

Although Chengdu is the heart of the Land of Abundance and rich in products, the ancient of Chengdu people were unsatisfied dwelling on the relatively rich land; instead, they took the initiative to build the "Shu Roads" typified by plank roads on cliffs, ancient tea-horse roads, waterways running down east to the Yangtze River, and especially, the Southern Silk Road by overcoming many obstacles and hardships in transportation and information transmission. Together with the convenience of other silk roads, they have closely interacted with the outside world to realize the broader development of the "Land of Abundance" in communication and let the world listen to Chengdu's voice and feel Chengdu's influence. The diligence and wisdom of Chengdu's ancient and modern people and their courage and heroism of traveling around the world have made Chengdu a prominent position in foreign exchanges in history. This is the most vivid interpretation of the innovative and entrepreneurial characteristics of "Tianfu Culture," and the most precious cultural resource of Chengdu that has won the status of a national central city.

7. Immigrants from All Over the Country

Historically, Chengdu is a well-deserved "Land of Abundance." In the era of peaceful reunification, Chengdu is always prosperous, rich and vibrant. But it was probably because of this attribute that Chengdu always faced a wave of immigrants under two backgrounds, in addition to political immigration to control some special groups, whenever dynasties rose and fell, the country was split, or powerful enemies invaded in large numbers.

First, earlier or more serious chaos or turmoil happening in other areas may force a large

Chapter One
The Origin and Presentation of Tianfu Culture

number of officials and people (sometimes including emperors) to take refuge in the Chengdu Plain. For example, in the early Western Han Dynasty, the emperor ordered people in other war-torn areas to take refuge and "eat in the Shu-Han Regime"; when the country fell into disrepair and decline after the "An-Shi Rebellion" (785−783) in the Tang Dynasty, Emperor Xuanzong (685−762) and Emperor Xizong (862−888) took refuge in Shu, together with a large number of refugees from the Central Plains. History shows that Wang Jian (847−918), Emperor of the Former Shu, "cordially invited the service of many scholarly and noble families in the Tang Dynasty who took refuge in Shu then, and let them take part in the governance of state affairs, leaving the laws, rites, regulation and other valuable things with the legacy of the Tang Dynasty." After the War of Resistance against Japanese Resistance broke out in 1930s, a large number of territories fell into the enemy's hands and refugees poured into Sichuan and Chengdu.

Second, Chengdu suffering a huge population loss during a national war may cause a large number of people to migrate to and settle down in the Chengdu Plain either spontaneously or in an organized way after the war ends. Such a kind of immigration in the late Song and early Yuan dynasties and the late Ming and early Qing dynasties is very typical.

There have been at least nine large-scale migrations that had a significant impact on the composition of the original ethnic groups. Every big migration (including a large number of people from other places, provinces and foreign countries who have come to Chengdu since the Third-line Construction and the reform and opening-up) would bring about a reset of their economy, culture and even language, customs and social psychology in the Ba-Shu region with Chengdu Plain as the core. The relationship among immigrants and between immigrants and aborigines gradually changed from conflict to integration, from simple competition to mutual reference, learning and cooperation. Generations of immigrants and their culture have not only enriched the connotation of Tianfu Culture and added vitality to it, but also shaped the humanistic characters of the Land of Abundance −Innovation and Creation, Fashion and Elegance, Optimism and Tolerance, Kindness and Public Welfare. Chengdu is famous for a large number of beautiful women, delicious food and fine wine, which are all the result of the blending of immigrant genes and the exchange and gathering of skills in making delicious food

Tianfu Culture and the Modern Pursuit of Chengdu

and fine wine from their native places. Sichuan opera, gathering all the advantages of each school, is also the crystallization of organic integration of many outside drama elements.

Immigrants from ancient and modern times in Chengdu also include people from foreign countries (usually in prosperous times or historical turning periods) who have settled and started businesses in Chengdu because of opportunities or backgrounds such as residence, study, business, missionary work, and medical treatment. The typical example is Zen Master Wuxiang (648-742), Prince of Silla, who, by the order of Emperor Xuanzong of the Tang Dynasty, presided over the construction of and "established regulations" for the Daci Temple and finally died in a sitting posture here, making an important contribution to the Buddhist cause in Chengdu. Having a special preference to Chengdu, the three generations of Omar L. Kilborn (1867-1920) from Canada founded modern medicine and medical services here.

Today's Chengdu, as China's national central city, is inheriting and carrying forward this kind of humanistic character. With a broader mind and mechanism, Chengdu is attracting people from all directions who are willing to build Chengdu together to create a bright future for such a great city with extraordinary aspirations for modernization and internationalization.

8. The City's Name That's Never Changed

In human history, it is rare, if not unique, for large and medium-sized cities with a history of more than 2,000 years to keep their names unchanged. However, Chengdu stands out of them.

In Chinese literature, the word "Chengdu" is first used as a verb to refer to becoming a capital. The literature that "one year's dwelling brings about a village, two years', a city; three years', a capital" is a classic expression of a place that has successfully become a ruling center with larger scale and influence because of its enlightened king who is good at governance and accords with people's will. It can be traced back to Su Zhe (1039-1112), a great literary giant, who recorded in Volume 2 of the *Biographies of the Five Great Ancient Kings* that when Shun was a common people, he insisted on influencing with sincere filial piety on his father, mother and brother who persecuted him. "When Shun cultivated in Lishan Mountain, all the people there

Chapter One
The Origin and Presentation of Tianfu Culture

allowed him to farm on the riverside; when he fished in Leize Lake, all the people there agreed him to live there; when he made pottery on the riverside, there were no bad pottery products there. One year later, the place where he lived became a village, two years later, a small town; three years later, a city." Shun had his own chiefdom because of his moral perfection and popular support. Later when the Great King Yao heard of his moral integrity and ability, he chose him as his successor. Finally, Shun became one of the greatest emperors in history. According to *Records of the Historian*, after King Taiwang of the Zhou Dynasty (King Wen's grandfather) moved to Mount Qi, he experienced the same story because his countrymen loved him very much for his good deeds and righteousness. About 2,500 years ago, when King Du Yu of the ancient Shu State moved the capital from Pixian or Fan Township (now the junction of Pengzhou and Xindu) to the present site, he was inspired by King Taiwang and named it Chengdu, with the metaphorical meaning of the wise king and successful completion of the capital construction. Therefore, the beginning of the construction of Chengdu's main urban area today, according to the actual location of Jinsha Site excavated, can be traced back to 3,200 years ago.

Secondly, as a regional political center, this city is called Chengdu from beginning to end. Because of its distinctive historical context, the city has many bynames and stories. When Zhang Yi (?−309 BC) was responsible for the construction of Chengdu City after the Qin State destroyed the Shu State, the city wall always collapsed. Later, a big turtle came out of the river and walked along a great curve. The local wizard suggested following it closely and building the city wall in accordance with its route, and finally, the construction was successfully completed. Because large amount of earth was digged out for its construction, a large pool was formed, in which the turtle hid later. Therefore, Chengdu is also called Turtle City. Gao Pian (821−887), a famous general of the Tang Dynasty expanded the city in order increase its defensive functions, which people called Taixuan City or Luocheng City. In the Later Shu Dynasty, a city named Yangma with defensive functions was built outside Luocheng City. As Emperor Meng Chang (919−965) doted on the beautiful and literary lady Huarui, he ordered to plant hibiscus all over the city wall in order to win her favor. When in full bloom, the flower looks splendid. Therefore,

Tianfu Culture and the Modern Pursuit of Chengdu

Chengdu is called Hibiscus City or Rong City. With the development of brocade industry in the Han Dynasty and exporting of Shu brocade products, Chengdu began to have the nickname of "Jincheng" (City of Brocade). During the Three Kingdoms period (220-280), with the increased importance of Shu brocade to the national economy and people's livelihood in the Shu-Han Regime, an official was appointed especially responsible the management of brocade industry. Therefore, Chengdu is also called Jin Guan City (City with Brocade Officials). However, no matter how many and elegant these nicknames are, its official name has remained unchanged.

The name of this city has remained unchanged for more than 2,000 years for the following reasons:

Zhang Yi's initial choice of the city site was impeccable. This ensured that either the expansion or contract of the city would be conducted only within its original site, regardless of its rises and falls in history.

The city and its jurisdiction are always vivid memories that Chengdu was one of the five capitals of the Han Dynasty, the most prosperous city only next to Yangzhou in the Tang Dynasty, the "Southwest Metropolis" of the Song Dynasty, the "Capital City" of the Kaiming Dynasty and the national capitals of several subsequent political regimes.

The common memory and psychological consensus have been formed by the praise and boast of many well-known literary and artistic works.

In history, it has rarely become the center of the national political and military struggle, so it has not encountered any forced changes in position and name as many other cities did.

No change of its name since the completion of its construction shows that Chengdu has at least 2,300 years of consistent cultural traditions and people here are full of self-confidence and pride. This is very conducive to the inheritance and promotion of urban culture, and in the process of building a national central city that fully embodies the new development concept, it encourages future generations to emulate or surpass their ancestors in all aspects, dare to be the first and pursue excellence.

Chengdu hasn't changed its name for 2,300 years. It has the China-renovated status of

Chapter One
The Origin and Presentation of Tianfu Culture

the material and spiritual highland of the "Land of Abundance," where the people are naturally full of confidence in and pride of their regional culture, and have a strong sense of subject and responsibility for national and regional culture. One of the outstanding manifestations is that it is not only the birthplace of Chinese local chronicles, but also the cultural resort with the most developed cause of local chronicle compiling. Liang Qichao (1873–1929) had a very fine exposition of the unique value of local chronicles in Chinese culture, "China is so big that a place has its own characteristics deeply influenced by its heredity and environment; however, it is the concept of loving the homeland that is one of the key factors for the progress of unity of the people... The formation of local style of study is a solid foundation for the academic community."

Professor Liu Fusheng (1948–) of Sichuan University pointed out, "China has a long tradition of compiling local historical records, in which Sichuan occupies a unique position. The ancient history and culture of Sichuan have long attracted the attention of the local people... the compilation of local chronicles has become a tradition of Sichuan local culture. In the Ming Dynasty, *General Records of Sichuan* was compiled four times, and Cao Xuequan wrote *Shu Zhong Guang Ji*, in which all the stories and anecdotes of the Shu region were collected. In the Qing Dynasty, *Records of Sichuan* was compiled three times." Sichuan experienced great natural and man-made disasters in the late Ming and early Qing dynasties, and the extreme scarcity of aborigines almost led to the "cultural disruption." In the early Qing Dynasty, immigrants from more than a dozen of provinces came to Sichuan one after another, and quickly regained their consciousness as the cultural subject after they became masters of the land. According to the *Joint Catalogue of Chinese Local Chronicles* edited by the Beijing Observatory of the Chinese Academy of Sciences, 4,889 records were compiled in the Qing Dynasty, accounting for about 60% of the records compiled in previous dynasties. Sichuan ranked first with 416 records in the Qing Dynasty. In addition, of the 1,164 existing annals edited during the 50 years of Tongzhi, Guangxu and Xuantong reigns, Sichuan still tops the list with 121 records. This regional cultural character, which cherishes its own historical and cultural memories, has always been a strong support for the city's spirit of Innovation and Creation, Fashion and Elegance, Optimism and Tolerance, Kindness and Public Welfare.

Tianfu Culture and the Modern Pursuit of Chengdu

The Unique Charms of Tianfu Culture

"Culture" is a concept with ambiguous connotation and extension. It includes material, institutional and spiritual aspects, but its core should refer to human spiritual activities mainly represented by values and lifestyle. "Culture" is actually short for "humanity and edification" in Chinese. "Humanity" is the foundation and tool, including all kinds of material and non-material heritages carrying cultural genes and cultural connotations, as well as languages and characters; "edification" is the real focus of this phrase. Its main function is to establish the popular mainstream values and lifestyle, and to build and continue the personality and characteristics needed for the healthy development of a country or region. As far as the construction of cultural individuality is concerned, it is necessary to meet the requirements of strengthening the internal cohesion and external competitiveness of each country or region's own culture in today's globalization trend, and strive to form the core competitiveness and communication power of culture. Chengdu, which aims to build a world-famous cultural city, certainly has such a pursuit.

Effective expression and dissemination are indispensable for any culture to exert its power. This book holds that the distinct personality and special charm of Tianfu Culture should be recognized from the following seven aspects.

**Chapter One
The Origin and Presentation
of Tianfu Culture**

1. Chengdu with Confucianism – To Endow Later Generations with Determination, Persistence and Ambition to Make Contributions and Achievements

In September 2014, Chairman Xi Jinping pointed out in his speech at the International Academic Seminar held in the Great Hall of the People in Beijing to commemorate the 2565th anniversary of Confucius's birth, "The doctrine of Confucianism founded by Confucius and the Confucian thoughts developed on this basis have had a profound impact on Chinese civilization and are an important part of Chinese traditional culture. Confucianism, together with other thoughts and cultures produced in the process of the formation and development of the Chinese nation, records the spiritual activities, rational thinking and cultural achievements of the Chinese nation in its struggle to build its homeland since ancient times. It reflects the spiritual pursuit of the Chinese nation and is important nourishment for the Chinese nation's continuous growth and development. The Chinese civilization has not only had a profound impact on China's development, but also made significant contributions to the progress of human civilization."

The Confucian culture, which was created by Confucius (551-479 BC) in the Spring and Autumn Period and has eventually become the core value system of the Chinese nation and even the entire East Asian ethnic groups, was the first in the world history to construct the sense of a community with a shared future for mankind, on the basis of which each nation develop its own education and academic culture. Confucianism emphasizes the value of human life, human dignity and ways to realize them. Facing all internal and external troubles, natural and man-made disasters of his ethnic group, he should stand up and actively respond. The loyalty, filial piety, integrity, benevolence, propriety, wisdom and faith it advocates have become the value pursuit of the national stability of China and East Asian countries. Confucianism became the country's highest ideology through the efforts of the great scholar Dong Zhongshu (179-104 BC) and others during the reign of Emperor Wu of the Han Dynasty (156-87 BC). Almost simultaneously, it was introduced to the Shu region when Wen Weng (156-110 BC) came to Chengdu to govern the Shu Prefecture and establish schools. Wen Weng became the founder

Tianfu Culture and the Modern Pursuit of Chengdu

and principal of the first local government school in Chinese history. Because of this great deed of his and beneficial to next generations, the great historian Ban Gu (32−92) commented in *Han Shu (History of the Han Dynasty)*, "The Ba-Shu has been so refined thanks to Wen Weng's edification with Confucianism."

Zhong Zhaopeng (1925−2014) of the Chinese Academy of Social Sciences even compared the status of Wen Weng to that of Confucius in the education history. He said, "Confucius established a private school to extend education to the common people. Wen Weng established schools in the Shu Prefecture, and later schools were established in almost in all the counties and prefectures in China. Confucius and Wen Weng are both memorable figures in the history of education." Professor Shu Dagang of Sichuan University further pointed out, "Wen Weng started the history of schools run by local governments, which has not only promoted the rapid Confucianization of Sichuan, but also promoted the spread of Confucianism throughout the country... It was the most representative achievement of the 'Shu Studies' in the Han Dynasty that among the 'four *Han Fu* schools,' there were three from the Shu region, and Sima Xiangru, Yang Xiong and Wang Bao were all famous *Ci Fu* writers and skilled scholars... In particular, the core values of 'nature-obeyedness, morality, benevolence, righteousness and norms of etiquettes' put forward by Wang Bao, Yan Zun, Yang Xiong and others have basically laid the foundation for the combination of theory and practice, the unity of spiritual and material worlds, especially the integration of studies of Confucianism, Taoism and other schools in the Shu Studies of past generations."

The profound cultural heritage of Confucianism has produced many leading talents in Chengdu, who keep pace with the times in the enrichment, development, efficient education and dissemination of Confucianism in China. Professor Su Pinxiao (1969−) of Sichuan University, through his systematical combing and study of Chengdu Official School in the Song Dynasty, pointed out, "Chengdu Official School became the largest local school in the country at that time. That's why Historian Li Xinchuan (1166−1243) wrote more than a decade later, 'Chengdu has the best school.'" The "Three Treasures of Shu Studies" greatly praised by scholars and scholar-officials in the Song Dynasty is the sign that the spread of Confucian theories and thoughts in Chengdu has grown into a unique towering tree, especially benefiting from the sustained and healthy development of Chengdu Official School in the Song Dynasty.

Lü Tao (1028-1104), a well-known official, praised and said, "The Shu Studies is so flourishing and famous in China as to pass on to one generation after another. There are three things worth of mentioning, one is Shishi School funded by Wen Weng, another is the Ritual Hall of Zhougong, and the third is the Nine Classics on the Stone Wall." Shi Shi School and the Ritual Hall are the brilliant palaces of Confucian education and cultural dissemination in the Han Dynasty in Chengdu, while the "Nine Classics on the Stone Wall" refers to the unprecedented stone-carving project of the main Confucian classics presided over and completed by Prime Minister of the Later Shu Dynasty, Wu Zhaoyi. With the joint efforts of officials and people of Chengdu in the Southern and the Northern Song dynasties, the "Thirteen Classics of Shi Shi" engraved in Shishi School was finally completed with a far-reaching influence. When Song Ningzong (1168-1224) was in power, Chengdu Prefect Wu Lie (1130-1213) built the ancestral hall of Zhou Dunyi, Cheng Hao and Cheng Yi, three famous officials of a Confucian school of idealist philosophy, together with the worship of Zhu Xi and Zhang Shi. These are all important creations in the construction, enrichment, development and dissemination of Chinese theories and thoughts.

As for the humanistic landscapes that advocate to the general public the core values of loyalty, filial piety, integrity, propriety, benevolence, righteousness, courtesy, wisdom and faith, apart from various single memorial buildings, memorial archways and inscriptions, there are countless examples from Wen Weng Stone Chamber to the Temple of Marquis Wu, from Du Fu's Thatched Cottage to Xinjin's Chunyang Temple, from Xindu's Guihu Park, Sheng'an Ancestral Hall to Yang Yuchun's General Office in Chongzhou, from Zhuxi Ancestral Hall in Longquanyi District to Confucian Temple in Yanhua Garden of Chongzhou.

Supported by developed education, scholarship, enlightenment and talents, Chengdu has, in fact, contributed countless emotional worlds with love and loyalty as the core to China since

Tianfu Culture and the Modern Pursuit of Chengdu

the Han Dynasty, and nurtured a lot of talents who took the achievements of perfect virtues, good deeds and immortal works as the basis of their outlook on life, and ancient classics, arts, and education as their main interest and hobbies, such as clean officials, scholars, literati, masters of classics, loyal ministers, righteous men, Confucian businessmen, village sages, and famous doctors, as well as skillful craftsmen, filial sons and virtuous grandchildren, and virtuous women who could benefit the native place and set a good example for local people.

In the history of China, regarding the most touching chapter expressing the core values of Confucianism, "Memorial on Sending Out the Troops" by Zhuge Liang and "Memorial of Pettitions" by Li Mi (224-287, from Sichuan) of the Western Jin Dynasty are regarded as rare and most sincere words in the world and a model of "loyalty" and "filial piety." Zhao Yushi, a scholar of the Song Dynasty said in "Notes of Guests' Departure" that those who read the former without tears must not be loyal, while those who read the latter without tears must not be filial. These two articles were both completed in Chengdu.

As the old saying goes, more often, generals were from the Ba area, while scholars from the Shu region. It is correct on the whole, but it cannot conceal the fact that Chengdu also saw the emergence of a group of outstanding commanders in the Qing Dynasty, such as Yue Zhongqi (1686-1754), Yang Yuchun (1761-1837) and others, who were not only good at strategies, but also brave and made outstanding contributions to quell the country's serious internal and external troubles. Yue Zhongqi, a native of Chengdu and the 21st generation of Yue Fei, was the main hero in quelling many separatist rebellions in Southwest and Northwest China (rebellions from Cewang Arabotan of Kingdom Jungar, Rob Zangdanjin of Tribe Heshuote, and the Chieftains of Great Jinchuan, etc.) in the three reigns of Kangxi, Yongzheng and Qianlong, and successively served as Sichuan Prefect and Shaanxi-Gansu Governor. In his whole life, regardless of his honor or disgrace, he was loyal to the king and devoted himself to serving the country. In his later years, he entertained himself in his poems and fields. He was really a typical general of Confucian grace. Yang Yuchun, a native of Chongzhou, Chengdu, was born in a military family. He was ordered many times to pacify rebellions and mutinies all over the country

**Chapter One
The Origin and Presentation
of Tianfu Culture**

with immortal merits, especially as a commander in chief to pacify Jaganir's (?-1828) rebellion, supported by Britain and trying to split Xinjiang from China. He was also a model of Confucian loyalty and courage in serving the country. Today, his former residence is preserved relatively intact in Chongzhou.

In the Second World War, facing the invading of Japanese fascism, Sichuan people devoted themselves to serving the country, made great sacrifices for the Chinese nation and made irreplaceable contributions by providing more than 3.5 million soldiers and taking part in almost all the important battles in the front battlefield as an important role at the price of the wounded and dead of more than 640,000. Among the Sichuan generals who died for their country, General Wang Mingzhang (1893-1938, from Chengdu Xindu) (Fig.13), who established extraordinary achievements in the Battle of Taierzhuang (1938), told his superior in the cable, "Determined to fight to death for the country!" What supported General Li Jiayu (1892-1944 from Pujiang, Chengdu) in the battlefield was his fervent cry at the expedition conference: "When the nation is in crisis, every man should stand out to fight to death as a soldier." They, inclusive of the above-mentioned Yin Cangling, are permeated with the Confucian character of sacrificing one's life for the sake of national safety.

In a word, the determination, persistence and ambition to make contributions based on the strong national feelings of Confucianism are the most important spirit of Tianfu Culture and the main basis for Chengdu to be full of creativity and fighting spirit all the time.

Fig. 13 General Wang Mingzhang

2. Chengdu with Buddhism – To Cultivate Later Generations' Feelings of Compassion, Kindness and Equality Toward Their Fellow Countrymen

Buddhism was introduced to China and Chengdu in the Eastern Han Dynasty. After a stormy journey from the Eastern Han Dynasty to the Wei, Jin and Southern and Northern dynasties, it was basically Sinicized in the Sui and Tang dynasties. Buddhism is the study of governing the mind. Its values of compassion, equality of all living beings, law of karma, purified mindedness, boundless benevolence, the cycle of death and rebirth, etc. have become an important supplement to Chinese culture because they advocate people's cleanness, peace and kindness. Because of its unique wisdom and function in solving the relationship between people and their hearts, it also has important influence on Chinese traditional philosophy, aesthetics, literature, art and the life way of some Chinese people. In the long history of nearly 2,000 years, Chengdu is the center of Buddhist activities and spread of Buddhism in the upper reaches of the Yangtze River, has created brilliant Buddhist cultural and artistic achievements, and in turn, Buddhism has also greatly enriched the connotation of Tianfu Culture. Compared with other cities, Buddhism in Chengdu has the following characteristics.

(1) A Long History with Many Famous Temples

As the center of the Land of Abundance, and located in the best geographical and transportation position along the Northern and the Southern Silk Roads and the Yangtze River Economic Belt, Chengdu has witnessed the development history of Buddhism theories and studies from its taking root, sprouting and growing almost completely synchronized with that of the Central Plains and the South. Professor Duan Yuming (1958–) of Sichuan University pointed out, "Chengdu, with its unique geographical advantages, is one of the earliest areas where Buddhism was introduced, and had long attracted the special attention of experts and scholars such as P. Pelliot and Liang Qichao. Buddhism in Chengdu had made great progress during the two Jin dynasties, and 'become an independent and regular popular faith.' To the Southern and Northern dynasties, the continuous disputes and turbulences in the Western Regions and the

Chapter One
The Origin and Presentation of Tianfu Culture

Central Plains brought about greater opportunities for the development of Ba-Shu Buddhism in the remote Southwest. With countless eminent monks who fled chaos and came to the Shu region, the Buddhist level of local monks was improved unprecedentedly and the number of temples, monks, nuns and believers soared. Based on this background, Buddhism in Chengdu area developed rapidly and became one of the famous Buddhist cultural centers in the country." This position was further strengthened in the Tang and Song dynasties, and has been basically maintained since the Yuan and Ming dynasties.

During the Song and Yuan dynasties, when Zen School of Buddhism became the mainstream of Chinese Buddhism, Zen in Chengdu was a very important component of Chinese Buddhism, with its great arhats in large numbers and far-reaching influences. There are countless Buddhist temples in history, which form an important part of the spiritual home, urban life and urban and rural landscapes of ancient and modern officials and common peoples. All the existing Buddhist temples have a long history and are of high status. Daci Temple in Chengdu was called as "The Biggest Habitat of Monks in China" and so named after a plaque written by Emperor Xuanzong (685-762) of the Tang Dynasty. According to Song Zhipan's *Comprehensive History of Buddhism*, when Emperor Xuanzong took refuge in Chengdu, Eunuch Gao Lishi reported, "Monk Ying Gan was offering porridge to the poor at the street corner in the south of city, saying, 'May the national fortune be back again and the territory restored. I would like to set up a temple in the east of the city to pray for my country.' The emperor was pleased, granted the plaque together with 1,000 *mu* of land, and ordered Wuxiang, a Zen master from Kingdom of Xinluo (Koryo), to establish rules and regulations for it."

Later, when Emperor Wuzong of the Tang Dynasty suppressed Buddhism, the temple survived just because of the plaque. Zhaojue Temple, known as the "First Buddhist habitat in Western Sichuan," was the base where Zen Master Keqin (1063-1135) of the Song Dynasty carried forward the practice of sitting in meditation of Yang Qi Branch of Linji Sect of Zen Buddhism, which is still regarded as the ancestral court by the Japanese Linji Sect. Shijing Temple in Longquanyi of Chengdu was the center of spreading Duanqiao's meditation method of Linji Sect of Zen Buddhism in the early Ming Dynasty, also a place to practice the Vajracchedika-sutra, a holy place for both esoteric and exoteric Zen sects. Wenshu Temple and Baoguang Temple were among the four great Buddhist temples in the Yangtze River Basin and highly respected. In its heyday, there were more than 100 temples in Mount Tiantai of Qionglai, and the "Religious Court" was even more conspicuous. Tiexiang Temple was the only place for nuns to practice the Vajracchedika-sutra among the seven places founded by Master Nenghai in modern times. Aidao Nunnery is a famous Buddhist nunnery in modern times, and the center for female Buddhist believers in the western Sichuan Plain to conduct Buddhist services or rituals. Located in the south of Chengdu, E'mei Mountain, one of the four famous Buddhist mountains in China and reputed as "Silver E'mei," is the bodhimandala of Samantabhadra Bodhisattva (a place where Samantabhadra Bodhisattva propagated Buddhist doctrine).

(2) Eminent Monks Emerging as the Models for Ages

Since Buddhism was introduced to Chengdu, there have been countless eminent monks of all ages. They have made outstanding contributions to Chinese Buddhism with their wisdom, merits and virtues. In addition to the legend of Monk Baozhang, which is difficult to accurately identify, the first eminent monks who lived in Chengdu should be Sengsheng and Huichi during the Eastern Jin Dynasty (317-420). The former's secular surname was Yuan, born in Pixian County of Sichuan. Buddhist literature claimed that he became a monk when he was young and was famous for his asceticism. Later, at the request of Song Feng and others in Chengdu, he became the master of Sanxian Temple, reciting "Hokkekyo" and practicing meditation. It was said that tigers came to listen to him and the gods guarded him on the both sides when he was chanting sutras in the mountains. He died a man of great ambition and encouragement. The latter's secular surname was Jia, born in Loufan County of Yanmen Prefecture (now Ningwu, Shanxi). He was the younger brother of the famous monk Huiyuan. At the age of 18, he became a monk with his brother Huiyuan, practicing Buddhism under Shi Daoan, well reading various Buddhist and other religious classics. Later, he went to Lushan Mountain with Huiyuan to study

Chapter One
The Origin and Presentation of Tianfu Culture

"Hokkekyo" and Abhidharma. In the 3rd year of Long'an in the Eastern Jin Dynasty (399), hearing that in the Ba-Shu, land was fertile, people were rich, and Mount E'mei was beautiful, Huichi desiring to expand his outlook, went west to Chengdu and stayed advocating Buddhism in Longyuan Temple. The prefectural governor Mao Qu (?-405) highly praised him. At that time, there were some monks, like Huiyan and Senggong, who had gained quite a reputation in Chengdu, but after Huichi came, all the monks and laymen in the Shu region showed respect and admiration towards him. Anyone who could visit him in the temple hall was called "Climbing Longmen" (metaphorically, to increase one's value through the reception or introduction of famous people).

During the Northern and Southern dynasties (420-589), thanks to the efforts of a large number of eminent monks represented by Sengya and Baoyu, Chengdu had the same level of Buddhist doctrine studies as that of the Northern and Southern areas where Buddhism was prevalent. More typically, the famous monk Chen Xuanzang (602-664), who went west to India to seek scriptures, studied and later was initiated into monkhood in Chengdu's Daci Temple between the ages of 18 and 22. Chengdu became the birthplace of his Vijnanamatrasiddhistra (Everything in the world is only what one thinks), and the place where the foundation for his general Buddhist system of encyclopedia style was laid. Xuanzang chose to study Buddhist disciplines for five years in Chengdu, for at that time there gathered eminent monks from all directions. In fact, it was a metropolis where Buddhism of various sects and the Northern and Southern cultures mingled, providing Xuanzang with favorable conditions for "benefiting from many famous masters" and blending various cultural materials. From the Sui Dynasty to the Song Dynasty, the political situation in Chengdu was relatively stable and the society was peaceful. Monks from all over the country went to Sichuan to avoid chaos and Buddhism in Chengdu continued to develop. After Zen came into being, the contribution of Sichuan monks was even greater. Men of insight said, "Those who would talk about the Shu region must know about Zen, and those who would judge Zen must know about the Shu region."

Many eminent monks, such as Xuanjian, Daoyi, Zongmi, Fayan, Qingyuan, Keqin,

Tianfu Culture and the Modern Pursuit of Chengdu

Chongxian, Shifan, Zhuxian, Daolong, Qingliao, Shaoqi, Chuiwan, Haiming, etc., are all shining in history, who created Buddhism schools, founded temples, promoted Buddhism or spread it to foreign countries. Interestingly, the saying that Chengdu is a city "you will never want to leave once you come" was also applicable to eminent monks then. Many monks from other provinces and foreign countries chose to settle in Chengdu. For example, in the Former Shu Dynasty, Guan Xiu (832–912), a famous poet monk and painter from Lanxi, Zhejiang Province, met his vigorous period of creation in Chengdu and was finally buried in the East Zen Temple of Chengdu. Zen Master Wawu Nengguang, a Japanese, came to Chengdu in the Later Shu Dynasty and lived in Biji Square for more than 30 years. In the Tang Dynasty, the "golden prince" from the royal family of Silla crossed to China and stayed at Dechun Temple in Zizhong, Sichuan to study the southern sect of Zen from the "Tang monk" Chuji, and later lived in Jingzhong Temple in Chengdu, where he founded the Jingzhong Zen Sect; later, his disciple Wuzhu established Wuzhu Zen Sect. Wuzhu Zen Sect of Baotang Temple was once spread far to the Qinghai-Tibet Plateau and influenced Tibetan Buddhism.

During the Ming and Qing dynasties, with the overall downward shift of the focus of Buddhism, Buddhist monks showed far greater enthusiasm in benefiting the world than that of the study of Buddhist theories and self perfection, and there were fewer eminent monks and great master than those of the previous dynasties, and the level of their Buddhist theories was not as high as that of the previous dynasties. In spite of the difficult maintenance of Buddhism, eminent monks and famous masters, though they were few, still played a very important role in pushing forward the sustainable development of Buddhism. Among them, the eminent monks in Chengdu, such as Shaoqi, Tongzui, Chegang, Jueling, etc. were the standouts as a highlight of recent Buddhism in Chengdu, forming the Chushan and Zhangxue Zen systems centered on Shaoqi and Tongzui respectively, which have deeply influenced the development of Buddhism in Chengdu.

Since the Republic of China, Buddhism in Chengdu has still seen the emergence of eminent and great Buddhist monks and masters, such as Master Foyuan (1853–1926), who initiated the expansion of Buddhist influence and reform in modern Chengdu; Master Xuecen (1841–1914), who wrote the first Buddhist history textbook *A Brief History of Buddhism* in the period of the Republic of China; Master Liu Zhuyuan (1875–1950), who brought the expounding of Buddhism texts and research in Chengdu to a new high; Master Nenghai (1886–1967), who made the focus of Buddhism in Chengdu move from Buddhist theories only to the combination of theory and practice; Master Fazun (1902–1980), who was reputed for being "Good at both Han and Tibetan cultures"; Master Taixu and Lay Buddhist Ouyang Jingwu, who, with their disciples of Wang Enyang, Meng Wentong, Han Wenwa, etc., created and promoted the doctrine of Vijnanamatrasiddhistra (Everything in the world is just what one thinks); Famous Lay Buddhist Yuan Huanxian (1887–1966), who aimed at the integration of the three religions with many writings and the influence of Weimo Temple he presided over for many years with his disciples of Nan Huaijin, Yang Guangdai, Xu Jianqiu, Wu Suonan, Tian Zhaopu, etc. In 1930 and 1938, the Buddhist and secular circles including various famous schools in Chengdu ceremoniously welcomed Master Taixu (1890–1947), the pioneer of the modern Buddhist reform in China and the most famous eminent monk in the Republic of China, to Chengdu to propagate Buddhism (staying in Wenshu Temple). And this event is a vivid portrayal that Chengdu has always been the fertile soil for breeding and attracting eminent monks and great masters.

(3) A Missionary Center for Admirable Propagation of Buddhism

From the Tang Dynasty to the Qing Dynasty, Chengdu was the center of missionary works and dissemination of Buddhist doctrines in Sichuan. Professor Duan Yuming pointed out, Buddhism and Chengdu's social life had been closely linked in the Sui and Tang dynasties. With a number of famous temples such as Konghui Temple, Jingzhong Temple and Daci Temple as the core temples, the constant propagating Buddhist doctrines by eminent monks and great masters became the main content of the belief life of Chengdu's scholars and ordinary people. According to Buddhist documents, as early as in the Xiao Liang's Reign (502–557) of the Southern Dynasty, there were so many missionary works and activities in Chengdu that

Tianfu Culture and the Modern Pursuit of Chengdu

three or four events were often held at the same time, when "one lecture came after another in competition with deafening drum sounds." When Master Huishao held lectures on Buddhism in major temples after he stationed in Chengdu, the audience was very large and like an endless flow of rivers. On this basis, Huishao also organized a special group of followers, who chanted the sutras and gathered several times a year. Following this tradition, eminent monks Huijing, Daoji, Bao Siam, Daoxian, Daozhen and others also held Buddhist lectures respectively in major temples after they came to Chengdu during the Sui and Tang dynasties, "with hundreds of people under the platform." This attracted not only a large number of Chengdu believers, but also the Xuanzang brothers and others to Sichuan. Typically, Daoyin's lectures on the *Vimalakīrti Sutra* in Chengdu often attracted more than 1,000 people. Therefore, some scholars believe that by the time of Sui and Tang dynasties, Chengdu had become one of the centers of Buddhist propagating.

In the heyday of the Tang Dynasty, Zen Master Wuxiang would propagate Buddhism in Chengdu's Jingzhong Temple in the first and last months of each year with the audience of about "ten thousand of followers." In the Middle Tang, Master Zhixuan was invited to propagate Buddhist sutras in Daci Temple by Du Yuanying (775–838), Prime Minister during his inspection of the Shu State. He was attended by a large number of monks and laymen of up to ten thousand, and was called "Bodhisattva Chen." Obviously, listening to eminent monks' propagating Buddhist doctrines in temples and joining in some organizations of followers or taking part in Buddhist activities became a way of life of Chengdu scholars and people. At the same time, as a rare public space in ancient times, temples with magnificent buildings and deep courtyards were gradually becoming leisure and entertainment places for them.

The magnanimity of Chengdu culture is also clearly reflected in missionary works; for example, a kind of theory can be taught by different people and in various ways at the same time in Chengdu. In the Southern Dynasty, Monks Baohai and Baoyuan from Langzhong and Zhifang from Zizhong were giving lectures on the "Satyasiddhisastra" in Chengdu at the same time at Xiexi Temple, Luotiangong Temple and Longyuan Temple respectively. During the Song

**Chapter One
The Origin and Presentation
of Tianfu Culture**

Dynasty, there were as many as 73 long-term lectures given by various courts of Daci Temple (Fig. 14-1, Fig.14-2). In the Song Dynasty, Chengdu Zhaojue Temple got great development because of Yuanwu's two stays, especially his special relationship with officials and celebrities, as well as his rich experience in temple construction and management accumulated from his stays in various temples, and he himself was referred to as the "Buddhist Saint." Masters of Huiyuan, Baoyin, Wenyan, Daozu, Daoyue, etc. were all his disciples during his second stay in Zhaojue Temple. It can be seen how the relaxing environment promoted the flourishing of Buddhism and its studies in Chengdu at that time.

Fig. 14-1 Daci Temple

Fig. 14-2 Daci Temple

(4) The Everlasting Exquisite Art and Literature

The exquisite art and literature are the characteristic of Chengdu Culture, and this is the same to Chengdu monks. For example, during the Five Dynasties, Chengdu, as the capital of the Former and the Latter Shu States, was in a relatively stable environment. The kings in that period also highly praised art and advocated culture and education. As a result, a group of so-called "poem monks" and "art monks" appeared, among whom Guanxiu (832-912) was the most famous, significantly influencing the history of Chinese art and representing another development type of Chengdu Zen monks. *Bi Yan Ji* by Yuanwu Keqin (1063-1135) in the Song

Chapter One
The Origin and Presentation of Tianfu Culture

Dynasty, praised by Japanese Zen circle as "the first sutra of Zen Buddhism," with each word a gem and full of Zen flavor. Up to then, the Literal Zen had reached its peak. Zhangxue Tongzui (1610-1695), the abbot of Zhaojue Temple in the Qing Dynasty, wrote *Records of Zen Temples Along Jinjiang River*, the only records about temples of a province. Yin Bangzhi referred to Zen master's literary talent as "Literary Character," as he put it, "From the standpoint of Zen, 'Literary Character,' different from the general 'expounding the texts of Buddhism,' refers to the method of practicing Buddhism through classics and writings… Without the 'Literary Character' of Zen masters in the Ba-Shu, the history of Chinese Zen would be rewritten." It can be concluded that it has made contributions in religion, history and culture.

Even Chengdu lay people were also inclined to writing as Buddhism upholders; for example, Fei Changfang in the Sui Dynasty wrote *The Three Treasures of Past Dynasties*, Zhang Shangying (1043-1121), Prime Minister of the Song Dynasty, wrote *On Custody of Buddha Dharma*, and Yang Shen (1488-1559), a top scholar in the Ming Dynasty, wrote *Poetry Anthology of Zen*, all of which advocated that Buddhism was beneficial to popular feelings and helpful to civilization.

Chengdu is one of the cradles of engraving printing. The earliest extant printed article in the world is the *Dharani Sutra* of the Tang Dynasty unearthed in Chengdu. A stone tablet of sutras of the Tang Dynasty was found at Lingyan Temple in Dujiangyan, Chengdu. The unearthed stone tablets have inscriptions on both sides, including the *Mahaparinivana Sutra*, the *Moon Lamp Samadhi Sutra*, the *Abhiseka Sutra*, etc. In the 4th year of Kaibao's Reign (971) of the Northern Song Dynasty, the *Tripitaka Sutra* began to be carved in Yizhou (Chengdu), and was completed in 983, with 130,000 wooden plates. This is not only the first official-carved *Tripitaka Sutra* in the history of Chinese Buddhism, but also the first wooden version of the *Tripitaka Sutra*, and therefore, called *"Kaibao Tripitaka"* in history. Its neat layout, excellent carving and beautiful writing have exerted a great influence on its various editions of Koroy, Khitan, Zhaocheng and Kasuga of Japan.

Temple towers in Chengdu also have their own characteristics. The towers built in the Tang Dynasty still exist today, such as the 17-layer square dense-eaves brick tower in Longxing Temple of Pengxian County, the pagoda of Baoguang Temple in Xindu, etc. The stone tower in Dabei Temple of Qionglai was built in the Song Dynasty, with beautiful curves and in unique shape. The modern Sarira Pagoda in Longxing Temple of Pengxian County, built in imitation of India's Buddha Pagoda, is very distinctive. Baoguang Temple with a layout of the early legacy of China and its Arhat Hall with 577 marvelous and famous sculptures are the best-preserved architectural complex and statue group of the Qing Dynasty in Sichuan, representing a very high level of Buddhist art development in Chengdu. During the Song and Qi Kingdoms, famous monk Xuanchang traveled west from Jingzhou to Dashi Temple in Chengdu and painted 16 pictures of Guhyapāda vajrah (Buddha's warrior attendants). Thousands of murals in Daci Temple are world-famous. More than 60 first-class painters such as Wu Daozi, Lu Lengjia, Huang Quan and his son have all painted exquisite masterpieces, representing the highest level of Chinese painting in the Tang and Song dynasties. In the Tang and Song dynasties, the murals of Longyuan Temple were also very famous. Murals completed in 1468, the fourth year of Chenghua's Reign in the Ming Dynasty, still remained intact in the Guanyin Hall and Pilu Hall in Guananyin Temple, Xinjin (Fig.15-1, Fig.15-2). Today, there are many murals of the Ming Dynasty in the main hall of Yongquan Temple in Pengxian County, Longzang Temple in Xindu County and Jiangshahe Temple in Pujiang County. Chengdu murals are rich in content and of high artistic value.

(5) Integrating with Life and Nourishing Local Customs

Buddhism is closely related to the material and spiritual life of Chengdu officials and citizens in various forms, and with rich connotations and regional characteristics. Together with Confucianism and Taoism, Buddhism has shaped the city's humane character of magnanimity, relaxation and charity. In particular, together with Taoism, it has jointly built a broad platform for Chengdu's leisure culture and greatly enriched the connotation of leisure culture (including leisure politics).

Chapter One
The Origin and Presentation of Tianfu Culture

Fig. 15-1 Murals completed in 1468 in the Guanyin Hall   Fig. 15-2 Murals completed in 1468 in the Guanyin Hall

In the special chapter of "Buddhism and Chengdu's Social Life" in *General History of Buddhism in Chengdu*, Professor Duan Yuming listed many historical facts and pointed out, "During the Sui and Tang dynasties, Buddhism and Chengdu's social life were already closely linked... Obviously, listening to eminent monks' propagating Buddhist doctrines in temples and joining in some organizations of followers or taking part in Buddhist activities became a way of life of Chengdu scholars and common people. At the same time, as a rare public space in ancient times, temples with magnificent buildings and deep courtyards are gradually becoming leisure and entertainment places for them." "In the Five and Song dynasties, Buddhism had more close relationship with the social life of Chengdu people, from which many unique folk

Tianfu Culture and the Modern Pursuit of Chengdu

customs of festivals developed." Taking Daci Temple as an example, he pointed out, "From the Tang and Five Dynasties and to the Song Dynasty, Daci Temple was not only a famous Buddhist temple in Chengdu, but also the center of the social life of Chengdu's scholars and common people. Its close relationship with the cultural, economic and leisure life of Chengdu people further shows the details of the influence of Buddhist culture on Chengdu people's social life."

The magnificent and beautiful buildings and various treasures and artworks in Daci Temple, including the unique and fine murals, the sculptures of man and Buddhist "God" in coexistence, and Buddha's metacarpal relics – one of the five treasures of the Buddha, have made it a museum of art. In this way, Daci Temple is no longer a sacred space for Buddhist followers, but also a cultural space shared by Chengdu scholars and common people, occupying an indispensable position in the cultural life of Chengdu people in the Song and Yuan dynasties. Daci Temple in the Song and Yuan dynasties was always one of the largest markets in Chengdu. At the same time, Daci Temple Market was also a center of sources of knowledge and culture, because people of all kinds mingling there would inevitably bring to it information, knowledge and cultural exchanges. People in the Song and Yuan dynasties would seek different news from one another. Master Qiaokai, famous for his erudition and indifference to fame and wealth, went to find unheard-of knowledge at Daci Temple every day to enrich his own; therefore, he was known as "Daci Immortal" for his extensive knowledge. When the brothers Cheng Hao (1032–1085) and Cheng Yi (1033–1107), masters of Neo-Confucianism, were in the Shu region, they were taught in studies of *Book of Changes* in Daci Temple. Daci Temple, as one of the most bustling places of entertainment in Chengdu, endowed people with various forms and connotations of activities, including listening to sutras and worshipping Buddha, visiting temples and statues, buying things and watching plays, dining and drinking, drinking tea and gossiping, watching lamps and the moon, watching the city from the high towers, enjoying the cool there in summer. It can be seen how deeply and comprehensively Buddhism integrated into the life of the ancient people and nourished the local customs in Chengdu.

As for the influence of Buddhism on the personality and charm of Chengdu city, Professor

Chapter One
The Origin and Presentation of Tianfu Culture

Duan Yuming made a wonderful summary: "Buddhism is a religion that teaches people how to be merciful, 'Be merciful to all living creatures, whether they are related to you or not.' Buddhism is also a religion that teaches people to how to be free and easy, 'Do it when you think it right to do, without consideration of personal gains and losses.'" Taking a bath of nearly 2,000 years of Buddhist grace, Chengdu has had a compassionate, free and easy urban cultural character. When a disaster came, people of the whole city helped one another; after a disaster, they still lived free and easy, neither blamed fate and others nor showed off their deeds. This rare cultural character is not only an expression of Chengdu's maturity, but also a confidence for a better future... In the academic history of China, the Shu Studies shined brilliantly every time the academic circles in the Central Plains were in trouble. Nourished from it, Chengdu has a calm, self-confident and inclusive cultural character, which has brought to Chengdu a very valuable gift – Never worship foreign things, nor be blindly arrogant."

In a word, in Chengdu, a particularly open and tolerant city, Buddhism and Confucianism developed and spread in parallel, which not only shaped the humane and religious feelings of compassion, kindness and equality among compatriots, but also greatly increased the optimistic tolerance of the city and the happiness index of the production and life of officials and citizens. In addition, public welfare and charitable undertakings in ancient and modern Chengdu could not do without the participation of Buddhist organizations, eminent monks and believers, who have played an important role in it.

3. Chengdu with Taoism – To Achieve the Romantic, Free and Leisurely Lifestyle of Individuals

Different from the Central Plains, where Buddhism worship was the mainstream besides Confucian culture, the "Tao" was popular in Chengdu area. Mount Heming, located in Dayi, Chengdu, is the birthplace of Taoism. Till today, it has kept a strong touch of Taoist culture. Taoist holy places such as Qingcheng Mountain and Mount Heming are also popular tourist destinations for Chinese and foreign tourists. Compared with Confucianism and Buddhism,

Tianfu Culture and the Modern Pursuit of Chengdu

Taoism and Taoist culture in Tianfu Chengdu are basically in the same position, and this fact has not only made the Chengdu Plain the center of the spread of Chinese Taoist culture and produce many important Taoist leaders and preserved Taoist classics, but also deeply integrated with the values and lifestyle of the people there. The accompanying martial arts, medicine, health preservation, music, food and wine with Taoist flavor and strength of character have enriched the unique connotation of the Ba-Shu civilization and culture. The city's character expressed in Chinese words of leisureliness, open-mindedness, optimism, elegancy is deeply rooted in the Ba-Shu civilization, and condensed and specifically manifested in Tianfu Culture; that is, it calls for love of and closeness to nature, individual's physical and mental freedom, a flexible life attitude, and a leisurely life and work style. Literati and scholars generally have extraordinary imagination and creativity characterized by thought of "immortality." Romantic literature and art masters and their brilliant works constitute the most personalized landscape of the innovation and creation, fashion and elegance of Tianfu Culture, which is always the best example in China. Meanwhile, it forms the simple, generous and inclusive customs and styles of the officials and people there. The above-mentioned humanistic resources closely related to Taoist Schools and Taoism are the cultural and social psychological foundation of the lifestyle with higher happiness index for the common people, and the creative source of popular and elegant works by officials, scholar-officials and celebrities on the basis of their knowledge of Confucianism and Taoism.

For example, it has been a major feature of Chengdu people since ancient times that they are close to nature and like sightseeing sceneries in mountains and rivers. For example, Su Shi (1037-1101, from Meishan, Sichuan) wrote after visiting a silkworm market in Chengdu (an old custom in Sichuan. In spring, 15 silkworm markets would be open for people to sell and buy silkworms, flowers, trees, fruits and medicinal materials, and to play as well), "Visitors here were too delighted to go home." After observing the life of Chengdu people, he and his younger brother Su Zhe (1039-1112) described, "People are tired of the high city walls; noisily, they rush out in the early morning." Feizhu, from Shuangliu in the Yuan Dynasty wrote in *Records of Local*

Chapter One
The Origin and Presentation of Tianfu Culture

Customs, "Chengdu is more popular in recreational activities than other places of the western Sichuan, thanks to its custom of entertainment and its vast territory and rich resources." Popular entertainment is a major feature of the Ba-Shu people, and played to full in Chengdu. Therefore, the Ba-Shu people had formed its tourism custom earlier, which reached its peak in the Tang and Song dynasties. As far as Chengdu was concerned, there were 23 regular recreational activities throughout the year then, such as river tours, mountain tours, temple tours, and country tours, and they often gathered out with singing, dancing, entertainment, sports, and business activities all the time, with rich cultural connotations and good economic benefits.

Chen Yuanliang, a Fujian native of the Southern Song Dynasty, wrote in his book *General Records of Festivals*, "According to the customs in Sichuan, the second day of the second month of the traditional Chinese calendar was the Country Sightseeing Festival, when all the people went out in an endless stream for sightseeing, singing and drinking behind the curtain, and scattering everywhere in the suburbs." This recreational custom of being close to and returning to nature has been passed down from generation to generation, developed into the largest leisure tourism industry in China – Farmhouse Resorts (Agritainment) represented by Peach Blossom Festivals of Sansheng Township, Nongke Village and Longquanyi District and integrated with sightseeing natural scenery, tasting local flavors and protecting animals and plants. It has become the most popular business card of Chengdu for its innovation, entrepreneurship, kindness and mutual assistance, the inheritance of historical context, rational use of resources, embodiment of the green development concept, and manifestation of the grass-rooted quality of the city.

Another example is the well-developed and profound Doctrine of Immortality in the Western Shu, which mainly came from the beliefs of Taoist Schools and Taoism to pursue the realm and goal of achieving physical and mental freedom, prolonging life, and even being immortal through practice of various disciplines. The theory and practice of its fairylands, immortals and ways of achieving immortality first appeared in Western Shu, namely Chengdu. According to the conclusion of Scholar Feng Quanghong (1931–), "The doctrine of immortal life came from Shu."

Tianfu Culture and the Modern Pursuit of Chengdu

According to the research of Meng Wentong (1894-1968), *Shan Hai Jing* (*Legends of Mountains and Seas*), the earliest geographical and mythological book in China, was probably written by ancient Shu people, whose representative figures and works could be found in the Ci and Fu poems, theories of Yellow Emperor and Lao Zi and astronomy as far back as to the Qin and Han dynasties. Shu people have cultural creativity and imagination characterized by "Thought of Immortality," and the doctrine of immortal life is also one of the main features of Tianfu Culture. The immortal system offered by Taoism has met almost all of people's requirements and needs, showing two major transcendences over death and life dilemma. Immortals are endowed with endless life, the ability to do as they please, and living an enviable life. The characteristics of immortality thought that cherishes freedom, romance, personality, and naturalness have nourished one generation to another, and produced many cultural giants, such as Sima Xiangru, Yang Xiong, Chen Ziang, Li Bai, Su Shi, Yang Shengan, Zhang Wentao, Li Tiaoyuan, Guo Moruo, whose articles with romanticism as the main style are the best in the world. Taoist School was closely related to the Chengdu Plain, and Taoism was born in Chengdu, and went on in parallel with Confucianism and Buddhism. They have played an important role in the construction of romantic and elegant personality of Tianfu Culture beyond the reach of other cities and regions.

Chengdu is one of China's best cities, where the three religions go parallel and complement one another. It has injected great vitality into the city's personality, formed a spiritual home for its officials and people, and ensured a free and leisurely urban cultural atmosphere for thousands of years.

4. Chengdu with Abundant Water Resources – Nurturing the Humble, Tender and Tough Temperament of Chengdu People

Chengdu is surrounded with mountains, and in the west of the plain is a windward slope of the southeast monsoon in the mountainous area with the annual rainfall of about 1,600-2,000 mm, where dozens of rivers are formed. This land nourished by these rivers has become the

Chapter One
The Origin and Presentation of Tianfu Culture

cradle of Baodun, Sanxingdui and Jinsha civilizations. The ancient Chengdu people were able to make full use of the advantages and avoid the disadvantages of abundant water resources, because they had a deep understanding of the nature of water early on and devoted themselves to water conservancy construction. The ancient Shu Kingdom was moving forward in ever-closer contact and interaction with Minjiang River, Tuojiang River and other rivers, leaving behind many amazing cultural relics and historical records.

In the late period of primitive society in China, when Yao and Shun, leaders of the tribal alliance, were in power (about 4,200 years ago), there was a global flood. Yu, who, together with the ancient Shu people, came from the Western Qiang, was entrusted by Shun to quell the flood of Minjiang River and Yellow River mainly by means of dredging. Finally, he brought a peaceful life to the people and enjoyed a high prestige, laying a foundation for the founding of the Xia Dynasty by his son Qi. In the last year of the Shu King Du Yu's period (who lived about 4,000 years ago), when a huge flood hit the Shu region, he appointed Bieling from Jingdi (now Hubei and Hunan) as Prime Minister to take charge of water control. Bieling cut off Mount Yulei (now Chaping Mountain at the junction of Dujiangyan City and Wenchuan County) to build an artificial channel, which diverted the surging flood from the upper reaches of Minjiang River to the Tuojiang River in the east. Water control was successful. During this period, because Du Yu had an affair with Bieling's wife, he felt ashamed and gave the throne to Bieling. Then Du Yu went to the Western Hills and lived in seclusion. Folklore says that after Du Yu's death, his soul turned into a cuckoo bird. Later, when Shu people heard the cuckoo bird singing, they mourned and recalled the former king and his merits in guiding farming.

In 316 BC, seeing the mediocrity of the king of the Shu State, the Qin State sent Zhang Yi and Sima Cuo to annex the Shu State. From 256 to 251 BC, when Li Bing was appointed as Governor of Shu Prefecture (now Chengdu area) by King Zhaowang of the Qin Dynasty, he led and relied on Chengdu people to create the Dujiangyan Project on the basis of inheriting the successful experience of Dayu and Bieling in water control. Thanks to this marvelous water conservancy project that embodies the spirit of "Harmony Between Man and Nature" and

Tianfu Culture and the Modern Pursuit of Chengdu

"Following Nature" and combines flood control, irrigation and shipping into one, together with the annual maintenance system, Chengdu has become the city that benefits most from water for the longest time in the world.

The Dujiangyan Project guarantees a very close relationship between Chengdu Plain and water, and has exerted a great impact on Chengdu's urban and rural features, lifestyles and human characters. For example, due to the abundant water resources, a large number of people in Western Sichuan can live in Lin Pan. This kind of harmonious and comfortable human settlement highly unified in nature and humanity, production and life, forms a unique style and custom of western Sichuan farmers. Because water resources are available everywhere through ditches in the plain, Chengdu has been full of lakes, gardens, parks, shrines and various recreational places with luxuriant vegetation and full of flowers since ancient times, "Surrounded with tress, the Qin Inn stands; around Chengdu, the spring flow goes," "The city is stacked up with beautiful houses, winter sees green trees towering," "Where is the temple of the famous Premier, in a deep pine grove near the City of Silk. With the green grass of spring colouring the steps, and birds chirping happily under the leaves." These verses by Li Bai and Du Fu are the clear evidence. Because of the abundant and clean water of Jinjiang River, with which the ancient people must rinse Shu brocade products, this river has the good name of Zhuo Jin Jiang (Colorful Brocade River). Famous lakes, rivers and towers such as Maha Pool, Jiang Pool, Longyue Pool, Jinhe River, Yuhe River, Xieyu River, Huanhua River, Xiyuan Garden, Xilou and Wangjiang Towers are all the necklace pearls of the Water City of Chengdu.

In order to cherish and make good use of water resources, Chengdu people have successfully implemented the Funan River Comprehensive Improvement Project since the 1990s. In 1998, Chengdu won the "Habitat Scroll of Honour Award," and subsequently won the "Regional Environment Design Award," "Excellence on Waterfront Award," "Local Government Innovation Award" and "Habitat Business Award." This project is a bold innovation in the coordinated development of human beings and nature and the better utilization of water resources, which started at the end of 2002 and has achieved great results, has realized

Chapter One
The Origin and Presentation of Tianfu Culture

diversion of rain and sewage of more than 300 small and medium-sized streets within the Second Ring Road, and dredged more than 50 rivers within the Third Ring Road. The city's sewage treatment rate has increased from 36% at the start of the project to more than 80%, and water in its main river courses reached the National Surface Water Environment Quality Standard III.... Chengdu vigorously promoting the construction of a "park city" in recent years, success or not, still relies on its benign interactive relationship and achievements with water. In short, thanks to water, Chengdu is born, flourishing, beautiful, happy, innovative and pioneering, gentle, humble, tender and tough.

It is inevitable in history that Taoism was born in the Chengdu Plain and has a profound influence on the values and lifestyle of the officials and people there. One of the fundamental reasons is that Taoism advocates the attribute and character of water. For example, Lao Zi said in Chapter 8 of *Tao Te Ching*, "The best is like water, which benefits all things without distinction and settles into the lowest places without deliberation. So it is the potential of all things." Water seems to be soft, but it can erode hardness. Therefore, Lao Zi continued in Chapter 78, "Nothing in the world is so soft as water, but it is the most powerful in cutting and eroding the hard. Everyone seems to know it that the weak could subdue the strong and the flexible outlasts the rigid, but only a very few can practice it." The soft, tender and tough attribute and character of water have been integrated into the graceful and generous ways of local people's conducting themselves in social life, the leisurely and magnanimous attitude in innovation and entrepreneurship and the well-grounded life choices. Especially when the country, the nation and the compatriots are in difficulties and have great needs for justice, the people here have always shown their unyielding characters and the spirit of selfless dedication. From their support of Li Bing's construction of the Dujiangyan Water Conservancy Project, Zhuge Liang's solemn and stirring cause of restoring the Han Dynasty and reunifying China with his six expeditions to Qishan Mountain, the regimes of Tang and Song dynasties to cope with various great internal and external troubles, the central powers of the Ming and Qing dynasties to quell various disturbances in Southwest China, to the heroic performance of the Sichuan troops and Chengdu people in resisting fascism during the War of Resistance against Japanese Aggression, it is

sufficient to prove that the people in this land rich in literary and artistic masters and all kinds of outstanding talents have the human character nurtured by the tough character and attributes of water.

5. The Poetic Chengdu – Nourishing the Passionate, Romantic and Smart Feelings of Future Generations in Dwelling and Traveling

Moistened with the fine rain and dew of Sichuan civilization and nourished with the sweet spring water of Tianfu Culture, Chengdu has been the highland of Chinese literature and art and the spiritual home for literary and art masters since ancient times, where they felt just like a fish in water and physically and mentally happy. Nurtured and nourished by its nature, humanity, and edification, literary and art masters have emerged shining like stars. In many periods, they have represented the highest level of Chinese literature and art, endorsing and spreading the values, lifestyle, spirit of the times, joys and sorrows of the Chinese nation, including Chengdu and Sichuan. They have made audiences at home and abroad feel the beauty of Chinese clothing, the magnificence of rituals and the charms of the Ba-Shu landscapes and humanity. Especially in the creation, appreciation and dissemination of poems and songs, Chengdu has a rich accumulation of first-class in China and even in the world and with its prominent feature that not only the fertile soil of Tianfu gave birth to many first-class poets such as Sima Xiangru, Yang Xiong, Zhuo Wenjun, Xue Tao, Madame Huarui, Yang Shen, Huang E, Li Tiaoyuan, Liu Shahe, Wei Minglun, etc., but also Chengdu is very suitable for poets to live and create poems because of its urban resources and personality, and has a large number of bosom friends and fans of outstanding poets and their works. Therefore, "As long as one was a poet, he would come to Sichuan in the ancient times"; for instance, Wang Bao, Chen Ziang, Li Bai, Du Fu, Su Xun, Su Shi, Su Zhe, Liu Yong, Lu You, Fan Chengda, Li Tiaoyuan, Guo Moruo, Yu Guangzhong....

They all left deep footprints in Chengdu, and created a large number of excellent poems, expressing their feelings or enlightening the coming. Its content covers almost everything from the sun and moon in the sky to the landscapes and life stories on the earth, from family feuds

Chapter One
The Origin and Presentation of Tianfu Culture

and national hatred to personal love and sorrow, from romance to homesickness, and from imperial courts to the secular society. However, the "Poetic Chengdu" mentioned in this book refers more to the harmony between poetry and the city from the imperial court to the secular society. For example, some places of interest, such as Du Fu's Thatched Cottage (Fig.16-1 to Fig.16-3) by the side of Huanhua River, Yanhua Garden in Chongzhou and others, are mainly for commemorating the great poets who were not born but stayed in Chengdu, while others, like Guihu Park (in memory of Yang Shen and his wife) in Xindu and Qintai Road (in memory of Sima Xiangru and Zuo Wenjun) in Chengdu Downtown (Fig. 17), are the landscapes to commemorate local poets. The two sorts add radiation and beauty to each other and Chengdu people never favor one more than the other. This shows that Chengdu has a special respect for poetry and poets beyond any utility. The custom of "traveling to Du Fu's Thatched Cottages on

Fig. 16-1 Du Fu's Thatched Cottage

Tianfu Culture and the Modern Pursuit of Chengdu

Fig. 16-2 Du Fu's Thatched Cottage

Chapter One
The Origin and Presentation of Tianfu Culture

Fig. 16-3 Du Fu's Thatched Cottage

Tianfu Culture and the Modern Pursuit of Chengdu

Fig. 17 Qintai Road (in memory of Sima Xiangru and Zuo Wenjun)

Man's Day" originated in the Tang Dynasty has made Chengdu City full of poetic flavor at the beginning of spring every year. In the first half of 2017, the conference called "I Love Chengdu: Chengdu Poetry Conference" was held in Chengdu and Du Fu's "Rejoicing in Rain on a Spring Night" was selected as the most beautiful poem about Chengdu. More than one million people took part in the online voting. The following chanting activities triggered a wave of poetry recitation throughout the city. The "recitation pavilion" set up at an important landmark attracted many men, women and children to line up in front of the pavilion for recitation.... This strong poetic atmosphere even amazed Danish Poet and Sinologist Marianne Larsen repeatedly. "People here love poetry so much that its flavor can be felt everywhere in bookstores and

Chapter One
The Origin and Presentation of Tianfu Culture

newspapers, and the government also attaches great importance to cultural development. This good poetic ecology is extremely rare in Denmark and even in other European countries." These are vivid examples of Chengdu's romance and charm due to poetry.

Chengdu's officials and citizens are accustomed to and good at expressing various emotions with poems. Apart from the well-known poetic works expressing and praising Chengdu's beautiful landscapes, prosperous economy and easy and warm life, and the firm, warm and elegant singing of such talented women as Zhuo Wenjun (175-121 BC), Xue Tao (768-832), Lady Huarui (883-926) and Huang E (1498-1569), there are also countless poems expressing that Chengdu's officials and citizens share weal and woe with the country.

Take the popular songs in the late Qing Dynasty as an example. When studying popular songs in Chengdu in his article "Promote the Study of Shu by Digging Deep into Historical Materials," Historian and Professor Hu Zhaoxi (1933-) recorded Wen Shouren's memory: "Since the Opium War in Daoguang's Reign of the early Qing Dynasty, the state was weak, big powers were pressing on the border with fierce and greedy eyes, compensations by ceding territories came one after another, and the state completely lost its dignity. Facing the fatuous and incompetent court, the Reform Revolution broke out. At that time, those who best reflected the indignation and injustice of the people turned out to be popular songs. When I was a child, I read the notebook left by my dead father about things during decades since 1902, including more than ten popular songs in Chengdu, saying that they were solemn and stirring. With the time passing by, I cannot remember them all. Only one of them 'When We Wake Up' can be remembered intermittently, 'The 400 million people are numb, the neighboring powers are aggressive, Ryukyu was abandoned and Taiwan ceded.... Who is the arch-criminal? Who forced to sign the covenant? When do we wake up?'" This poem clearly and strongly expresses the national feelings and worries of Chengdu people.

Zhong Shuliang (1916-2009) was a famous scholar and poet in Chengdu in the 20th century. The Ba-Shu Publishing House published *Selected Poems of Zhong Shuliang* in 2005. He wrote more than 3,000 poems in his life, covering a wide range of contents and is praised

Tianfu Culture and the Modern Pursuit of Chengdu

as a contemporary dean of poets and "Du Fu of today." Among them, the poems about the War of Resistance against Japanese Aggression are the "Poetic History" of justice. For example, it can be said that the poem "40 Lines in Mourning of June 11" reflecting the Japanese bombing of Chengdu is written in words of blood and tears to warn the descendants, "On June 11, 2nd year of the Republic of China,... Big fires were seen soon after the explosion. Half of the red sky seemed dyed with compatriots' blood... Mother and son cried to each other, husband and wife held together in tears.... Then I knew Yanshikou had become the sea of fire; Pifang and Shuncheng streets were only left burned columns and broken walls; the survived were mutilated and the dead found everywhere.... We were only meat on the enemy's chopping block. With the irreconcilable family feud and national hatred for the enemy, we'll keep in mind this piece of bloody history." Again, in "60 Lines in Mourning of July 27th," he wrote, after he returned from the bombing shelter at Luojia Mill, "Seven or eight miles back to home, a miserable scene was found along the field road. The dead lay in the open air silent, and the wounded moaned bleeding. Crying was too horrible to be heard, and the wind added more sorrow to it. A cow fell to the ground and a child lay in blood.... Mr. Huang had a young lady, and she was 17 or 18 years old only. I happened to having met her once, how beautiful and quiet she was! So deeply and warmly they loved, but with grievance they were lost.... How can I make known my loyal heart? On the silk piece I play to the full my poetic art."

Of course, the poet not only mourned for the dead compatriots and the broken country, but also had the determination of revenge on the Japanese fascists and the encouragement and praise for the soldiers of the Sichuan troops who left Sichuan to fight against Japanese aggression: "Blood debts must be paid off with blood, and no tolerance could be given to war criminals." "Generals sang the Song of Expedition, fervently started to the battle field as heroes of the nation. With the reports of victory pouring in, the whole Sichuan people celebrated their successes ceremoniously." This author worked with Mr. Zhong in Chengdu University, listened to his teachings many times, and presided over the "Symposium on Zhong Shuliang's Academic Thoughts and Alumni Symposium of Wenxin College (Chinese Department)" to celebrate his

Chapter One
The Origin and Presentation of Tianfu Culture

92nd birthday. Every time when he felt the poet's lifelong loyalty to the country, his infatuation to create for the people, and his simple and quiet lifestyle with great goals, this author always seems to meet a good rain after a long drought, feel warm in the spring breeze, and be able to ascend a height and enjoy a distant view in spring.

The so-called poetic Chengdu especially refers to that poetry is not only the family and national hatred or romantic love of poets, but also a way of life for many ordinary people in the city. Famous Writer Xiao Fuxing wrote in his *Poetry and Chengdu*: "Compared with some other cities, Chengdu has a special feature in its relationship with poetry."

There have been many native poets in Chengdu since ancient and modern times, and poets who have been to Chengdu in past dynasties are even more. No matter how beautifully their poems may be written or combined, they are not enough to show that Chengdu is a poetry city. The only thing that can prove it is the influence of poetry on the city and the moistening and popularization of poetry like water spreading in the city.

Once in Chengdu, teahouses were most popular, where there was also the enthusiasm of the people to write poems spontaneously. Some busybody liked to post in the teahouse the poem he had written. The next day when he went to see it, it had attracted a lot of responders, who took up the challenge through composing poems to reply in turn, and the guests were all commenting on the pros and cons. Poetry made people enjoy themselves. There was no place like Chengdu teahouses where people could find such a lively scene of poetry. Imagine that it could keep up with the poetry contest as described in Grand View Garden of *A Dream of Red Mansions*.

Only in a grass-rooted city can poetry be pulled down from the elegant palace and placed on an equal footing with itself. Only in a city with the tradition of poetry can poems bloom like flowers everywhere.

Chengdu's tradition of poetry owes much to Du Fu and his thatched cottage. However, the tradition of poetry is a cultural heritage, which cannot be achieved overnight, but accumulated and polished over a long period of time, and then poetry has become the blood and genes of

Tianfu Culture and the Modern Pursuit of Chengdu

this city.

Perhaps the story that Sima Xiangru (c. 179-118 BC) and Zhuo Wenjun (175-121 BC) in the Han Dynasty married through poetry and music and passed the love crisis is a classic expression of this tradition.

According to historical records, Sima Xiangru, born in Chengdu, once lived in Peng'an, Sichuan. When he was a child, he liked reading and fencing, and was called Quanzi (dog's son) by his family for being naughty. He admired Lin Xiangru, a wise and magnanimous Zhao politician who was loyal to the imperial court and protected the country during the Warring States Period, so he named himself Sima Xiangru. When he was young, his family donated money to the imperial court in exchange for his position – an aide who was waiting by the emperor's side to attend affairs of driving and hunting. Feeling bored, he left by pleading illness and went to King Xiaowang of the Liang State, the younger brother of Emperor Jing of the Han Dynasty, for Xiaowang liked literature. After a few years of happy and free life in the Liang State, he published "Zixu *Fu*" and began to have a certain reputation. After Liang Xiaowang died, he had to return to Chengdu; but at that time his family had nothing but bare walls in the house. Wang Ji, County Magistrate of Linqiong (now Qionglai County, Chengdu) and a good friend of his as well, offered him some favors, letting him live in the official guesthouse of Linqiong and visiting him every day after work. A local steel magnate named Zhuo Wangsun decided to entertain Wang Ji and his precious guest.

At that time, Zhuo Wenjun, the apple of Zhuo Wangsun's eye, was also a literary youth. Her husband died shortly after his marriage. When Sima Xiangru came, Zhuo Wenjun was very concerned about his behaviors. In the party, Sima Xiangru played the ancient musical tune "The Male Phoenix Seeks His Mate" with beautiful lyrics and melodies, which moved Zhuo Wenjun. So they eloped to Chengdu. Since Zhuo Wangsun flew into a rage and refused to admit their relationship, the two earned their own living by opening a tavern with Xiangru as the waiter and Wenjun as the businesswoman of wine. Finally, Zhuo Wangsun admitted the marriage and gave 100 servants and millions of copper coins. Emperor Wu of the Han Dynasty liked literature,

Chapter One
The Origin and Presentation of Tianfu Culture

one day when he happened to read "Zixu *Fu*" and learned that Sima Xiangru was in Chengdu, he recruited him to Chang'an as a very close literary aide of his. Xiangru wrote "Shanglin *Fu*," "Daren *Fu*," "Changmen *Fu*" and "Meiren *Fu*" one after another to play up the strength and magnificence of the grand Han Dynasty, which brought him a nation-wide fame. His proses such as "An Official Declaration for the Ba-Shu People," "Refute and Question My Fellow Countrymen in Sichuan," "The Memorial of Remonstrate Hunting," "Feng Chan Wen" and so on, are all famous literary masterpieces and have been handed down so far. Later, he returned to Chengdu as a military officer in charge of the security of the royal palace, and together with Tang Meng, subdued the southwest barbarians in Yunnan, Guizhou and Southern Sichuan. Famous as Sima Xiangru was, he turned his affection to a beauty in Maoling. Therefore, Zhuo Wenjun wrote a poem and an article to save their love.

Her poem "Bai Tou Yin (To a Faithless Husband)" reads:

Love should be as pure as snow on the mountain, and as bright as the moon in the clouds; knowing that you have two hearts, I came to you for a break. Today we wine for the final party, and tomorrow we will leave apart. Along the ditch I was slowly moving, the love is gone like the river away flowing. When I decided to elope with you, I didn't cry like an ordinary girl so sad. I expected I'd married a single-minded man, and we could love each other forever. Love should be just like fishing rods light, soft and long, or like fish so lovely and happy. A man should be particular about loyalty, and no treasure can compensate the sincere love lost.

Her article reads:

In spring, flowers are full bloom, and the plain color is covered in a colorful world. The *guqin* is still there, but the player has been changed! There are mandarin ducks swimming in pairs along the Jinjiang River, and the lingering branches stretching in Han Palace. None

Tianfu Culture and the Modern Pursuit of Chengdu

of them ever left their partners. I have to sigh for people who are inextricably bogged down in beauty and tired of the old! The strings have been broken; the mirror, incomplete; the morning dew, dry; the flowers, faded; the grey-haired begin to lament how sad the departure is. Hope you eat well and don't let me lie in your heart. Swear to the mighty Jinjiang River, saying goodbye to you forever!

In comparison, the former poem mainly shows not only her disdain for Xiangru's affection shift, but also her wish of his returning from the wrong path. The latter shows her firm stand that no matter how painful she was, she would not compromise with those who betrayed love. In the history of Chinese love literature and women's literature, they have all become eternal songs of women's wisdom and firmness. Today, Sima Bridge, Qintai Road in Chengdu and Wenjun Well in Qionglai are all important landmarks of the couple's romantic story.

In a word, Chengdu has been a city with poetry as its blood and gene for more than 2,000 years, and worthy of the title of the most elegant one in the world. In the history of mankind, Chengdu has always been the beautiful realm of "man's poetic dwelling in the earth," which is sincerely yearned for by the famous German poet Holderlin (1770–1843). Chengdu, as a famous poetry city, moistens the enthusiasm and romance of future generations in dwelling and traveling, supports Chengdu to generate endless creative inspiration, adds more grace to people's lifestyle and promotes people's happiness index. This is undoubtedly the warmest and charming touch of Chengdu, a city with unlimited creativity.

6. The Music Chengdu – Building an Elegant, Exquisite and Leisurely Home

"Music" here refers to both happiness and music itself. For human beings and life, Confucianism and Taoism are full of the sense of happiness. The secularized Buddhism also makes people relaxed with a particularly pure mind when facing various difficulties. Because of its comparative prosperity and the nourishment of the three religions, Chengdu has been a happy city since ancient times, where officials and common people are optimistic and have

Chapter One
The Origin and Presentation of Tianfu Culture

kept a balance in production and life, material and spirit, creation and enjoyment. Therefore, whether they are the rich, the powerful, peddlers or servants, they generally have enjoyed a high happiness index. Today, people can see a large number of picture bricks in the museum, showing the colorful and dynamical life in Chengdu during the Han Dynasty. In 2017, *Chengdu Evening News* revealed through big data technology that the most frequently used words in describing Chengdu in Tang Poetry were brocade, clear, green, sweet, quiet, blue, drunk, joy, fragrant, and beautiful, all of which can prove that this city has left people many beautiful and joyful memories in the peaceful years. Professor Su Pinxiao (1969–) of Sichuan University wrote in the volume of "Five Dynasties and Two Song dynasties" of *General History of Chengdu*: "During the periods of the Former and Later Shu and the Southern and Northern Song dynasties (907–1279), with the development of economy and culture, Chengdu became increasingly prosperous, and the cultural life of its residents became more colorful. As a result, the recreational atmosphere developed further on the basis of that in the Tang Dynasty." Fei Zhu, an official and scholar of the Yuan Dynasty wrote in his book *Records of Local Customs*, "Chengdu is more popular in recreational activities than other places of the western Sichuan, thanks to its custom of entertainment and its vast territory and rich resources. On every festival or seasonal points, the prefect set tables for celebration, when crowds of people in colorful carts and clothes poured in and out with deafening drum sounds and vaudeville playing ahead. The streets were sandwiched with densely crowded people helping the old and carrying the young, frolicking and chasing one another, or just placing benches in public places to convenience the audience." In the Song Dynasty, the prefect often took the lead in recreational and amusement activities, in which he was called "Roaming Head," and the people following with their benches called "Roaming Bed." "Roaming for Fun" is the main feature of Chengdu's amusement culture.

Zhang Yong (946–1015), a well-known minister trusted by the emperor, served as Governor of Chengdu for two times in the early Northern Song Dynasty. As he had a deep feeling and experience of the customs and culture in Shu, he said in his poem of "Memorial of Shu,"

Tianfu Culture and the Modern Pursuit of Chengdu

Chengdu is largely populated with rich products, and its customs so frivolous and arrogant. The pearls and jewelries are so luxurious beyond words, and idlers are indulged in entertainment. A flying spring is sprayed from the Rainbow Bridge, and the red pavilion is blocked in the thick willows. Candle shadows cast by stars, and songs chase the moonset. Gamecocks attract gamblers over one million, and their joyful laughters can be heard so loud. Performance girls wear jade earrings, and fine horses are equipped with the golden bridle. The wine shops are open overnight, and the flower market is getting ignored.

From his description, it can be seen that Chengdu's amusement life in the Song Dynasty was rich and colorful, including not only singing and dancing, but also cockfighting and horse racing, drinking and gambling, spring outing in the suburbs and flower watching in the streets. The trend of recreation not only spread to major commercial streets in the region, but also manifested in the great extension of residents' leisure and entertainment in time and space. There were not only the mass carnivals on folk festivals, but also the entertainment service by restaurants and teahouses throughout the night. Chengdu in the Song Dynasty could be called the city that never slept. Another minister Tian Kuang (1005−1063) also said that in those years, officials in charge of Sichuan all regarded people's recreation as an important part of their administration for the people. Therefore, in his poem "Chengdu's Roaming for Fun," he mentioned several times that so many people rushed out for roaming events, leaving most alleys empty, and the numerous tourist boats were shuttling back and forth in Jinjiang River.

In the Song Dynasty, the prosperity of Chengdu and the optimistic lifestyle of the officials and people were highlighted in the trade fairs (markets) held every month throughout the year, interwoven with entertainment activities and gathering elements. According to *Chengdu Chronicle*,

Chengdu Prefecture holds the trade fair every month each year: Lantern Market in the first lunar month, Flower Market in the second, Silkworm Market in the third, Brocade Market in the fourth, Fan Market in the fifth, Incense Market in the sixth, Antiques Market in the seventh, Fragrans Market in the eighth, Medicine Market in the ninth, Wine Market in

Chapter One
The Origin and Presentation of Tianfu Culture

the tenth, Plum Market in the eleventh and Taofu Market in the twelfth.

Among them, there is a complete description about letting the lamps go on the Lantern Festival of the first lunar month, which was very famous in the Tang Dynasty. The myth has been passed down to this day that legendary Taoist Ye Fashan (616–720) guided Emperor Minghuang (685–762) of the Tang Dynasty to Fuchun Square in Chengdu to drink wine and watch lanterns. In the second year (969) of Kaibao's Reign in the Northern Song Dynasty, it was ordered that three days would be set for letting the lamps go on the Lantern Festival next year. Later, it became a custom: To open the textile Market and light up the lanterns on the 14th, 15th and 16th days of the first lunar month every year. At that time, Zhaojue Temple was the brightest place lit by lanterns in Chengdu (Fig. 18-1, Fig. 18-2).

In the Song Dynasty, Chengdu Prefect Tian Kuang said in his poem "Chengdu Lantern Fair on Lantern Festival," "All over the country I was once traveling, people were fond of funny parading. Yet it reached its climax in the entire Shu region, rich in products and heavily populated there. Lanterns were lit at the spring night, and Jinli was full of the smell of burning incenses." Lu You also chanted in a poem, "The deafening gongs and drums saw boiling crowds at the city gates, and the lanterns piled up like hills even moved the dusk." This is the evidence of the highlights of Chengdu's Lantern Festival. During the Lantern Festival, the tourists gathered, so there was almost the complete supply of

Fig. 18-1 Chinese New Year Lantern Festival show in the Temple of Marquis Wu

Tianfu Culture and the Modern Pursuit of Chengdu

Fig. 18-2 Chinese New Year Lantern Festival show in the Temple of Marquis Wu 2

effective drugs, famous flowers and rare goods. The Flower Market in the 2nd month has arisen since the Tang Dynasty. Xiao Lu's poem "Chengdu" says, "At dawn I heard of the closing of the Flower Market, but saw so many bamboo rafts still bustling on the quiet river." In the early years of the Northern Song Dynasty, Chengdu's prefect Zhang Yong, on the Spring Outing Day on the 2nd day of the 2nd lunar month, went out of the Wanli Bridge in dozens of colorful boats with officials and guests, and called it "Little Tour to the River." In a poem, he said, "For Spring Outing families go in thousands, and lovely ladies are as beautiful as flowers. So slim and graceful they're standing in the flowers, as if they'd ride the clouds." Xue Tian also described in his poem "A Hundred Lines for My Experiences in Chengdu," "The beaded curtain was rolled up at the willow riverbank at night, swinging in the spring breeze from the Flower Market." It can be seen

Chapter One
The Origin and Presentation of Tianfu Culture

that the Flower Market in the Tang Dynasty was set up beside Jinjiang River and bamboo rafts as its transporting tools. From the "Little Tour of the River" starting from the Wanli Bridge in the Song Dynasty to the "Flower Market" and "willow bank" in Xue Tian's poem, it can be roughly seen that the flower Markets in Chengdu in the Tang and Song dynasties were set between the Qingyang Palace to the Yuju Temple, along the Jinjiang River from the west to the east.

Happy cities are more creative and more peaceful. As far as the ancient Chinese political civilization is concerned, Confucianism always advocated that kings should "share happiness with the people." This is also part of the "benevolent governance" that Confucianism aspires to. Its most successful local governance practice is the leisure politics created by outstanding scholar-officials in charge of Chengdu during the Tang and Song dynasties. They conformed to Chengdu's regional culture and local customs by initiatively designing, creating conditions and taking the lead in participating in various recreational, amusing activities and dinner parties that could realize the best psychological and emotional communication between officials and people and enhance the sense of the community of shared-futures for mankind. Most of the governors of Chengdu in the Northern Song Dynasty were fond of amusement. In the Song Dynasty, when Emperor Renzong (1010-1063) wanted to appoint Song Qi (998-1061), a romantic gifted scholar and the "Red Plum Minister," as Governor of the Shu State, the civil officials thought it inappropriate because of the contrast between the luxurious style of the Shu State and Song Qi's preference for recreational activities. Since the emperor himself was versatile, this did not disturb him. After Song Qi arrived in the Shu State, he followed Chengdu's folkway, avoided harsh governance, and kept on his life accompanied by music, singing and dancing, poetry, wine and recreation; however, the social governance became more effective. Later, when Tian Kuang (1005-1063) succeeded him as Prefect of Chengdu, he also enjoyed it very much and wrote *Chengdu's Roaming for Fun* of 21 chapters to "record the real Chengdu." When Xue Kui (967-1034) took up his post, he called himself "Xue Chunyou" (Xue Spring Outing) and created 10 chapters of poem *Where the Good Spring Tour Is*. When Zhao Bian (1008-1084), a frugal and honest official was the prefect of Chengdu, he even thought that the dinner parties and

Tianfu Culture and the Modern Pursuit of Chengdu

amusement activities were closely related to the governance of Chengdu and could never be abandoned. Therefore, he spared no public money to support these activities. Because of this, these festival events prevailed in Chengdu during the Song and Yuan dynasties and became one of its political and civilizing traditions. These "officials fond of amusement" achieved the overall harmony of the officials, people and the society by means of amusement and recreation that were best in line with the human nature, which was not only a brilliant idea in stimulating economic development but also a pioneering undertaking in maintaining the city's happiness index. Therefore, Chengdu's recreation and leisure economy since ancient times has been not only a wealth creation and enjoyment activity in which all social strata participate, but also a humanistic landscape and political practice full of wisdom.

Chengdu, advocating freedom and full of leisure, imagination and creativity, is also naturally the capital of China's music and performing arts, with many famous musical talents, works and activities in history. Judging from the history of Chinese music, the Shu region and Chengdu are undoubtedly the most important sources and one of the regions with the greatest vitality, creativity and influence. Changhong, a Shu native, who lived in the Spring and Autumn Period, served the Zhou royal family for 50 years, and left behind an allusion to "Loyal-hearted," was one of the earliest musicians recorded in Chinese history. Even Confucius once asked him for music knowledge. This shows the early accumulation of music in Chengdu. During Kaiming Dynasty (about the middle of the 7th century to the end of the 4th century BC), the king of the ancient Shu Kingdom was good at music and composed a series of songs, such as *Dongping, Yuxie, Longgui, Yiwu, Youling*, etc. According to *Records of Shu* Volume III of *Chronicles of Huayang*, a mountain spirit in the Shu Kingdom turned into a beautiful woman. When the king saw her, he loved her and accepted her as his concubine. Not accustomed to the living conditions, she wanted to leave. The king tried his best to retain and please her with the song of Dongping. A few days later, when the concubine died, the king was deeply saddened. Then he erected a large stone in the north of the city as her tomb (now Mount Wudan in the north of Chengdu), and composed songs of *Yuxie* and *Longgui* to express his yearning. It can be seen

Chapter One
The Origin and Presentation of Tianfu Culture

that music played an important role in the spiritual life of the upper-class society represented by the royal family. Academics believe that the history of music popular in the Chengdu Plain and its surrounding areas during the ancient Shu period can be roughly divided into three periods.

The early representative form was secular music that spread among the people. People sang with the beats produced by tapping natural objects, daily necessities and labor tools. All kinds of natural and artificial products also had the function of musical instruments. The medium-term representative form was religious music for various sacrificial occasions. Musical instruments made of jade, stone, copper and other materials produced resonance sounds through striking, shaking and collision to shock the mind and create a solemn atmosphere. Typical musical instruments include the stone chimes, copper bells, and copper pendants unearthed from Sanxingdui Site, and chimes, copper bells from Jinsha Site, etc. The late representative form was the imperial court music used by nobles of ancient Shu kingdom in important ceremonial places and daily life. It was mainly played with large-scale combination of musical instruments with exquisite workmanship and harmonious melody. Typical musical instruments include the chime set unearthed from the ancient Shu boat-coffin tomb in Shangye Street of Chengdu, the chime set from the Tomb of Shu King in Xindu, the bronze chime set of the Warring States Period in Jinsha Lane, etc. The ancient Shu music, originating early and rich in musical forms, is closely related to the music culture of Shang and Zhou dynasties in the Central Plains and the Jingchu music culture in the middle and lower reaches of the Yangtze River.

Since the Han Dynasty, all kinds of public and private activities and gatherings including teahouses and wine shops in the city have always been accompanied by beautiful music, dances, operas and performances in peacetime. Chengdu is therefore full of interest, elegance and fashion, and its cultural soft power is thus lively and prosperous. As the famous story goes, when the great literary giant Sima Xiangru (c. 179−118 BC) attended a private party in Linqiong (now Qionglai, Chengdu), he impressed Zhuo Wenjun, daughter of Zhuo Wangsun, the "Steel Magnate," with a song of "The Male Phoenix Seeks His Mate" he played. They then eloped and

Tianfu Culture and the Modern Pursuit of Chengdu

eventually got married. Such a kind of elegance and romance of his is rare. Today's Qintai Road in Chengdu is where they earned their living by selling wine after they eloped. After their tavern was closed every day, it was indispensable with Sima Xiangru's beautiful guqin melody. In "San Du *Fu*," Zuo Si (c. 250–305) in the Western Jin Dynasty described the Chengdu customs of the Shu-Han Regime as follows: in various banquets, there were abundant wine and delicacies, "people competed for a toast, and music was played; local ethnic girls plucked the strings, while Han women beat time. The sound of the West Qin rose through pressing the frets; the song of "On the River" was given in high pitch. Waving the long sleeves, they were dancing; their posture and movements were so beautiful and nice. People sat closer to drink together, and drank up as the penalty one cup after another. How nice to drink tonight, who'd care about getting drunk for months?" This shows how prosperous and wonderful music activities were at that time.

The poet-sage Du Fu (712–770) of the Tang Dynasty extremely admired Chengdu full of music in his poem "Gift to General Qing," saying, "The tune I heard in your mansion is so melodious, Half floating with river breeze, half wafting above clouds; Such a tune can be from nowhere but the imperial palace, For it is hardly played in common households." Although the poet was well informed and versed in music appreciation, the music he heard in Chengdu seemed almost like the best to him in the world. In addition, Du Fu wrote in "Chengdu Mansion," "These tiered walls are filled with splendid houses, in winter's last month the trees are gray-green. Full of noise, this famous metropolis, pipes playing mix with reed organs. Though lovely indeed, I have no one to turn to, I lean gazing at the river bridge." Here, "pipes playing mix with reed organs" is obviously from a band, so beautiful that the poet didn't know how to praise it. In the 12th year (753) of Emperor Xuanzong's Tianbao's Reign of the Tang Dynasty, when Li Bai stayed in Xuancheng (now Anhui), he wrote the famous five-character poem "Listening to a Shu Monk Playing the Lute," after Li Bai met a monk from Sichuan playing the lute, which reads, "This monk with his lute came from the land of Shu, In the west, from the high Emei Mountains. Plucking the strings, he played for me. I heard murmuring pines in many valleys. Like flowing water, the music cleansed my heart, leaving its echo in the frosty bell. Dusk came unnoticed to

Chapter One
The Origin and Presentation
of Tianfu Culture

these green hills, as the autumn clouds grew darker and darker." The whole poem compares the superb skills of the Shu monk in playing the lute to the flowing clouds and flowing water, so bright, smooth and charm. While praising the beautiful sound of the lute, it also reflects the superb performance level of musical instruments and the close ties between religious life and music in Chengdu in the Tang Dynasty.

Chengdu once had the highest level of Chinese musical instrument production. For example, in the Tang Dynasty, there was a Lei's family, who improved and made the traditional ancient *qin* into the best-quality "Lei's Qin" during the period from the Kaiyuan to Kaicheng reigns of the Tang Dynasty, lasting for about 120 years. Nine family members of three generations were famous craftsmen, including Lei Shao, Lei Zhen, Lei Xiao, Lei Wei, Lei Wen, Lei Yan, Lei Jue, Lei Hui, Lei Xun. As an old saying goes, "Lei's Qin is the best in the Tang Dynasty, and Lei's nine people from Shu bestride the line." Lei Wei's "Fuxi-style" *guqin* with "fine ornaments worn at the waist," now in the Imperial Palace Museum, is the most representative piece of Tang *qin* handed down from ancient times and is known as the "fairy product" of *qin*.

Other important musical achievements in Chengdu are as follows.

The relief sculpture of 24 musicians unearthed in Yongling Maosoleum of Emperor Wang Jian (847–918) of the Former Shu Dynasty is a comprehensive expression of the mutual integration of Chinese native music and foreign music, is an exquisite and unique cultural relic in the history of music and has special and important value for studying the music culture of the Tang and Five Dynasties.

Wang Zhuo, a writer and scientist in the Southern Song Dynasty, lived in the Miao Sheng Yuan of Biji Square in the north of Chengdu in his late years. He wrote *Biji Manzhi*, a book of great value, incisive insights and unique skills. It is a lyric note and music review of ancient Chinese music theory, and has a high position in the history of literature and music.

Originated in Chengdu and its surrounding areas in the Song Dynasty, Dongjing music is a music gene played with traditional stringed and woodwind instruments while chanting the Taoist scripture "Wencang Dadong Xianjing" (after Ming and Qing dynasties, with its further development and prosperity, this kind of music began to spread widely to other areas in Sichuan and Yunnan). Today, Dongjing music is still very popular in Sichuan Province, Han-inhabited areas in Yunnan, Naxi and Yi minority-inhabited areas such as Lijiang and Chuxiong. With the approval of the State Council in 2014, Dongjing Music was included in the fourth batch of national intangible cultural heritage lists.

"The Flowing Water," created and composed by Zhang Kongshan, a Taoist priest in Qingcheng Mountain and a famous guqin master in the Qing Dynasty, is not only popular in China, but also spread abroad. In 1977, it was recorded as a gilded disc in the United States, and taken by the space shuttle Voyager II into space and the depths of the universe.

During the Republic of China, Ye Bohe (1889-1945), a Chengdu native who studied in Japan, wrote and published the first *Chinese Music History*. Wang Guangqi (1892-1936), also a Chengdu native, went to Berlin University's Music Department for further study in 1917 and later employed by the Oriental College of Bonn University to teach literature and art. In June 1933, he received his doctor's degree in musicology from Bonn University for his thesis "On Chinese Classical Opera" and became the earliest Chinese musicologist who won honor for his motherland in Europe. And *Chinese Music History* he wrote was the first book that marked the successful transformation of the discipline of Chinese ancient music history into a modern academic discipline.

On the other hand, there are two precious cultural relics of Chengdu's unique rap art that can vividly express the process of creation, appreciation and popularization of music. In 1957, the drumming and rapping figurine of the Eastern Han Dynasty was unearthed from the Tianhuishan Han Tomb in Chengdu (now stored in the China National Museum). In 1963, the standing rap figurine was unearthed from the Eastern Han tomb at Songjialin in Pixian County, which vividly demonstrated the active situation of rap performance in Chengdu area in the Han Dynasty.

The music genes of Chengdu have kept the city warm and calm, honest and romantic. When the Frenchman Mair, Victor H. traveled to Chengdu in 1898, he wrote the article "Chengdu

Chapter One
The Origin and Presentation
of Tianfu Culture

in the Eyes of the French" during the Reform Movement of 1898 about the city and officials' life. "People of wealth sweep the streets every day, while learned men carry water and push carts." He was somewhat surprised that those of high social ranks actually engaged in ordinary physical labor calmly. Obviously, Chengdu was different from the places he observed such as Guangdong, Shanghai, Chongqing and Beijing. In fact, this has been only the normal lifestyle and taste of Chengdu literati since ancient times. In Chengdu's urban civilization of more than 2,000 years, there are a variety of factors that have created its humanistic character of a "downward-looking" concern for and expression of the joys and sorrows of ordinary people in most of the time (especially during the Ming and Qing dynasties). For example, ordinary people are most of the audiences and consumers of the material and spiritual products introduced by Sichuan Opera, Sichuan cuisine and Sichuan tea. That is to say, in this city, the relatively wealthy people have their own happiness, and the ordinary people also have their own happiness and satisfaction, and people in this city can coexist harmoniously. The factors behind it are abundant products and easy livelihood, the profound influences of Tao School and Taoism that stress on freedom and of Confucianism that pays attention to spiritual life, and the repeated immigration that has made it difficult to form a monopoly class of long economic, political and social status.

In the 20th century, Chengdu had a bumpy development, but in the 40 years since the reform and opening-up, Chengdu has passed on its own cultural genes and achieved various scientific and sustainable developments. Chengdu has become a "post-modern" city with sound economy, active culture and comfortable life, and has been continuously rated as the city with the highest happiness index in China by the media in recent years.

The story of a romantic couple, a Chengdu boy Zhou Xiaolin and a Beijing girl Yin Jie, may manifest the connotation of this happiness index. In 1986, on his way to Jiuzhaigou, Zhou Xiaolin, a part-time tour guide, fell in love with Yin Jie, a Beijing girl visiting Sichuan, at first sight. In his words, the moment he saw Yin Jie, he decided that she would be his future wife. But Yin Jie did not like this diligent and enthusiastic young man at first, because the Sichuan young man in front of her was not her ideal partner in consideration of geography, family, age or other various factors. However, Zhou Xiaolin did not think so. He pursued Yin Jie through various means and even went to Beijing by train to propose marriage to Yin Jie. As the saying goes, "The utmost sincerity can melt even a metal and stone heart." Zhou Xiaolin moved Yin Jie, they fell in love and married. They lived successively in Beijing and Guangzhou. Traveling in Danba, Ganzi Tibetan Prefecture, Sichuan, the couple hoped to introduce its charm to the world. Overcoming many obstacles of mountains, rivers and weather changes, they took a large number of photos, published the photographic album *Beauty of Danba Valley*, wrote the essay "The Initial Experience of Distinctive Danba," and got the photos of Danba Diaolou exhibited at the United Nations with the help of their French friends. With their efforts, Danba was rated the first of "Most Beautiful Ancient Villages and Townships in China" in October 2005. As Yin Jie loves flowers, one day she sighed, "When will we have a home with a small garden?" Zhou Xiaolin spent all his money in building for her a 1,200 *mu* rural garden in a beautiful valley in Daqiao Village, Zhuanlong Township, Jintang County, 66 kilometers away from Chengdu Downtown. Then the couple lived their favorite life here. They planted more than 390 varieties of hollyhock because of their special love. With his daily concentrated studies, Zhou Xiaolin classified the hollyhock. At the same time, the two started to compile the *Atlas of Chinese Hollyhock Varieties*.... After the story was broadcast by *Reader* hosted by Dong Qing, a famous CCTV program anchorwoman, it had touched countless audiences. This is the most beautiful scenery with Chengdu temperament.

7. Chengdu Integrated with Ethnic Groups – Creating a Magnanimous, Inclusive and Open Mind for the Common Life of All

"Group" here refers to ethnic groups and mainly refers to immigrants and aborigines. The so-called "integration" refers to the integration of different ethnic groups and their influence. In fact, Chengdu has recorded a history of common struggle between aborigines and immigrants since the construction of the city led by Zhang Yi. For more than 2,300 years, due to wars

Chapter One
The Origin and Presentation of Tianfu Culture

and various natural and man-made disasters, there have been many large-scale immigration activities in the Ba-Shu region in history, such as the migration of "thousands of Qin people" to the Shu region after the Qin swallowed up the Ba-Shu region, even including Lü Buwei punished by Ying Zheng, the king of the Qin State. They brought higher culture into the Shu region. After Qin Shihuang destroyed the six states, he forcibly moved the powerful and wealthy families of the six states to the Shu region, including Zuo Wangsun, a rich man of the Zhao State, who moved to Linqiong and became the steel magnate with his capital and iron smelting skills. These immigrants brought abundant capital, advanced production skills and management, and promoted the further prosperity of Chengdu's economy. With a large number of Han and minority immigrants to Chengdu during the period of the Shu-Han Regime in the Three Kingdoms Period and Cheng-Han Regime in the Sixteen Kingdoms Period, they greatly enriched the cultural connotation of Chengdu City. Therefore, *Biography of Xin Qingzhi* records, "Chengdu, as a local metropolis, is deeply influenced by out-coming customs." From the An-Shi Rebellion of the Tang Dynasty to the Five Dynasties, many officials and people from the Central Plains migrated to Chengdu, including the two fleeing groups represented by Emperor Xuanzong and Xizong of the Tang Dynasty (Wang Jian and Meng Zhixiang, the founders of the Former and Latter Shu dynasties, from Henan and Hebei respectively, migrated to Chengdu together with most of their ruling clique and armies). It was a great influx of the economy and culture of Guanzhong and Central Plains to the Ba-Shu region, especially Chengdu. A typical example was Du Fu's residence by Huanhua River. Only a few years later, there were more than 200 famous poems left, adding much fame to the holy thatched cottage. In the late Ming and early Qing dynasties, "Hunan-Guangdong Immigration to Sichuan" saw a large number of immigrants of tens of thousands of households come to Chengdu from more than ten provinces. In just a few decades, Chengdu stood up again in the thorny and ruined land infested by tigers and leopards, and picked up its former graceful bearing again. Dujiangyan Irrigation System, though severely damaged, also reached the highest level of irrigation area in the history after many times of annual repair and expansion by officials and peoples.

Tianfu Culture and the Modern Pursuit of Chengdu

In addition, westerners who came to Chengdu in modern times have generally been accommodated and treated well in the city. In this background, international friends, represented by Canadian Omar L. Kilborn's three generations and Lindsay (known as the "Father of Modern Chinese Dentistry"), founded the most advanced modern medical science and treatment cause in West China, represented by obstetrics and gynecology and stomatology in Huaxiba (Fig. 19). It is also the crystallization of the city's character of accepting all kinds of ethnic groups. The deep feelings of the three generations of Omar L. Kilborn towards Chengdu are enough to move the posterity deeply. (In 1919, when Omar L. Kilborn returned to Canada on vacation, he died of pneumonia at home. After the news reached Chengdu, many Chengdu people benefiting much from him held a traditional Chinese memorial ceremony in the Confucian Temple, expressing their respect for this Christian in a Chinese way.)

In short, many immigrations in history, either large or small, had a profound impact on Tianfu Culture, enriching the connotation of its values and lifestyles, and adding weight and charm to the city (including the aforementioned people in "As long as one was a poet, he would come to Sichuan in the ancient times" and "Almost all the scholars have had the experience of staying in Sichuan since the ancient times," some of

Fig. 19 Huaxiba

Chapter One
The Origin and Presentation of Tianfu Culture

whom or their descendants and relatives did not leave when they came). Especially, a large number of immigrations during the late Ming and early Qing dynasties, the War of Resistance against Japanese Aggression period, the Third Front Construction, and since the reform and opening-up have brought endless huge human, financial, and information resources and injected various factors and vitality needed for economic and social development to Tianfu Chengdu so as to achieve its re-emergence and sustainable development. Immigrants and their cultures (whose basic characteristics are equality, friendliness, openness, tolerance and hard work) have not only connected Chengdu with China and other parts of the world more and more closely, but also strengthened and enriched Tianfu Cultural connotation of "Innovation and Creation, Fashion and Elegance, Optimism and Tolerance, Kindness and Public Welfare" on a platform that constantly bring forth the new through the old with a broader vision and mind and a more peaceful mentality, and promoted the new start and new realm of Chengdu's career development. Inheriting and carrying forward the positive energy of immigration cultures, Chengdu will also continue to be China's most friendly and kindest city for immigrants (including the foreign immigrants needed by Chengdu) and all the guests and friends who temporarily live or stay here for studying, doing business, investing and starting businesses, traveling and sightseeing, artistic creation and even love. It will become this city's most beautiful spiritual temperament and a kind of cultural soft power with great competitiveness.

With the combined effect of the above eight "sources of living water" and the seven charms of Tianfu Culture, Chengdu has also nurtured two outstanding endowments.

First, Chengdu is a lucky place for women to live and start businesses in. Since ancient times, women have had a high status here. Girls are well nurtured and outstanding women are generally respected; therefore, they are full of confidence and aplomb both at home and in the workplace. They are a unique style of Tianfu Culture and a special driving force for the city's "innovation, entrepreneurship, fashion and elegance." Whether it's rich in beautiful blue stockings and talented women, or those lovely beauties are both the main characters and highlights of the numerous amusing tours attended by almost all the people here; whether the

Tianfu Culture and the Modern Pursuit of Chengdu

records of customs *in Chengdu County Annals* in the Jiaqing's Reign reads, "It is the worst custom to drown a new-born daughter, but the Sichuan people, rich or poor, do hope to have a daughter. This is a good custom," or Chengdu men show to their wives the courtesy, respect and love represented by the contemporary dialect comedy *Happy Soft Ears*; they can prove that Chengdu is the most suitable place for women, especially intelligent women, to start businesses and live in. Equality between men and women and respect for women are one of the connotations of modern civilization. In this regard, Chengdu is undoubtedly the most gentlemanly and leisurely.

Second, with its gentle and friendly urban and rural style in peacetime and its long tradition of helping each other and being public-spirited in face of difficulties, Chengdu has been a city full of love and mutual aid since ancient times. In ancient times, there were countless stories of outstanding scholar-officials, rural sages, and folk righteous people who were enthusiastic about public welfare, benevolent and charitable, and helped the weak and the needy. It is the most proud memory that many times in history, Chengdu stretched its arms to accept and help the people or individuals who came to take refuge or survive in Sichuan due to various natural and man-made disasters. Since modern times, Chengdu has been especially outstanding in friendly public welfare. Take the philanthropy for example. From the late Qing Dynasty, because Sichuan, with a large population, entered the process of modernization late and there were the disputes caused by multiple factors between the parties and the warlords, many people lived a hard life, and many vagrants and beggars gathered in Chengdu. According to Tan Luying's statistics, from 1920 to 1940, there were nearly 400 charitable organizations successively in Chengdu, most of which were small in scale and few of official background, with the funding mainly collected from the private. In spite of the main managers composed of squires and rural sages and the weak social capital, Chengdu saw Yin Changling, the "First Chinese Charity Man" (Fig. 20) and his business Cihuitang with the function of self-hematopoiesis, as well as the "Chinese and Western Charity Association" jointly organized by social sages and Chinese and Western churchmen. They were all outstanding people of Chinese charitable causes at that

Chapter One
The Origin and Presentation of Tianfu Culture

time. In addition, it is worth mentioning that Chengdu was the most gentle and friendly city to the Man and Mongolian Banner people who lived or were left in the city after the 1911 Revolution (only Chengdu and Guangzhou solved the remaining problems in the mildest way at that time). Not only did there not occur the storm of "Anti-Manchus" like many other cities in China at that time, but also the issue of the Manchus' leaving or staying after the birth of the Republic of China was resolved through peaceful negotiations. In addition, during the Republic of China, the Sichuan local government in Chengdu also set aside special funds and set up charitable organizations to provide relief and assistance to the original Banner peoples who were not good at

Fig. 20 Yin Changling, the First Chinese Charity Man

economic activities fell into poverty, and this policy lasted for more than 20 years until the outbreak of the War of Resistance against Japanese Aggression. Chengdu has been such a warm city that is always full of love. In the "5.12" Wenchuan earthquake in 2008, the Chengdu people took positive actions sharing weal and woe with the people in the stricken areas with generous donation and selfless contributions, and many epic stories of great benevolence and love came one after another. Together with the relief and reconstruction of the disaster areas by the people of the whole country and the international communities under the direct leadership of the Chinese government, Chengdu people have written in human history a touching chapter that people love each other and stand together through thick and thin.

Chapter Two
Chengdu from the Perspective of Tianfu Culture

Throughout the history of human civilization, the city has always been a distinctive symbol of human civilization. The unique culture of a city creates and maintains people's spiritual hometown. The distinctive human characteristics and cultural tension also make many cities shine like stars in the world. In a word, the culture is the heart and soul of a city.

Tianfu Culture and the Modern Pursuit of Chengdu

Origin of Civilization

Along the upper reaches of the Yangtze River where rich ecosystems develop, one can locate the vibrant Sichuan Basin. Surrounded by mountains, it is inlaid with webs of rivers that wrap around at their center – the beautiful and fertile Chengdu Plain. Since ancient times, local human beings have worked hard to build homes and wealth here, forming the base of the Tianfu Kingdom (Land of Abundance), which has later attracted various neighboring cultures. Eventually, the prosperous Shu civilization came into being, and generated the everlasting Tianfu Culture (Fig. 21, Fig. 22).

Fig. 21 Cultural relics unearthed from Sanxingdui Site – Bronze Human Head

Chapter Two
Chengdu from the Perspective
of Tianfu Culture

1. Legends of Ancient Kings and Tribes of the Shu Region

The early Shu civilization equals a remarkable ionic pillar in the temple of the Chinese civilization. During the Neolithic Age of about 4,500 years ago, on the land of China there were a number of tribes and ethnic groups – the Yandi Tribe in the Wei River Valley, the Huangdi Tribe in the Yellow River Valley, the Baiyue on the Yunnan-Guizhou Plateau, and the Di and Qiang on the Tibetan Plateau. Along the upper reaches of the Minjiang River, a clan named "Shushanshi" thrived, the earliest ancient tribe named after the Chinese character "Shu." From it, the arteries of the ancient history of the Shu culture began to take shape.

Another notable ancient Shu tribe on the Chengdu Plain, Xiling Kingdom, is famous for a woman named Lei Zu. Married to the Yellow Emperor from the Yellow River Basin, Lei Zu was crowned as "The imperial concubine of the Yellow Emperor"; one of her good deeds was to teach people rearing silkworms, and won her the popular title "Notre Dame of Silkworm." Her

Fig. 22 Cultural relics unearthed from Sanxingdui Site – Figure with Human Head and Bird Body

Tianfu Culture and the Modern Pursuit of Chengdu

son, Changyi, married a woman named Changpu from the Shushanshi Clan. The couple gave birth to a boy named Gaoyang, who became Emperor Zhuanxu later. After Zhuanxu bestowed his descendants and relatives with titles and land of the Shu region, the Shu region grew into a kingdom west to the Central Plains.

Dayu, a renowned ancient historical Chinese figure, was the offspring of Lei Zu and the Yellow Emperor. It is said that he was born from a giant stone named Shi Niu located near Beichuan County. With much perseverance and valiance, he drew from previous failed experiences and led the innovations to effectively dredge floods. The success of water control in the Sichuan Basin and the spirit of battling natural disasters have made Dayu a hero, inspiring many in the Chinese history. After death, Dayu was honored as "King Dayu."

The curtains of the Shu agricultural civilization were raised with the legend unfolded of three Shu Kings' successive great ventures into the Chengdu Plain, resulting in the founding of the prosperous and unified Shu ethnic society. Eventually settling down in Chengdu, people of the Shu region lived a plowing and weaving lifestyle.

The earliest King of Shu was called Cancong. The tribe he ruled was one branch of the Di Tribe. According to legend, Cancong was a later blood of Emperor Zhuanxu and the first ancient Chinese person to domesticate wild mountain silkworms. His successor was Baiguan, who is said to have lived near where the Dujiangyan City lies today and engaged in farming. Some argue that Baiguan was originally leader of the Shushanshi Clan and lived upon the upper reaches of the Minjiang River. The clan thrived and afterwards founded a powerful chiefdom. Then it migrated to the Chengdu Plain, ruling the Shu region for hundreds of years. The third king was Yufu, originating from the upper reaches of the Minjiang River. He gradually unified clans on the Chengdu Plain and then established the first ancient Shu Kingdom at Sanxingdui (today at Guanghan, Sichuan). Since then, the ancient Shu civilization has started toward its flourish. A folklore named "King Yufu Battling at Yinma River" records the history of Yufu unifying and founding the kingdom.

Toward the end of the ancient Shang Dynasty, a man named Du Yu gained respect from

Chapter Two
Chengdu from the Perspective of Tianfu Culture

people for his knowledge of farming. They made him King of Shu, calling him "Emperor Wang." During his reign, floods frequented the Chengdu Plain; he heard of a tale about a man named Bieling from Jing (Hubei Province), whose body after death went against currents and even resurrected when it reached Chengdu. Du Yu summoned this man and learned that he knew of water. Soon, the king appointed him the official in charge of battling floods. Under the leadership of Bieling, the people of Shu successfully tamed the flood by carving through Mount Yulei and diverting the water of the Minjiang River into the Tuojiang River. The success of Bieling's water control created the basic conditions for the ancient Shu people to migrate to and settle in Chengdu. Later, he established the Kaiming Dynasty, the last dynasty in the history of ancient Shu and moved to Chengdu, starting a glorious history of the construction of "Chengdu City." In 316 BC, the Qin State conquered the Shu State and implemented the governance system of prefectures and counties, and the ancient Shu civilization gradually merged into the unified Chinese civilization.

2. Layout of Chengdu City during the Pre-Qin Period

Chengdu is the cradle of the ancient Shu civilization. Since the Shang and Zhou dynasties, it had been the political, economic and cultural center. Meanwhile, Chengdu had played an important role as the hub of cultural exchanges between the ancient Shu Kingdom and the Central Plains, the Middle and Lower Reaches of the Yangtze River, South China, Southwest China and Northwest China. From 2500 to 1700 BC, the Baodun Culture on the Chengdu Plain constructed a series of ancient city structures. A discovery of a complete house structure of bamboo-reinforced mud walls at the ancient Baodun Town ruins in Xinjin County gives a clue of what life could be at the time. The year of 2000 BC witnessed the birth of Sanxingdui, a giant city of the ancient Shu Kingdom. Around 1400 BC, the Chengdu Plain walked into the Bronze Era, and started the ancient Shu civilization with a resplendent culture composed of many bronze vessels, cities and big religious architectures. The archaeological excavation of the Sanxingdui Ruins reveals numerous material records that congregate the cultural traits of the

Tianfu Culture and the Modern Pursuit of Chengdu

Cancong Dynasty, the Yufu Dynasty, and the Du Yu Dynasty. In 1300 BC or so, the embryo of the city of Chengdu began to take its shape, with its core areas located approximately around Jinsha Village and Shi'erqiao today in the western part of Chengdu.

The Qin Empire, after conquering the Shu State, decided to launch a city construction in Chengdu area according to the city plan and system of Xianyang, the imperial capital. In total, it took 30 years to build the cities of Chengdu, Pixian, and Linqiong successively, constituting the grand "Chengdu City." Yet, problems arose during the construction, as Chengdu is not geologically identical to Xianyang because it is rich in water and wetlands. Thus, even picking up a location for constructing the city walls presented challenges. In a legend, Zhang Yi (?−309 BC), an official, made multiple attempts but failed in constructing the city walls, which collapsed immediately. In frustration, he saw a giant turtle floating over the river, circling a piece of wild land for several miles till reaching to the southwest of the city before it died. Following the turtle's trace, Zhang Yi successfully completed the construction of the walls. Such is the legend of Turtle City, which has become a nickname for Chengdu with a historical sense. Since the Qin Dynasty, Chengdu's city structure has remained almost unchanged for over 2,000 years, and become one of the established types of Chinese city structures in history. It is a rare case in the history of the Chinese cities that neither the name nor the location of Chengdu has been changed for thousands of years…

Chapter Two
Chengdu from the Perspective of Tianfu Culture

Chengdu's Grand Pattern in Han and Tang Dynasties

Since Li Bing (c. 302-235 BC) built Dujiangyan Irrigation System in the Qin Dynasty, the Chengdu Plain has been known as the Land of Abundance with rich soil stretching thousands of miles. In Western Han Dynasty, Wen Weng entered the Shu region and founded a school that became a cultural icon: The Stone Chamber. Since then, Chengdu has gained popularity nationwide.

When Liu Bei (161-223) and Zhuge Liang (181-234) came to the Shu region, they created the best political and cultural landscape during the Three Kingdoms Period. People in the Shu-Han Regime pushed the Confucian core values to the peak. Ideas such as Liu Bei's "Morality," Zhuge Liang's "Wisdom," Guan Yu's (?-220) "Righteousness," Zhang Fei's (166-221) "Courage" and Zhao Yun's (?-229) "Loyalty" all contributed a great deal to the systematic composition of China's theory of ethics.

Therefore, the once secluded, barbarian Chengdu has come onto the map as a top-tier metropolis and gradually become the strategic fort for national defense, sending workforce, money and goods to fight against outside enemies and taking in migrants during the nation's tough years.

1. Wen Weng's Enlightenment of the Shu Region

During the reign of Emperor Wu in the Han Dynasty, with the effort of iconic Confucian practitioners like Dong Zhongshu, Confucianism gradually became the nation's highest ideology; almost simultaneously, this school of thinking also spread to Chengdu as Wen Weng (156–101 BC) established the Stone Chamber to spread knowledge in the Shu region. Wen Weng brought literary education to the Shu Prefecture and founded the earliest local official school in Chinese history – Wen Weng Stone Chamber. Wen Weng created the tradition of advocating education and academics in the Shu Prefecture, bringing huge revolutionary changes of the regional cultural habits and promoting the rise of the Shu Studies as an important component of Chinese academics. Over 2,000 years after that, despite the ups and downs, and several changes of the name of Wen Weng Stone Chamber, the school has never stopped operating nor changed its location. In a way, with its history of more than 2,150 years, it is qualified as a long-standing epic and a miracle in the world's history of education. (Fig. 23)

Fig. 23 Wen Weng Stone Chamber

Chapter Two
Chengdu from the Perspective of Tianfu Culture

2. The Capital Construction in the Shu-Han Regime

In the splendid and deep-running Chinese culture, the culture of Three Kingdoms was one of the most energetic and celebrated subcultures; and Chengdu was a pivotal joint in the pan-Three Kingdoms cultural realm. People naturally connected that culture with Chengdu, Sichuan, and the legendary tales of Sage Zhuge Liang and his dedicated peers who formed an unbreakable bond in the Peach Garden. Liu Bei, the leader of the Shu State, was a famous, untamed politician with great ambitions in the Three Kingdoms Period, modest and kind, considerate and respectful to men of talent and gallant men as well. Hustling amid the troupe of the princes, Liu recovered Jingzhou and its surroundings after the Chibi Battle and entered Western Sichuan. At that time, the Central Plains were caught up in chaotic warfare that almost crumbled the economy, but Western Shu was relatively safe with sustainable economic and cultural development. The Chengdu Plain's thousand miles of rich soil provided a firm foundation for establishing the Shu-Han Regime. In the tripartite confrontation of the three kingdoms, Liu Bei unified the Ba-Shu region and took Chengdu as his capital. Centered on what is known today as Qinglong Street, Liu carried out a large-scale urban construction on the city, whose location and layout had remained unchanged until the eve of the founding of the PRC. (Fig. 24)

3. The Establishment of a State in the Cheng-Han Regime

In 304, Li Xiong (274-334) became the King of Chengdu and created seven legislations to lower taxes, reduce military services and build schools. With the help of Fan Changsheng, a hermit in the Qingcheng Mountain, and others, Li Xiong's power grew stronger day by day. Two years later, he came to the throne in Chengdu. Li Xiong had a generous temperament, modesty and humility. He loved using talents to their best potential. He was lenient on criminals and ran a lean government. In the three decades of his ruling, the Shu region saw good harvests, a safe society and empty jails. Since Li Xiong emphasized education, lessened taxes and military spending, the Shu region was peaceful during his reign and residents lived in abundance. In 338, Li Xiong's nephew Li Shou (300-343) proclaimed himself Emperor. To facilitate regional

Fig. 24 The Temple of Marquis Wu

monetary circulation management, the Cheng-Han Regime made a unified currency called Han Xing money, using the name of the initial year, Han Xing, to mark the inception of a new reign. This unprecedented invention of Cheng-Han Emperor Li Shou marked the transition from currency named by its weight to that named after the title of a reign. Since then, each emperor in Chinese history had been issuing currency named after the title of his reign to claim his legitimate ruling.

4. The City Expansion by Yang Xiu

In 347, General Huan Wen from the Eastern Jin Dynasty ended the Cheng-Han Regime and

Chapter Two
Chengdu from the Perspective of Tianfu Culture

lit Chengdu City on fire because he was not satisfied with Cheng-Han's luxurious lifestyle. The fire destroyed Shao Cheng (the smaller city in a larger city) north and south of Chengdu, leaving only the Kongming Temple intact. After the chaos of the Northern and Southern dynasties, Chengdu received little to no restoration. It was not until Yang Xiu was appointed King of Shu Prefecture that Chengdu, the central city of the Shu region, started undergoing reconstruction. Yang Xiu rebuilt Shao Cheng, historically known as Sui City, with its northern wall stretched to the north of the old urban area of Chengdu and to the south of the Wudan Mountain, and enclosing the original western and northern walls of the city. It was known as Shao Cheng of the Sui Dynasty. Shao Cheng that spanned a total of 10 miles or 17 miles if you take the old urban area in consideration was historically known as "Expansion of the Smaller City Within a Larger One." Unfortunately, Chengdu was repeatedly war-torn and the city built by Yang Xiu got destroyed many times. Because another wall was built around the city wall of Shao Cheng in the Tang Dynasty and there was big massacre of the whole city at the end of the Ming Dynasty, Shao Cheng is nowhere to be found. Yang Xiu built the city with the soil nearby and turned the leftover pit into a garden pond. He also built a tower in the East Gate of Chengdu – legend has it that it was where fairies scattered flowers from heaven. It was thus named "Flower Scattering Tower."

5. The Shu Region as the Refuge

Surrounded by mountains, the Shu region was called "The Blocked State." During the era of cold weapon, Sichuan, because of the strategic position, was relatively easy to defend. Due to the traffic occlusion, it was able to maintain a stable society and prosperous economic development, and to avoid destruction from war as well. Numerous visionary strategists such as Zhang Liang and Zhuge Liang regarded the Shu region to be the foundation of the empire. During the middle and later Tang Dynasty, Emperor Xuanzong (685–762) and Emperor Xizong (862–888) both chose the Shu region as the refuge during the rebellion of Guanzhong area. Chengdu, in their eyes, was where the banquet was gathered, lives were enjoyed, and they

might be content to retain sovereignty. Emperor Xuanzong stayed in Chengdu for a year and had huge influence on the political situations of the region. From then on, the Shu region changed from the strategic supplier of the Tang Dynasty to the place where rule and powers were competed. Officials, scholars and literati who followed Emperor Xuanzong to Chengdu had promoted the economic and cultural development of the region; therefore, people believed that Chengdu was the most prosperous city only next to Yangzhou.

6. Gao Pian's Construction of the City Wall

From the middle Tang Dynasty, population of Chengdu increased substantially, crowding the city wall. Because of soil quality, the city wall of Chengdu gradually collapsed. During the era of Emperor Xizong, the insufficient defensive ability of the city wall of Chengdu manifested itself with numerous attacks from the Nanzhao State, and with people in rural areas pouring into the city to take refuge, the disadvantage of lack of defense and small size of the city worsened its situation even more. When Gao Pian (821–887) was the governor of the prefecture, he built another city wall to reinforce the defense of the Shu region and to maintain the stability and soundness of the social economic development by extending the city wall to 12.5 kilometers long (16.5 kilometers if including outer urn cities), 10 meters high and surrounded with a long dike; therefore, it was called "Luocheng" (also called "City of Taiyuan" and "City of Taixuan"). From its scale of engineering and completeness, Luocheng has surpassed the former construction, setting up the foundation of the construction of city wall of Chengdu for the following dynasties. In addition, the city wall built during the Qin Dynasty and Sui Dynasty was based on soil, which was not stable due to the soil quality in the region. However, Gao Pian used the more solid brick as the building block. It was the first-time that brick was used to build city wall of Chengdu, a method used by later generations thousands of years to come.

7. Chengdu – the Capital of the Former and the Later Shu Dynasties

In 888, Wang Jian attacked the Shu region, and was appointed as Governor of the Shu

Chapter Two
Chengdu from the Perspective of Tianfu Culture

region 3 years later. In 907, Wang Jian proclaimed himself as the emperor after the fall of the Tang Dynasty, and named his dynasty as "Qian Shu" (the Former Shu). Although Wang Jian was not educated, he was a merciful emperor who was willing to listen to advices and respect brilliant minds. For example, when Wang Jian founded the Former Shu Dynasty, he still adopted the system of the Tang Dynasty and appointed many officials from the Tang Dynasty who were looking for refuge in the Shu region, and this policy provided strong support to and enabled the Former Shu to become a stable and wealthy state at that time. During his reign, Wang Jian not only respected talents, but also spent great efforts to govern the city, develop agriculture and silkworm produce, reduce taxes, conduct water conservancy, increase production and carry out a policy of "recuperation for all." As a result, prosperity and stability were restored, and the Shu region became the wonderland in the chaotic time.

In 934, Meng Zhixiang (874–934) became the emperor and named his dynasty "Hou Shu" (the Later Shu Dynasty). In the same year, Meng Chang (919–965) succeeded. He was a hardworking, simply dressed individual who focused on water conservancy, agricultural development and implement of the policy of "recuperation for all." As a result, the Later Shu became a powerful state and was able to extend its sphere of influence to Chang'an. Meng Chang was talented and elegant. He established "Han Lin Academy of Art," the earliest imperial art academy in China. He himself drafted the first Spring Festival Couplets in Chinese history: "The New Year welcomes the blessings of the past; the happy festival intones the long-lasting of the spring." Chengdu was also called a "City of Hibiscus" because of Meng Chang. According to the legend, Meng Chang had a concubine called "Madame of Pistil," who loved peony. Meng Chang then opened up a "Garden of Peony" and ordered citizen to plant peony, too; Meng Chang wanted Chengdu to become the city with more peony than that in Luoyang. He also ordered people to plant hibiscus trees around the city wall of Chengdu. Every fall, flowers blossomed like brocade; therefore, Chengdu was also called the "City of Hibiscus." Whenever hibiscus blossomed, Meng Chang would order to drive him to watch them with a bevy of beautiful young girls.

Chengdu's New Look in the Song, Yuan, Ming and Qing Dynasties

From the Song and the Yuan till the Ming and the Qing dynasties, Chengdu stood out for its characteristic cultural and spatial styles, even within the Chinese cultural territories. In the realm of humanities, Chengdu's cultural spirit developed in line with the city's burgeoning prosperity, witnessing the thriving of Shu Studies that blended local culture and the Central Plains' culture, and integrated the Three Doctrines—Confucianism, Buddhism, and Taoism, the influence of which extended beyond the Ba-Shu region. The Yuan Dynasty saw the people of Chengdu resisting with bravery and bursting patriotism against the invasion of the Mongolian army. On spatial layout and transformations, Chengdu went through a vassal state during the Ming Dynasty with the construction of the Prince Shu's Residence to the formation of the north-south axis of the city, and this process has made far-reaching influences on today's layout of Chengdu; in addition, with the construction of the Manchu City, Chengdu saw the appearance of double cities.

1. Shu Studies

In the Han Dynasty, Wen Weng established the school in the Shu Prefecture teaching and spreading Confucianism. The efforts had reduced barbarism considerably and cultivated an educated class and a number of talents. The literature works they created were not in the least inferior to those of the Central Plains Culture. Famous literary authors are Sima Xiangru

(c. 179−118 BC), Wang Bao nicknamed "Deep Clouds" (90−51 BC), and Yang Xiong (53 BC −18 AD). Their works had garnered fame throughout history. Meanwhile, they were also versed in Confucian classics. During the Tang and Song dynasties, the famous "Eight Great Men of Letters of the Tang and Song dynasties" included three from the Shu region – Su Shi, Su Xun, and Su Zhe. In historiography, out of the ten existing historical works left before the Sui Dynasty, there were two written by the Shu people; the Shu region took the lead in historical writings after the Tang Dynasty. In the study of Confucian Classics, Cheng Yi, a notable scholar, left behind a famous saying, "Sichuan is the best in studies of *Book of Changes*." In the following decades, a series of achieved Sichuan scholars showed up – Zhang Shi, Er Jiangjiu, Wei Liaoweng, etc., who further developed Shu Studies into a nationwide popular school of thought with unique advantages of Sichuan Regional Culture in Chinese academic researches.

2. War Against Mongolians

During the twelfth and the thirteenth century, the Mongolian cavalrymen from Northern China swept more than ten military powers around the world, stretching its territories east to the Pacific Ocean, north to Lake Baikal, west to the Black Sea and south to the South Sea. However, its intrepidity had been intercepted in the Shu region for 52 years while the troops went on attacking the Southern Song Dynasty. The Shu region was in fact the first battlefield Mongolians picked up against the Southern Song Dynasty. During the wars, Chengdu experienced several attacks, two times breached, so Yu Jie (1199−1253), an official, learning the lesson from the experience of self-defense of a single village, came up with a strategy to build citadels and villages on the mountains functioning as bastions so as to from a complete defense system in which the bastions were able to support and communicate one another through rivers and government-financed roads in fighting against Mongolian troops for a long run. The war brought about tremendous pain and disasters to the Shu region, causing a sharp reduction of population, economic recess and miserable lives.

Tianfu Culture and the Modern Pursuit of Chengdu

3. Prince Shu's Residence of the Ming Dynasty

In 1378, the first emperor of the Ming Dynasty, Zhu Yuanzhang (1328–1398) conferred titles of nobility on his eleventh son Zhu Chun (1371–1423) as King of the Shu's State, with his fiefs in Chengdu. In 1383, Emperor Zhu sent Cao Zhen (?–1393) to construct the Prince Shu's Residence, which took eight years to complete, costing considerable labor and materials. The residence embodied the typical Ming imperial style (Fig. 25). Zhu Chun immediately moved into the grand manor located right inside Da Cheng of Chengdu, at "the south of the Wudan Mountain." Three layers of walls surrounded the vast and splendid place stretching north to the Eastern and Western Imperial Rivers, south to Hongzhaobi, east to Donghua Gate, and west to Xihua Gate, inside which the gates of "Courtesy," "Wisdom," "Justice" and "Kindheartedness" were erected, and the Chengyun Gate, the Chengyun Hall, the Yuan Hall, and the Chengxin Hall stood magnificently, together with numerous resplendent pavilions, terraces and towers. Like many

Fig. 25 Prince Shu's Residence of the Ming Dynasty

historical Chinese architectures, the place faces south with the back to the north. One legend tells of the big fire on the whole city by the leader of an insurrectionary army, Zhan Xianzhong, which unexpectedly lasted for three months.

4. Immigrants from Hunan and Guangdong to Sichuan

Chengdu is a typical immigrant city. Immigrants were introduced to Sichuan after the Qin conquered the Ba-shu region. The Zhuo's from the Zhao State, the Cheng and Zheng's from the Qi State, as well as Lü Buwei the sinner, all migrated to Chengdu during this period. Refugees flooded to Sichuan from the late Eastern Han to the Western Jin dynasties, as well as in the Northern Song Dynasty. Immigrants from southern provinces such as Hubei came to Sichuan during the transition from the Yuan to the Ming dynasties, and from the Ming to the Qing dynasties. The tale "Immigrants from Hunan and Guangdong to Sichuan" refers to the special period in history when a major migration happened and lasted for more than a hundred years from the late Yuan Dynasty to the Tongzhi's Reign of the Qing Dynasty. Immigrants had very profound impact on the culture and conventions in Sichuan. In the beginning, the immigrants maintained their original customs in religion, culture, dialect, marriage, clothing, food, housing and transportation, enriching the immigration society with various and prosperous cultures and conventions. The widely spread immigrants' guilds and associations are vivid demonstrations of the immigration culture. Guildhalls, usually sponsored by immigrant merchants, served as major venues for worships, performances, communications and celebrations (Fig. 26-1 to Fig. 26-3). Backed by its large population, the immigrant community came to be so powerful that even some local people started to fake the settler identity for protection and support; thus appeared the phenomenon called as "Sichuan is full of people from Chu (ancient name of Hubei Province)." This large-scaled immigration brought to Chengdu different cultures and lifestyles from various geographies and vitalized Tianfu Culture with freshness. It is fair to say that it is the immigration culture that has resulted in the unparalleled appeal and inclusiveness of Chengdu. The immigration history of Chengdu, including the "Third Front Construction"

Tianfu Culture and the Modern Pursuit of Chengdu

Fig. 26-1 Guildhalls in Luodai Historic Town

era after the establishment of People's Republic of China, and the large population coming to Chengdu from all over the country and world after the opening-up policy, could all be viewed as the recombination of economy, culture, language, custom and social psychology happening in Ba-Shu region with the Chengdu Plain as the center. The relationship within immigrants, between immigrants and locals, gradually transformed from conflict to integration, from simple competition to mutual learning and cooperation. Generations of immigrants and their culture have not only enriched the meaning of Tianfu Culture, but also added to its vibrance, and have eventually produced the optimistic, inclusive, friendly, charitable, innovative and enterprising humanistic character of Chengdu.

Chapter Two
Chengdu from the Perspective of Tianfu Culture

Fig. 26-2 Guildhalls in Luodai Historic Town

Tianfu Culture and the Modern Pursuit of Chengdu

Fig. 26-3 Guildhalls in Luodai Historic Town

Chapter Two
Chengdu from the Perspective of Tianfu Culture

5. Construction of the Manchu City

Shortly after the Qing Dynasty put down the rebellions in Sichuan, the court sent Zhang Dedi (?-1683) to Sichuan as governor. After arriving, he saw disastrous impacts of war to this ancient city and pondered renaissance of culture and reconstructions. He soon ordered soliciting immigrants to develop agriculture and economy, transforming the war-torn city into good homes. Local dignitaries actively joined in the reconstructions of the city and its cultural landscapes with capital and finance. Meanwhile, the Temple of Marquis Wu and Du Fu's Thatched Cottage were being rebuilt. The River View Pavilion, a historical landmark in today's Wangjiang Park, was constructed during that time, a building created out of the hands of Qing people by making use of traditional local resources. Eventually, Chengdu regained the lost reputation of "Land of Abundance," after the successive constructions of more than a hundred years. As a result of this long-run effort, Chengdu had expanded to its unprecedented scale, with a rigorous and complete layout. Among many emerging cultural phenomena, the most interesting is the birth of the Manchu City. According to literature, the Manchu City was 16 kilometers in perimeter and 10 meters in height. One would walk 4.7 kilometers to go through the city. Thus, the city won the nickname a "4.7-kilometer city." Of the five giant gates, the grand East Gate was the most splendid with two plaques hanging on it saying, "Former Site of Shao Cheng" and "Comeliness and Loftiness." Not far from it was a drill ground. The Manchu City, from a bird-eye view, was like a centipede; the office of the general was the head, Changshun Street, the body; several alleyways, the feet. In its peak, there were 20,000 some Manchu solders ("Eight

Tianfu Culture and the Modern Pursuit of Chengdu

Banner Soldiers") and almost the same number of their family members. The city's population reached the scale of a town. For a considerable time, the city did not allow the entrance of the Han Chinese or the random egress of the Manchu people, making the place almost a small Manchuria state. Toward the end of the Qing Dynasty, the Manchu City opened to the outside world. In Republican China, the city dissolved into Da Cheng of Chengdu.

Chapter Two
Chengdu from the Perspective of Tianfu Culture

Revolutions in Chengdu and Its Peaceful Liberation

In the People's Park of Chengdu stands the Monument to the martyrs of the Railway Protection Movement built by the then Sichuan Railway Company in 1913 for commemorating the brave men who sacrificed their lives in the Movement in Sichuan. Outside the east gate of the People's Park is the Monument to the Sichuan Army Martyrs in the War of Resistance against Japanese Aggression, portraying a soldier with a gun in his hand and advancing northeastward, the direction the Sichuan troops headed for when they went on the expedition. Both monuments are witnesses of the courage, perseverance, loyalty, and pioneering spirit Sichuan people showed in the revolutionary wars.

1. Railway Protection Movement

In 1907, the previously government-run Sichuan-Hankou Railway Company was taken over by merchants in Sichuan. In 1910, the Qing government attempted to forcefully take back the railway building rights as well as the funds pooled for building the railways from merchants, despite of strong opposition from patriots and people in provinces including Sichuan, Hubei, Hunan, and Guangdong. This action triggered strong opposition especially among people in Sichuan, and activities calling for local development of railway projects scaled up. The stubbornness of the Qing government intensified the contradictions, and protests organized by the Railway Protection League emerged across Sichuan Province. On September 7th, General

Tianfu Culture and the Modern Pursuit of Chengdu

Governor of Sichuan, Zhao Erfeng (1845–1911) arrested the leaders of the Railway Protection League, including Pu Dianjun (1875–1934) and Luo Lun (1876–1930), and shot unarmed civilians on the scene. This was the shocking "Bloody Massacre of Chengdu." The news soon got around the province. Branches of Railway Protection League in other places headed to the capital city Chengdu and encircled the city with armed force. Then, the anti-Qing armed uprisings were in full swing. Later, under the leadership of Chinese Alliance, the massive railway protection movement triggered the outbreak of the Revolution of 1911 in Sichuan. Since the majority of Hubei New Army was dispatched to Sichuan to repress the uprising, revolutionaries in Wuhan were presented a golden opportunity to launch an uprising. On October 10th, Chinese Alliance successfully initiated the Wuchang Uprising, the democratic revolution led by Sun Yat-sen (1866–1925) spread quickly across the country, and finally overthrew the Qing Dynasty. To memorize the martyrs in the Sichuan Railway Protection Movement, Sichuan Railway Company built a magnificent 30 meters-high monument in the People's Park of Chengdu (Fig. 27).

Fig. 27 Monument to the martyrs of the Railway Protection Movement

2. Indomitable Sichuan Army

Chengdu has given birth to a multitude of heroes, who have played a vital role in leading the people to build up the country during its most difficult days and maintaining the stability of the country in peacetime, transforming China from a war-torn country to a modern socialist country enjoying long-term prosperity. In the early twentieth century, China suffered from the invasion of the Japanese imperialism and the survival of the Chinese nation was in jeopardy, especially after the Lugouqiao Incident on July 7th, 1937, when the Japanese aggressive forces occupied Northeast China (today's Heilongjiang, Liaoning and Jilin provinces) and part of Eastern China. The occupation forced the national government agencies, institutions of higher education and cultural organizations and groups, and refugees to move westwards. As the strategic base in wartime, Sichuan once again became the home for holding the national strength and hope. Confronted with the crazy attack of the Japanese military, China was on the edge of falling. To resist the Japanese military and save the country, different forces from various classes, factions, parties, and organizations in Sichuan united and formed the indomitable Sichuan army. During the years of the War of Resistance against Japanese Aggression, over three million young men in Sichuan joined the army and six army groups consisting of 400,000 Sichuan soldiers fought bravely in almost all the frontline battlefields. They left a solemn and glorious chapter in China's anti-Fascist war with their blood and lives, and were praised as the "Indomitable Army." In addition, known as the Land of Abundance, Chengdu naturally became the granary of the country, and provided food and supplies for the frontline and the home base, making great contributions in defeating the Japanese imperialism and achieving independence and liberation of the Chinese nation.

3. Peaceful Liberation of Chengdu

October 1st, 1949 saw the founding of the People's Republic of China. In November 1949, the First and Second Field Armies of the People's Liberation Army swept across Southwest China and headed straightly to Chengdu. Seeing its last stronghold in the mainland be losing, the national government led by Chiang Kai-shek (1887-1975) launched the Western Sichuan Battle, which failed as some influential Sichuan warlords chose to side with the Community Party of China at this critical moment. Different from the Chiang government, which impeded and took advantage of the Sichuan warlords, the CPC had done sophisticated United Front Work ever since the War of Resistance against Japanese Aggression. With their understanding of the CPC, these warlords had confidence in the future of China led by the CPC. Therefore, in December 1949, when Chiang was hesitating to leave Chengdu, Liu Wenhui (1895-1976), Chairman of Xikang Province of Kuomintang, Deng Xihou (1889-1964), and Pan Wenhua (1886-1950), deputy directors of the Southwest Civil and Military Authority, released a joint declaration in Pengxian County that they would support the leadership of the CPC Central Committee and the People's Government, and stand with the CPC and the Chinese people. Influenced by the peaceful uprising of Liu, Deng, and Pan, the majority of high-rank officials of Kuomintang launched uprisings with their troops, which promoted the peaceful liberation of Chengdu. On December 13th, 1949, deprived of powerful force and isolated in Chengdu, Chiang signed the last "Alternative Plan" and escaped from Chengdu, indicating the failure of his recovery plan. On December 27th, Chengdu declared its peaceful liberation, which promoted the peaceful liberation of Yunnan and the peaceful liberation negotiation of Tibet. On December 30th, under the leadership of He Long (1896-1969), commander-in-chief of the Southwest Military Area and director of the Temporary Military and Political Committee of Northwest Sichuan under the CPC, led the nonmilitary personnel of the 18th Corps of the People's Liberation Army and his 60th Army into Chengdu. Therefore, Chengdu, a time-honored city, escaped from destruction of war and has kept its layout from the Qing Dynasty.

Chapter Two
Chengdu from the Perspective
of Tianfu Culture

Famous Scholars and Sages in Chengdu

As the splendid culture has always produced a mountain of a man, many great minds, in turn, have made remarkable contributions to the development and prosperity of culture. Chengdu's sustainable development has owed a great deal not only to Tianfu Culture but also to so many famous scholars and sages who have always been the most brilliant stars in history.

1. Famous Scholars and Sages

(1) Li Bing

Li Bing (c. 302-235 BC), Governor of the Shu Prefecture in the Qin Dynasty, was a famous expert of water conservancy engineering in the Warring States Period. He knew astronomy and geography and had made great achievements in water conservancy, transportation, salt industry and other fields. When Li Bing served as the governor of the Shu Prefecture, he led the people of the Shu region to build Dujiangyan Irrigation System, the greatest and lasting water conservancy project in human history. As a result, the Chengdu Plain has become a "Land of Abundance," with its fertile grounds stretching thousands of miles. After the construction of Dujiangyan Irrigation System, Li Bing became well known and was honored as the "Lord of Sichuan" by the people of the Shu region. In order to commemorate Li Bing and his son, people built Erwang Temple nearby the Dam, which has also become a famous scenic spot in China today. The story of Li Bing's flood control in Dujiangyan was well known thousands of years ago and left many legends about Li Bing's struggle with the God of the river, one of which is about the stone rhinocero of Water-control God. It's said that when Li Bing was building Dujiangyan Irrigation System, in order to subdue the monsters in the water, he once ordered to carve five rhinoceros out of huge stones. In fact, they are the ancient water gauges to measure the water level, symbolizing Stone Gods of Water Control. It is said that two of them were transported to Chengdu, and the other three were put in the Minjiang River of Guanxian County. Of the two brought back to Chengdu, one was placed in the abyss in the outskirts of the city, and the other was placed in the Jianjiang River in the south of the city, hoping that they could forever protect Chengdu from floods. In 2014, archaeologists unearthed an 8.5-ton Warring States stone rhinocero in Chengdu, which was roughly identified as the stone beast Li Bing used to tame water.

(2) Wen Weng

Wen Weng (156-101 BC), an official and educator in the Western Han Dynasty, was appointed Governor of the Shu Prefecture in the last year of Emperor Jingdi. During his term of office, Wen Weng made outstanding achievements in promotion of education, development of talents and construction of water conservancy system. When he saw the local vulgar folk customs and backward cultural and educational conditions, he followed the principle of "Being rich before educated" to make effective governance in economy and social life, while promoting education in the Shu Prefecture and establishing the earliest local official school in Chinese history. As a result, learning became popular in the Shu region, and talents came forth one after another; in turn, they brought back to it the fame in Southwest China. Wen Weng was also the first official to expand the irrigation area of Dujiangyan Irrigation System. When Wen Weng first arrived in Sichuan, he met many victims in the streets of Chengdu. Knowing that Jianjiang River, originating in the Longmen Mountain, often caused disasters, he went to Fanxian County and Qiandi County to investigate the disaster on the spot and wrote to the court requesting for water control funds. At the same time, he began to collect money from local squires, and made great efforts to tame Jianjiang River by following Li Bing's methods of water control in the Qin Dynasty. Since then, Fanxian County had gradually become a rich and prosperous place.

(3) Sima Xiangru

Sima Xiangru (c. 179−118 BC), a native of Chengdu of Sichuan Province, Master of Ci and Fu in the Western Han Dynasty, was one of the outstanding representatives in the history of Chinese culture and literature. Talented and supported by his wife Zhuo Wenjun (175−121 BC), he was finally appreciated by Emperor Wu of the Han Dynasty with his works such as "Zixu *Fu*," "Shanglin *Fu*" and "Daren *Fu*." Later, he represented the court to communicate with the minority tribes in Southwest China, and his successful accomplishment of the task showed his outstanding military, political and diplomatic talents. Sima Xiangru is the founder of *Han Fu*, a literary form. His works are rich in words, grand in structure, and full of his extraordinary gifts in Fu. Ban Gu (32−92), a Chinese historian, and Liu Xie (c. 465−520), a literary theorist, called Sima Xiangru "Ancestor of *Ci*," and Wang Yinglin (1223−1296), with others of later generations, called him "Sage of *Fu*."

(4) Yan Junping

Yan Junping (86 BC−10 AD), also known as Yan Zun, was born in Chengdu, the Shu Prefecture in the early Western Han Dynasty. Yan Zun had been smart since he was a child. He devoted all his life to studies of *Book of Changes*, Confucianism and Lao Zi's School of Thoughts; he was familiar with the Four Classics of the Yellow Emperor, and was well informed through traveling all over the country. It's said that Yan Zun was proficient in the five elements of *Yin* and *Yang* and was good at divining the past and the future. At the end of the Western Han Dynasty, seeing that there would be chaos in the country, he was unwilling to be an official, so he lived in seclusion in Chengdu, and made a living by divination in Pixian, Chengdu, Pengzhou, Qionglai, Guanghan, Mianzhu and other places to help people solve their doubts. Therefore, in some folklore, "Yan Junping" was a symbolic figure with insight of something inexplicable. In order to commemorate him, later generations also named the street where he lived as "Junping Street." His divination conduction was special. As many people came to him, his business went very well; however, he was not greedy. Every day after earning enough money to live, he would close the stall and spend his spare time lecturing Lao Zi's thought. Yan Zun didn't involve himself in any official career in his whole life. After he was fifty years old, he mainly retired into Pingle Mountain, Pixian County, writing and teaching his disciples. During that period, he trained many top talents, such as Yang Xiong.

(5) Yang Xiong

Yang Xiong (53 BC–18 AD) from today's Pidu, Chengdu, Sichuan Province was a renowned scholar, philosopher, litterateur and linguist in the late Western Han Dynasty. Stammering when he was a little child, Yang Xiong felt it very difficult to communicate with others. He was determined to shock the world with his articles and to leave a permanent name in history. At that time, Sima Xiangru, a senior in Chengdu, was well known for his *Fu*, and Yang Xiong admired him very much. Thus, he devoted himself to study for decades. It wasn't until his forties that he went to Beijing with his literary creations "*Fu* of Sweet Spring" and "*Fu* of the East of Yellow River." After Emperor Cheng of the Han Dynasty (51–7 BC) read them, he praised Yang Xiong as Sima Xiangru's reincarnation and promoted him to be a close servant. From then on, every article Yang Xiong wrote would spread quickly and become popular. As a result, he became the most renowned *Fu* writer in China after Sima Xiangru. Yang Xiong's "*Fu* of the Shu Capital," taking the Shu capital and Shu history as the theme, created a precedent of such kinds of literature writings. Yang Xiong also wrote *Tai Xuan* and *Fa Yan* by imitating *Book of Changes* and *The Analects of Confucius*, so he was called "Confucius of the Han Dynasty."

(6) Zhuge Liang

Zhuge Liang (181–234), a native of Langya, Yangdu, Xuzhou, was a well-known statesman and strategist in Chinese history, a phenomenon with outstanding resourcefulness in the

Chapter Two
Chengdu from the Perspective of Tianfu Culture

Three Kingdoms Period, and was often regarded as the embodiment of wisdom. In Chinese history, Zhuge Liang was the first prime minister who dared to make public his own fortune. As Prime Minister, Zhuge Liang not only took the lead in clean government, but also taught his descendants to "cultivate moral character by frugal style." He regarded frugality as the basis of self-cultivation and good moral character, and thought that without frugality, there would be no virtue. Zhuge Liang took the clean government as an important political and legal construction, such as strictly controlling the scale of the Shu-Han Palace and Hui Mausoleum, carrying out strict clean government education and restriction on his later lord, the inner part of Shu Han ruling group and his descendants, etc., and finally created a political atmosphere of clean government and positive performance of official duties in the upper class of the Shu-Han Regime. Zhuge Liang finally won the long-term support and applause of the army and people of the Shu State with Chengdu as the center because of his outstanding wisdom, being entirely worn out in performing his duties, honest governance and discriminating in rewards and punishments.

(7) Li Bai

Li Bai (701-762), born in Jiangyou, Sichuan Province, was a great romantic poet in the Tang Dynasty and was hailed as the "Immortal Poet" by later generations. Li Bai spent his childhood in Jiangyou, Sichuan Province. When he was 20 years old, he wandered to Chengdu, the base of Taoism. Taoist thought and immortal theory had a great influence on the young Li Bai. The characteristics of Tianfu Culture also strongly influenced and cast Li Bai's character of pursuit of freedom, the elegant and distinctive way of thinking, and the romantic style of literary creation. His gorgeous and bright poetry and his rich imagination also benefited from that period of his life. At the age of 26, Li Bai left Chengdu to roam around the world. Later, he wrote many poems about Chengdu, among which "Chengdu seems like the Beauty of Heaven" was one of them, and the famous "Jiutian Tower" (Heaven Tower) in Chengdu was named thereafter.

Tianfu Culture and the Modern Pursuit of Chengdu

(8) Du Fu

Du Fu (712-770) was known as the "Sage of Poetry." In 759, in order to avoid the "An-Shi Rebellion," Du Fu abandoned his official position and moved to the bank of Huanhua River in Chengdu. As soon as he arrived here, Du Fu clearly felt that the rich and prosperous Land of Abundance was quite different from the turbulent North. Since then, he fell in love with the city. He built a thatched hut by the side of Huanhua River west of Wanli Bridge and lived here. This is the "Du Fu's Thatched Cottage." During that period, Du Fu wrote a lot of excellent poems reflecting the customs and human feelings of Chengdu. Four years later, Du Fu left Chengdu with his wife and offspring, and the thatched cottage was annihilated. When Wei Zhuang, the great poet, entered Sichuan, he found the old site of the thatched cottage, repaired it carefully, and presented it to the public again. Since then, in order to commemorate Du Fu, the people of Chengdu have continued to repair and expand the thatched cottage. Now the thatched cottage has been renamed as "Du Fu's Thatched Cottage Museum," and become a famous cultural "Holy Land" in Chengdu.

(9) Zhang Yong

Zhang Yong (946-1015), a native of Juancheng, Shandong Province, was an honest and upright official. As he was good at applying the carrot and stick judiciously, and conducting deeds benefitting the people, Shu people honored him as "the first able man to govern the Shu after Zhuge Liang." In 994, when Zhang Yong entered the Shu region for the first time, he managed the Shu region and people well. Coupling hardness with softness, and carrying out the policy of control through conciliation, he solved the chaos in Sichuan. In addition, Zhang Yong encouraged scholars to take part in the imperial examination and seek fame, thus greatly promoting the learning trend in the Shu region. In 1003, when a mutiny took place in the Shu region, Zhang Yong entered Sichuan again. When the people in Sichuan heard about it, they felt very happy. The situation in the Shu region was soon reversed under the governance of Zhang Yong. Zhang Yong also invented the first paper money recognized and issued by the

Chapter Two
Chengdu from the Perspective of Tianfu Culture

government in the world, "Official Jiaozi," for which he was also known as the "Father of Paper Currency."

(10) Fan Zhen

Fan Zhen (1007-1088) was from Huayang County, Chengdu Prefecture, and his family was an important academic and political family in Sichuan in the Song Dynasty. The Fan family had successively produced three renowned historians Fan Zhen, Fan Zuyu (1041-1098), and Fan Chong (1067-1141). Among them, Fan Zhen was the oldest. The three Fans successively passed the highest imperial examinations, and "Three Fans's Compiling Historical Literature" became a favorite tale among the historians' society. Fan Zhen was honest, loyal and humble, and did not talk about other people's faults in private. He was ready to die for loyalty and never gave in, even if facing fierce social criticism. Fan Zhen was devoted to practicing justice. A senior official like him had the opportunity to recommend his offspring to the court for appointment, but he always gave the opportunity to his people first, and then considered his own offspring. If the villagers could not marry or conduct funerals due to limited financial resources, he would also take the lead funding for them. About such a historically famous person from Chengdu, there are a lot of materials of his life for us to study.

(11) Zhao Bian

Zhao Bian (1008-1084) was a famous and honest official in China. Zhao Bian once served as Magistrate of Chengdu twice, and won the support of the people in Sichuan for his diligence in the administration and love of the people, selflessness and outstanding achievements. It is said that the Qingbaijiang River of Chengdu was named after his reputation as "clean and white." When Zhao Bian came to the Shu region for the first time, he vigorously advocated culture and education and explored talents. For example, Su Xun (1009-1066), the "Old Su" in the "Three SUs," was discovered by him, together with Ouyang Xiu (1007-1072) and others, in the period of his governance. In 1065, when Zhao Bian entered Chengdu again, he was really loved by the people of Shu because he adjusted measures to local conditions, made loose and simple policies, selected talents, respected etiquettes, and lived a simple life. In 1071, when the crisis arose again in Chengdu, Emperor Shenzong (1048–1085) of the Song Dynasty decided to use the 64-year-old Zhao Bian again. Knowing clearly the difficulty ahead, Zhao Bian resolutely entered the Shu region again. Since his prestige in the Shu region was very beneficial to his work of governing the Shu region, the political situation was soon stabilized.

(12) Lu You

Lu You (1125–1210), a native of Shanyin, Yuezhou in the Song Dynasty, was an official who advocated forcefully recovering the occupied half of the country. However, the minister who was ready to surrender transferred him to Chengdu to take up his duties. In 1172, the extremely depressed Lu rode a donkey to Sichuan. However, the colorful Chengdu soon pacified Lu You's frustrated mind. During his stay in Sichuan, Lu spent half of his time in Chengdu. He was infatuated with Chengdu's mountains and rivers, and loved Chengdu's life so much that he even liked to pose himself as a native of Chengdu sometimes. He called Sichuan "My Shu" and claimed, "I was bound to be a Sichuan people in my prelife." As the Chinese flowering crabapple in Chengdu was very prosperous, flower appreciation has become one of his most important entertainment activities in Chengdu. Lu You once marveled at the beautiful scenery of crabapple in Zhang's Garden and wrote many wonderful poems about it. After returning from the Shu region, Lu You also collected more than 1,100 poems recording Chengdu's beautiful scenery into the poetry collection to show his permanent yearning.

(13) Wei Liaoweng

Wei Liaoweng (1178–1237), or "Master Heshan" among scholars, was from Chengdu City, Sichuan Province. He was a famous Neo Confucian, Confucian classics scholar, educator, and master of Shu Studies in the middle and late Southern Song Dynasty. As a man of the Shu region, Wei spent most of his life in Sichuan serving as an official, giving lectures and propagating doctrines of the ancient sages. Wei once founded and recruited disciples in Heshan Academy in Pujiang and the northern part of Jingzhou, Sichuan Province, spreading the Neo-Confucianism through lectures and academic discussions. The education and academic activities of Heshan Academy had cultivated many talents for the prosperity of Sichuan geography and established Heshan School with the characteristics of Sichuan Regional Culture. Wei Liaoweng was good at writing poems and articles. His words are broad in meaning, clear and beautiful or solemn and stirring in style. Typical works include *Heshan Collection*, *Essentials of the Nine Classics*, etc.

(14) Huang Quan

Huang Quan (c. 903−965), a painter of the Five Dynasties of Western Shu, was a leading figure in the Academy of Western Shu Painting. He was good at painting of landscapes, figures, dragon and water, pine trees and stones, especially flowers, birds, grass and insects, and had created a new style of "the Huang's Luxury Style" that reflected the interest of court appreciation. He and his rival Xu Xi (dates of birth and death unknown) were called "Huang-Xu," who painted "in a bold and free manner" in the south of the Yangtze River. In style, "Huang's luxury and Xu's boldness" had a great influence on later flower-and-bird paintings. Huang Quan's paintings generally chose lucky animals and birds, rare flowers and different stones that could represent the magnificence of the palace and upper life as the theme. Before painting, he attached great importance to observing and understanding the shape and habits of flowers and birds. In painting of birds and insects, he pursued the unification of vivid images, substantial and neat background, rigorous and fine brushwork, exquisite and gorgeous painting style and magnificent colors. *The Lifelike Painting of Rare Birds* that remains today is one of the representative works. After the Mengchang, Emperor of the Later Shu Dynasty, surrendered to the Song Dynasty, Huang Quan joined the Painting Academy of the Northern Song Dynasty. Since then, the painting style of Western Shu School, represented by the Huang's family, was greatly accepted by the court of the Northern Song Dynasty. And his tradition also became the criteria of flower

and bird painting in the Northern Song Dynasty, and influenced the court painting style of the Northern Song Dynasty for nearly a century.

(15) Yang Shen

Yang Shen (1488-1559), from Xindu, Sichuan Province, knowledgeable and productive in writing, was called the "Three Great Gifted Scholars of the Ming Dynasty" together with the famous Xie Jin (1369-1415) and Xu Wei (1521-1593). In 1511, Yang Shen won the first place in the highest imperial examination in Beijing. Afterwards, Yang Shen was appointed as a scholar in the Imperial Academy, where he read a large number of ancient classics, and was known as "a scholar who reads every book available." Therefore, he was praised as the most widely-read scholar in the Ming Dynasty by contemporary scholars. Besides reading, Yang Shen devoted a lot of energy to academic creation and wrote more than 400 works in his whole life, making him one of the most productive writer in China in ancient and modern times. Today, in Xindu District of Chengdu, there is a beautiful historical garden – Sheng'an Gui Lake – to cherish the memory of him, which is not only the representative of Western Sichuan gardens, but also the only one in China that has preserved the remains from the Sui and Tang dynasties. The lake was formed in the construction of the city wall of Xindu County in the Sui Dynasty; in the early Tang Dynasty, Lu Zhaolin (636-695) built an official garden around the lake. When Yang Shen lived in Xindu in the Ming Dynasty, he planted osmanthus trees along the lakeside. Thus came the name of Guihu Lake (Osmanthus Lake).

2. Renowned Women

(1) Zhuo Wenjun

Zhuo Wenjun (175-121 BC), a native of Linqiong, Sichuan Province in the Western Han Dynasty, is deemed the most beautiful woman in the Ba-Shu region and one of the Four Talented Women in ancient China, good at drum and zither, melody, chess, painting, poetry and calligraphy. The story of "Wenjun Provoked by Qin" and "Elopement with Xiangru" in history is

Chapter Two
Chengdu from the Perspective of Tianfu Culture

a typical generalization about Zhuo Wenjun's courage to stand up to secular prejudice, pursue independent marriage and maintain marital equality. In legend, a street near today's Tonghuimen of Chengdu is the place where Zhuo Wenjun played Qin harmoniously with Xiangru, and thus named "Qintai Ancient Path," which has been extended and renamed Qintai Road. Zhuo Wenjun had the ability and wisdom to participate in and deal with family and social affairs independently. Her story, "Selling Wine," not only showed her courage to be the first in the world and her personality of advocating freedom and independence, but also obtained her father's final approval of her love choice and independent marriage. When Sima Xiangru was appointed as a court official for the second time, Zhuo Wenjun stayed in the countryside for a long time to help her father Zhuo Wangsun manage the property. With the help of Wenjun's management, Sima Xiangru didn't need to be distracted by making a living, let alone curry favour with somebody in authority for good salary, so he was able to express his mind and concentrate on writing *Fu*, and finally created a new era in the Chinese literary field of *Fu*.

(2) Xue Tao

Xue Tao (c. 768–832), a renowned poet of the middle Tang Dynasty, was originally from Chang'an. When her father Xue Yun (dates of birth and death unknown) was exiled to Shu, Xue Tao went to the Shu region with his father when she was a little girl and lived in Chengdu till death. She was on a par with Zhuo Wenjun, a talented woman in the Shu region, and later generations regarded her as one of the "Four Female Poets of Tang Dynasty" together with Li Ye (?–784), Yu Xuanji (c. 844–c. 871), Liu Caichun (dates of birth and death unknown). There were 11 governors of Western Sichuan – the top local military and political officers of Chengdu in history, most of whom had poetry exchanges with Xue Tao; many famous poets in Sichuan at that time also often sang with Xue Tao, such as Bai Juyi (772–846), Zhang Ji (c. 766–830), Wang Jian (c. 767–c. 830), Liu Yuxi (772–842), Yuan Zhen (779–831), etc. After she abandoned her career as a singing girl, Xue Tao lived by the Huanhua River in the western suburbs of Chengdu, where she carefully created a kind of exquisite, small and easy-to-write red notepaper

for writing poems. Later generations copied it and called it "Xue Tao Jian (Xue Tao Paper)." The appearance of Xue Tao Paper attracted many literati and poets. Later, someone drilled a well to draw water in the process of copying, and thus appeared Xue Tao Well, the Poem Reciting Tower, Huan Jian Pavilion, and today's Wangjiang Pavillion Park – the so-called "former residence of Xue Tao."

(3) Huang Chonggu

Huang Chonggu (dates of birth and death unknown), a native of Linqiong, Sichuan Province, was Zhuo Wenjun's fellow villager and a talented woman in the Shu region. Huang's father used to be an emissary in the Shu region. Huang received a good family education since she was a child. She was refined and cultured, skilled in poetry, literature, music, chess, calligraphy and painting. After her parents died, the family became poor and she was dependent on the old nanny for a living. Later, in adulthood, she often disguised herself as a man and travelled to Eastern and Western Sichuan to increase her experiences. It is said that she once disguised herself as a man and achieved the first place in the Imperial Examination. This legend, through the adaptation and creation in ancient and modern literature, was integrated with the real people and stories, and had a wide influence.

(4) Huang E

Huang E (1498–1569), born in Suining, Sichuan Province, was the first of the "Four Talented Women in Sichuan." She was well versed in classics and history, and good at poetry, writing, and music composing. Her talent and prestige were well known in the artistic and literary circles in Sichuan. Smart and studious when she was young, she began to write poems and composed music in her youth, which gave full play to her talent and brought her fame. After marrying to Yang Shen, she and Yang sang with each other and had strong love for each other. After Yang Shen was banished forever for no reason, Huang E lived in Xindu County for a long time, managing household chores. Feeling sad in the other corner of the world apart from Yang, she could only pour a cavity of love into the literary lines. As a result, Huang E's poetry and melody styles also changed greatly. It is worth mentioning that the creation theme of Huang E's *yuefu* poems was extended to boudoir stories. Those *yuefu* poems she wrote from the perspective of women became the pioneer of those created by boudoir groups, and she herself became one of the representatives in the development of Southern *Ci*.

Chapter Three
Many Firsts in the World or in China in the History of Chengdu

Chengdu has bred a number of remarkable achievements. To name a few, Li Bing, who guided the construction of the Dujiangyan Irrigation System; Wen Weng, who initiated the "Stone Chamber" and promoted schooling; Chang Qu's *Chronicles of Huayang* raised the curtain of compiling local chronicles, and the excellent works created by a lot of brilliant men of letters who followed Emperor Xuanzong and Emperor Xizong of the Tang Dynasty into the Shu region. A variety of cultural genes have composed a splendid page of the historical album of Chengdu, full of its cultural spirit of "Innovation and Creation, Fashion and Elegance, Optimism and Tolerance, Kindness and Public Welfare."

Tianfu Culture and the Modern Pursuit of Chengdu

Many Firsts in the World in the History of Chengdu

1. Dujiangyan Irrigation System – the World's First Water Conservancy Project

Dujiangyan Irrigation System, located along the Minjiang River in the west of the Chengdu Plain, was built in the 51th year of King Zhaoxiang of the Qin Dynasty (256 BC) and has remained the oldest irrigation system existent in the world.

The prefecture chief, Li Bing, from the Qin Dynasty, invented the "Fish Mouth-shaped Levee," a dam-free dividing dyke made of bamboo cages full of stones and with their tops in conical shape. When these cages were placed at the bottom of the river, the part above water resembled the mouth of fish. The "Fish Mouth-shaped Levee" makes use of slopes and stream courses, dividing the Minjiang River into an inner river and an outer river. The inner river receives water from the Minjiang River, guaranteeing usage of the irrigation water and the domestic water, and the outer river is wider, serving the function of water division because in flood seasons during summer and autumn, its water flow would be automatically higher than that of the inner one. The "Fish Mouth-shaped Levee" is the most important hub part of this project as well as flood control works on the Chengdu Plain. Li Bing then built the "Flying Sand Weir" 700 meters down from the "Fish Mouth-shaped Levee," and the "Bottleneck-shaped Water Inlet" 200 meters further down from the Weir. In flood, when the discharge of water of the inner goes beyond the capacity of the "Bottleneck-shaped Water Inlet," the "Flying Sand Weir" will divert the

Chapter Three
Many Firsts in the World or in China in the History of Chengdu

water into the outer river, which functions as water discharge control.

The Dujiangyan Irrigation System designed by Li Bing 2,200 years ago has more or less maintained its original look and function, nurturing the Land of Abundance, and winning the reputation "Top of World Records."

2. Boiling Salt with Natural Gas – the World's Earliest

The digging of well salt in Chengdu started as early as in the Li Bing's time. According to *Chronicles of Huayang*, when Li Bing was ruling the Shu Prefecture, he ordered people to dig salt ponds along the brine courses in Guangdu (today's Shuangliu County). In the Western Han Dynasty, more than twenty salt wells were successfully dug in places like Linqiong (today's Qionglai County) and Pujiang. Thus, with more salt wells dug, there emerged a number of wealthy families and businessmen who made exorbitant profits out of these wells and fishing fields.

The pan-region of Chengdu has been the first place to boil salt with natural gas in the world. During the period of Three Kingdoms in the Eastern Han Dynasty, burning wells or natural gas were found in Linqiong County. Firewood-boiled salt is of no comparison to that of the natural gas approach as the latter improves much the extraction rate of salt. In legend, Zhuge Liang valued natural-gas-boiled salt and went in person to survey the salt ponds. The high efficiency of natural-gas-boiled salt and the recommendation from officials stimulated the enthusiasm of private development of natural gas.

3. Shu Tea – the Start of World's Tea Culture

China has a long history of tea culture. In the Qin and Han dynasties, there was the custom of processing and drinking tea in Chengdu and nearby areas. According to *Tong Yue*, written by Wang Bao from the Western Han Dynasty, Wang Ziyuan, from Zizhong, stipulated the routine work the servant had to do in the indenture of buying and selling servants, including cooking tea, getting the clean tea wares ready, and buying tea at Wuyang. Such a record is the earliest in both China and the world regarding planting, drinking and buying tea.

Tianfu Culture and the Modern Pursuit of Chengdu

Sichuan has always been the fine region of tea production. Lu Yu, from the Tang Dynasty, mentioned in his work *The Classic of Tea*, that many places in Sichuan were rich in tea, such as the seven places of Pengzhou, Mianyang, Meishan, Qionglai, Ya'an, Chongzhou, and Guanghan, among which the tea from Mount Mengding at Ya'an was chosen as the royal tribute. Mount Mengding, located in the middle of the Qionglai mountains, surrounded by airy clouds and lush greens, provided the most suitable environment to grow tea. Tea from Mount Mengding has gained much fame over time and is frequently referred to in the Chinese literary works and poems (Fig. 28). Apart from the highest-grade tea of Ganlu and Huangya, it has several other brands, such as Leiming, Wuzhong, Queshe, Longtuan, Fengbing, etc.

Fig. 28 Shu Tea planted in Mount Mengding

Chapter Three
Many Firsts in the World or in China in the History of Chengdu

4. "The Bian's Family from Longchi Archway" – the World's Earliest Publisher

During the middle and late Tang Dynasty, Chengdu became the major printing center in the country. The Bian's family from Longchi Archway, Chengdu, was the earliest publisher from existent records. *The Tuo Ronnie Sutra Printed by the Bian's in Longchi Archway, Chengdu County, Chengdu Prefecture* (now preserved in the Museum of Chinese History), printed in the Tang Dynasty, was excavated from a silver bracelet at a Tang tomb near the River View Pavilion in Chengdu in 1944. "The original one was a piece of thin square paper – the Tang cocoon paper which was made from pulp of cocoon, mulberry leaves, skins, linen and sandalwood. Viewed under the light, it has some sheen on it, thin yet pliable and tough, with its frame 31 cm high and 34 cm wide, on both sides. Outside the frame is inscribed "Sutra printed and sold by the Bian's from Longchi Archway, Chengdu County, Chengdu Prefecture" (*General History of Chengdu*, p. 232). It is estimated that this article was published after the year 757. Woodblock printing went quite popular at that time in Chengdu, which reflected the prosperity and stability of the city. In the Tang Dynasty, Chengdu took a leading place nationally in politics, economy and culture.

5. Jiaozi – the World's Earliest Paper Currency

In the Tang Dynasty, Chengdu was already a prosperous metropolis of political, economic and cultural influence. In the Five Dynasties and the Song Dynasty, Sichuan's economy kept on thriving due to the stable political situation and the geographical advantages. Meanwhile, currency needs soared as circulation of commodities increased quickly. Thus, heavy iron currency was no longer a suitable option. In such new tendencies, the Shu people invented Jiaozi to ease commercial transactions, which in turn enhanced the credibility of paper bills. In case of bulk trade, one needed to deposit a huge sum of iron money into a money shop for a temporary custody at first, which, then, issued a bill of credit. Such a kind of bill was the earliest Jiaozi. Later, businessmen did not want to pay the management fee to the money shop nor carry a lot of iron money, so they applied Jiaozi directly in transactions, giving it the full function and role of paper currency. Therefore, Jiaozi is the inevitable result of the development of commodity economy to a certain extent.

Tianfu Culture and the Modern Pursuit of Chengdu

Many Firsts in China in the History of Chengdu

1. Chengdu – The Only City with Its Name and Location Unchanged for More than 2,000 Years in China

Two thousand years ago, the last dynasty of ancient Shu – the Kaiming Dynasty, moved its capital from Piyi or Fanxiang (today in Shuangliu County) to what is now the north of Chengdu's downtown area, naming the capital "Chengdu." In the fifth year of Emperor Shen's Reign of the Zhou Dynasty, the Qin State conquered the Shu State and set this city as one of the counties – Chengdu County. Since then, despite the rises and falls of dynasties, the name of Chengdu has remained unchanged.

The city scale of Chengdu has over time expanded, yet its general location has never changed for thousands of years. Among all cities in China, Chengdu has had the longest history of city construction. In the 27th year of Emperor Huiwen's Reign of the Qin Dynasty (311 BC), the court ordered Zhang Yi and Zhang Ruo to build the city of Chengdu. Later, when Li Bing was ruling the Shu Prefecture, he directed much engineering work on irrigation and city construction, resulting in the beautiful view of "Pi River and Jian River adorning the city" with "nine bridges across the river around it." In the Han Dynasty, when Emperor Wu developed the minority areas in Southwest China, the old Chengdu City built in the Qin Dynasty was further stretched to the north and the east. Zhuge Liang, from the Three Kingdoms Period, set up the base camps together with a lot of constructions in the southern and northern suburbs of Chengdu. Thus, the

Chapter Three
Many Firsts in the World or in China
in the History of Chengdu

city extended its borders relentlessly. Far from the Central Plains, where wars took place often and intensely, Chengdu enjoyed a relatively long peaceful time, and was seldom involved in the national political and military struggles.

2. Wen Weng's Stone Chamber – The Earliest Regional Official School in China

Weng Weng, born in Lujiang, Anhui, China, had picked up intellectual interests since childhood and was versed in *Spring and Autumn Annals*. In the last year of Emperor Jing's Reign of the Han Dynasty, he was appointed as the prefect of the Shu Prefecture. When he arrived in the Shu Prefecture, what came into his eyes was the lack of educational institutions and a society full of barbarous pulses. As a result, Wen Weng was determined to establish the Stone Chamber School, the very first regional higher education institution founded and run by local government in China's history, located at where the elite secondary school, Chengdu Stone Chamber Middle School is today. The "Stone Chamber" School recruited students from all counties of Chengdu. All the enrolled students were entitled to their families free of corvee, those of outstanding grades would be appointed as officials, and even those less outstanding granted laudatory titles of "Filial Piety" and "Able Farmer." Over time, the trend to receive education had been formed in the Shu region, which became a glorious lifestyle for young people to assume. Wen Weng and the Stone Chamber School laid the foundation of Shu Studies, revealing the curtains of this classic school of thought that would attain much influence in the history of China.

3. *Dialect* – World's First Treatise on Dialect

The full name of *Dialect* is *Interpretation of Other Dialects in Youxuan Messenger's Language*, written by Yang Xiong of the Western Han Dynasty. Youxuan was a convenience vehicle ridden by ancient court messengers. The corpus of *Dialect* was collected from local languages and dialects by Youxuan messengers or emissaries when they itinerated around vassal states and kingdoms. In content, *Dialect* covers a wide area, including almost all the territory of the Han Dynasty. Longitudinally, *Dialect* has recorded the change and development of vocabulary in about seven or eight hundred years, from as early as the Spring and Autumn Period to the Qin and Han dynasties. *Dialect* consists of 13 volumes, 675 items of vocabularies and around 11,900 words in total. It is hard to imagine that a linguistic work of such scale was congregated and completed by a single person (Fig. 29).

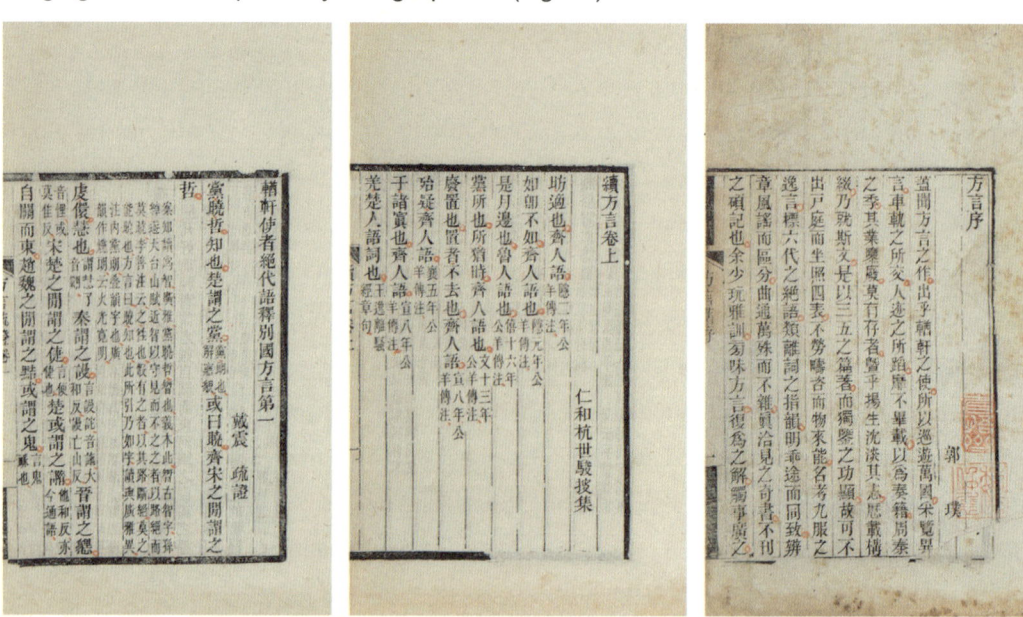

Fig. 29 *Interpretation of Other Dialects in Youxuan Messenger's Language*

4. Chengdu Lacquerware – China's Largest Official Lacquerware Production Base

From the Qin to Shu-Han dynasties, Chengdu's lacquerware production took a leading role with its high level of production process and painting skills nationwide, and the city became the largest base in China. The most representative was the "Shu Prefecture Handicrafts Section," which mainly produced lacquer utensils and parts of musical instruments, weapons, vehicles and horse ornaments. The lacquer painting process in Chengdu was one of the earliest in

Chapter Three
Many Firsts in the World or in China
in the History of Chengdu

China. As early as in the Qin and Han periods, Chengdu's lacquerware began to be coated in black, brown and red colors. The production of lacquerware peaked in Chengdu during the Shu-Han period. The Chengdu lacquerwares unearthed from the tomb of Zhu Ran of the Eastern Wu (a kingdom from the Three Kingdoms Period) in today's Ma'anshan Mountain in Anhui Province show a very high level of processing and are quite popular with people.

5. *Chronicles of Huayang* – China's Earliest Chronicle of Regional History

Chang Qu, or Daojiang, born in today's Sanjiang Township of Chongzhou, wrote *Chronicles of Huayang* in the Eastern Jin Dynasty. The name Huayang refers to the south of Mount Hua, which came from a sentence in the ancient book *Shang Shu: Yu Gong* – "Huayang and Heishui are two names only for one place – Liangzhou." As Liangzhou in the south of Mount Hua generally conforms to the Ba-Shu region, Hanzhong, and Nanzhong in Chang Qu's works, this work was so named. *Chronicles of Huayang* has twelve volumes, carefully recording the historical courses, geographical shifts, material cultures, local politics, regime changes, individual stories and so on. It is the first local chronicle in China's history and of high historical data value, providing precious historical literatures for studies and researches into the politics and culture of the Shu region before the Eastern Jin Dynasty as well as the economy, ethnicity and customs of the ancient Southwest China.

6. *Kaibao Tripitaka* – the World's First Officially Engraved Buddhist Tripitaka

Kaibao Tripitaka was completed in the Kaibao's Reign of Emperor Taizu of the Song Dynasty. The emperor, in the fourth year of the Kaibao's Reign (971), sent Zhang Congxin to preside over the engraving of the entire set of Buddhist scriptures in Chengdu. The project closed in the eighth year of the Tai Ping Xing Guo reign of Emperor Taizong (983), which was the first officially engraved Buddhist Tripitaka in Chinese in the world.

Tianfu Culture and the Modern Pursuit of Chengdu

Kaibao Tripitaka, based on the catalogues of Buddhist sutras collected in the Tang Dynasty's *Interpretation of Buddhism in the Kaiyuan Era*, consists of 13,000 engraved blocks, 5,048 volumes, 480 sets, and is in the scroll format. On each block there are 23 lines and 14 characters in each line, and with the title, the block number and the set number engraved at the top of each block and the engraving date and relative remarks at the end of each volume. After the completion of the first-stage engravings, more versions of translation joined in it. In the last few years of the Northern Song Dynasty, its set number rose to 653, the volume number, 6,628. Unfortunately, after the Jingkang Event broke out, the Jin army plundered the whole set of *Kaibao Tripitaka*. Today, the entirety of *Kaibao Tripitaka* has been lost, and even the only left volumes are incomplete. *Kaibao Tripitaka* is famous for its exquisite engraving, neat and rigorous typography, not only reflecting the wonderful craftsmanship and techniques of printing developed in Chengdu during the Song Dynasty but also containing highly precious and reliable Buddhist records and writings for further studies and researches of Buddhism.

7. "Shu Drama Crowning China" – the Earliest Dramas of Real Sense in China

Shu Drama has a long-life course, its origin possibly dating back to the ancient Zhou Dynasty (Fig. 30). A legend tells that during the reign of Emperor Xian of the Zhou Dynasty, the king of Shu married a mountain spirit. To delight her, the king composed a song named "Dongping," which started the tradition of amusing people with music and dance in the Shu region. During the Qin Dynasty, after Shu Governor Li Bing completed the construction of Dujiangyan Irrigation System, the local people would hold the sacrificial rite of "Water Discharge" accompanied with performances before the annual repair and maintenance of the Project. Such a kind of performance done with disguised wizards and music gods was the prototype of drama. In the Three Kingdoms Period, the king of Shu Kingdom, Liu Bei, asked people to play his literatis Xu Ci and Hu Qian, the scene derived from the case where the two men were debating and attacking each other. This was the earliest form of theater practices in the Shu region.

Chapter Three
Many Firsts in the World or in China in the History of Chengdu

Fig. 30 Shu Drama

Chengdu's "Zaju" (poetic drama set to music) in the Tang Dynasty was among the earliest forms of drama plays in the history of China.

From the last few years of Tang to the Five Dynasties, it was by no means fortuitous and isolated that Zaju came from Western Shu already with well developed drama performances of high standards. Please take a look at the skills of men playing women in the Shu region, who did much better than those in Chang'an, the capital. According to records, the best effect of theater designs and set designs was in the Shu region. Musical satiric plays in the Tang Dynasty were exquisite in both form and content, such as *Double Wheat Ears*, which also originated from the Shu region. Once more, the most committed actors and actresses of dance, music and martial arts were nowhere else except for the Shu region. (*On Tang Dramas and Tricks*, first half, p. 246)

Tianfu Culture and the Modern Pursuit of Chengdu

Thus, it is highly likely that poetic dramas set to music originated in the Shu region, particularly the ones played by both men and women.

8. Daci Temple – the Biggest Buddhist Art Palace in the Late Tang and Five Dynasties

Daci Temple is also called Great Sage Ci Temple. When Emperor Xuanzong of the Tang Dynasty took refuge in the Shu region, he ordered to construct Daci Temple, and wrote down four characters – "Great Sage Ci Temple." This temple as a royal Buddhist temple was the biggest one in Southwest China, where numerous sages and eminent monks chanted sutras and advocated Buddhism. The temple is more famous for its beautiful murals, which were the main carriers showcasing art, culture and religion of that age. Legend says that in Daci Temple, there used to be 8,524 various buildings in 96 yards with 1,215 murals of Buddha, 10,488 of Bodhisattvas, 68 of Śakro devānām indrah and King Brahama, 1,785 of Arhats and ancestral monks, 262 of Caturmahārājakayikas and Lord Shiva, and 158 about Buddhism stories and many god statues. In addition, there were murals of mountains, waters, flowers, birds, pavilions, dragons, and tigers. The total number of murals reached beyond 15,500, with many out of the hands of famous painters of the time. The murals in Daci Temple, either in the scale or in craftsmanship, would count among the grandest Buddhist art palaces in China in the late Tang and Five Dynasties.

9. Heming Mountain – the Birthplace of Chinese Taoism

Taoism is a Chinese-born region, originating at Heming Mountain near Chengdu in the Eastern Han Dynasty. The founder was Zhang Ling, from Feng County, Jiangsu. In the reign of Emperor Shun (142) of the Han Dynasty, Zhang Ling moved to Heming Mountain with his family and disciples, founding "the Doctrine of the Celestial Master," a Taoist school of practices and ideas. Through teaching and propagating the Taoist doctrines, Zhang Ling attracted quite a large number of disciples; hence the name of Taoism became popular in the Ba-Shu region.

Chapter Three
Many Firsts in the World or in China in the History of Chengdu

Taoism mainly carries out its religious theory through the application of *Fu* talismanic practices and alchemy, in which a series of elements could be closely connected to the Shu culture. For instance, the Taoist talisman characters have close ties to many Shu symbols. "The Shu Symbols" is the name given by the academia to the Shu pictographs, which are usually found to have inscribed on the bronze vessels and lacquerwares excavated in the Ba-Shu region. The Taoist talisman characters are at once motifs and characters, gradually derived from the formation, grammar, composition and meanings of the Shu pictographs.

10. "Shu Stone Classics" – The Earliest Assembled Collection of the "Thirteen Classic Works" in China

"Stone Classics" refer to the literature inscribed onto stones, usually organized and commissioned by imperial courts or feudal governments in pre-modern China (Fig. 31). The emergence of stone classics provided an officially accredited and unified version for people to receive regular and proper education. They also played an important role in publication, knowledge spreading and cultural preservation.

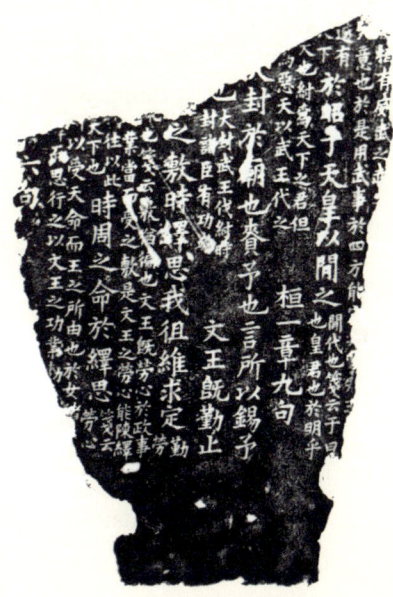

Fig. 31 Shu Stone Classics

As Meng Chang began to carve the "Shu Stone Classics" in the first year of Guangzheng's Reign of the Later Shu Dynasty, they were also named "Meng-Shu Stone Classics" or "Guangzheng Stone Classics," with the following characteristics: (1) The longest time. Starting in 938, the project was finished in the fifth year of Xuanhe's Reign of Huizong in the Song Dynasty

159

(1123), taking 112 years in total.¹ (2) Fine editions. The printing and engraving of "Shu Stone Classics" were based on "Kaicheng Stone Classics," whose original edition was edited by Kong Yingda and Jia Gongyan in the Tang Dynasty, and was officially released as an authoritative version of the imperial examination. (3) The earliest version of the Thirteen Classic Works in China's history. The Thirteen Classic Works were the core treatises of Confucianism. The six classics Confucius recommended were *Book of Changes*, *Book of Documents*, *Book of Songs*, *Book of Norms*, *Yue Jing*, and *Zuo's Commentary*. In the Han Dynasty, *Yue Jing* was lost, but several more like *Rites of Zhou* and *The Analects of Confucius* were added to form a group of nine classics at first, and finally to twelve classic works. In the fifth year of Xuanhe's Reign in the Northern Song Dynasty, with *Mencius* included into the Stone Classic Works², there were thirteen classic works in total, constituting of the first assembled collection of "Thirteen Classic Works" in the Chinese history. Thus, the "Shu Stone Classics" established the most stable norms and models of Confucian literature, playing an indispensable role in the development of systemic Confucian Studies.

11. *Materia Medica for Emergency from Classics and Historical Documents* – The Popular Pharmacopoeia of the Longest History in China

Materia Medica for Emergency from Classics and Historical Documents, written by Tang Shenwei, a Chengdu native from the Song Dynasty, was very popular and of the longest history in China. Tang Shenwei moved to settle in Chengdu in the Yuanyou's Reign of Emperor Zhezong of the Song Dynasty, and completed the book of 32 volumes from about 1097 to 1107.

---

1 Some scholars regarded Chao Gongwu's supplement of the *Book of Ancient Literature* (1168-1170) as the final completion of "Shu Stone Classics," thus believing that the time span of making "Shu Stone Classics" was around 230 years (*General History of Chengdu IV*, p. 305). Some other scholars took the fifth year of Xuanhe of Huizong in Song Dynasty as the closing year of "Shu Stone Classics," believing the time span of 112 years (Shu Dagang: "The Collection of 'Shushijing' and 'Thirteen Classics,'" *Zhouyi Research*, 2007, issue 6, p. 72). The book chose the second view.

2 The nine classics refer to the nine classics based on the five classics that were added to *Zhouli*, *Yili*, *Gongyang* and *Guliang*. "Twelve classics" refer to the twelve classics that were added to *Xiaojing*, *The Analects of Confucius* and *Erya* when the stone classics were completed. In the Song Dynasty, *Mencius* was added. Therefore, there are a total of thirteen classics.

Chapter Three
Many Firsts in the World or in China in the History of Chengdu

This pharmacopoeia is a collection of great achievements in the development of the Chinese pharmacology. It has two traits: (1) It is a work compiled with annotations. Many medical books Tang Shenwei referenced to have been lost today, but can be traced in Tang's pharmacopoeia. (2) The collection of medicines in the book was the largest in and prior to the Song Dynasty, for it gathered medicines of 1,746 kinds based on previous records and researches, five times the medicines of *Sheng Nong's Herbal Classic*.

According to the records, *Materia Medica for Emergency from Classics and Historical Documents* was in popular use for almost five hundred years.

12. Shu Brocade – the Highest Brocade Production in China in the Eastern Han Dynasty

Shu brocade, well known for its exquisite craftsmanship, lavish decorative patterns and fine colors and textures, was the favorite goods of the royals and aristocrats. In Western Han tombs such as the Mawangdui, Changsha, pieces of the beautiful Shu brocade were excavated. A few historical records mentioned as well that Shu brocade was held as imperial gift granted to neighboring countries.

Shu, the Chinese character, contains the character, "worm," originally meaning the silkworm in the hollyhock. As the main abbreviated name of Sichuan, the character implies that since ancient times, Sichuan has been prolific with a large scale of silkworm breeding and mulberry growing. Furthermore, the legend of King Cancong leading the ancient Shu in silkworm breeding further tells of the close ties between Chengdu and silk weaving. Since many of the patterns on Shu brocade are drawn from myths and legends, divination inscriptions, historical figures, landscapes, flowers and birds, etc., they are carrying special or unique metaphors. Shu brocade thus is the vivid historical material of the Chinese applied arts. The production of Shu brocade involved complex and artful processes, starting from patterns creating, silk yarns dyeing, then looms setting, and finally hand embroidering. In 2006, the craftsmanship of Shu brocade was included in the first batch of the National Intangible Cultural Heritage List, with the approval of China's State Council.

Tianfu Culture and the Modern Pursuit of Chengdu

13. The First Couplet in China

Couplets, also known as pair of antithetical phrases, are "the combination of antithetical sentences, door gods and peach wood charms against evil." The antithetical couplet is a unique form of literature and art of the Han nationality in China, and part of the brilliant national cultural heritages in China. "The New Year welcomes the blessings of the past; the happy festival intones the long-lasting spring" written by Meng Chang, King of the Later Shu Dynasty is the earliest couplet in the Chinese history.[1] It is a typical Spring Festival blessing couplet, which raised the curtain of the Chinese couplet culture. Since then, in the Song and Yuan dynasties, both literati and the rustic poor created antithetical couplets as their taste; in the Ming and Qing dynasties, Zhu Yuanzhang, the emperor of the Ming Dynasty, advocated antithetical couplets; in the Qing Dynasty, Emperor Kangxi and Emperor Qianlong preferred antithetical couplets. During that time, the antithetical couplets were more abundant in content and more diverse in form, and many famous couplets were handed down to this day.

The above mentioned world's firsts and China's firsts in the history of Tianfu Chengdu, reflect that Chengdu has made remarkable achievements in ideological culture, education, handicraft industry, agriculture and other aspects with Tianfu Culture "innovation and creation, elegance and fashion, optimism and tolerance, friendship and public welfare" as its spiritual support and power source. Chengdu is known as the "Land of Abundance" not only for its fertile land and rich products, but also for its innovation development leading the world and China, which has laid a solid foundation for Chengdu to become a world-famous cultural city.

---

1 Although at present suspected couplets are found in the pedigrees from Tang Dynasty and posthumous papers from Dunhuang, the earliest couplets recorded in the official history are Meng Chang's Spring Festival blessing couplet. Therefore, this book argues that this couplet is the first couplet ever recorded.

Chapter Four
Chengdu in the Literary Works of the Past Dynasties

Neither the name nor the site of Chengdu has ever changed for more than 2,000 years. In the thousands of years of history, Chengdu has gradually developed into a political, economic and cultural central city in Southwest China, and a world-renovated "Land of Abundance."

Tianfu Culture and the Modern Pursuit of Chengdu

Chengdu in "*Fu*"[1] of the Han and Wei Dynasties

Under the pen of the literati of the Han and Wei dynasties, Chengdu boasted the historical features of the grand founding of ancient Shu State, the abundance of geographical products, the unique folk customs, and the bustling and hustling fairs. Through the literary masterpieces handed down, later generations can understand Chengdu in the Qin, Han, Wei and Jin dynasties.

1. Founding a State and Building the Capital

The origin of ancient Shu preceded that of the Yellow Emperor. According to Dr. Duan Yu, the kingdom should originate before 2500 BC. In the time of the Yellow Emperor, it began to enter the civilization era, during which the state regime began to form. At that time, there were three clans led by Cancong, Baiguan, and Yufu respectively. After Yufu eventually defeated the other two clans, he established the first ancient Shu Kingdom – Yufu Dynasty, setting its capital at Sanxingdui, Guanghan. In the "Shudu *Fu*" ("Ode to the Capital of Shu") written by Yang Xiong of the Western Han Dynasty, "Shudu" refers to Chengdu; around the early years of the Western

---

1 *Fu*: a literary form, sentimental or descriptive composition, often rhymed.

Chapter Four
Chengdu in the Literary Works of the Past Dynasties

Zhou Dynasty, Du Yu seized power, founded the second dynasty of ancient Shu, Du Yu Dynasty, and moved the capital to Chengdu.

A zealous construction wave rose in Chengdu after the Qin State occupied the Shu State. In the 27th year (311 BC) of Huiwang's Reign of the Qin Dynasty, Zhang Yi and others built Chengdu City for the first time. There were 18 gates in the city, and more than 400 grass-roots organizations of residents. The prefecture chief Li Bing of the Qin Dynasty dredged the "two rivers" passing by the city in the west and south respectively. There were seven bridges across the waters of the two rivers. In the second year (115 BC) of Yuanding's Reign, Emperor Wu of the Han Dynasty ordered the reconstruction of Chengdu City. On the basis of the seven bridges, two more bridges were added. At that time, nine bridges were the most important transportation hub connecting the living quarters in the west (called Shao Cheng or Smaller City) and the administrative areas in the east (called Da Cheng or Larger City). At the time of the Qin and Han dynasties, there were many waterways in Chengdu, and the main mode of transportation was water transportation. The two rivers and nine bridges were of great significance to the development of Chengdu.

Chengdu's urban landscape is determined by the potential of mountains and rivers and designed by human resources, with a wide construction pattern: the Minshan Mountain standing in the north, the two rivers flowing throughout the territory in the south, Da Cheng built in the east for decision-making over thousands of miles, and Shao Cheng designed in the west for the prosperous fairs and streets, all of which are favorable conditions for Chengdu to become a famous city in China. Since the ancient Shu period, Chengdu has been carrying on the cultural spirit of innovation, creation, optimism and inclusiveness. Many innovative urban constructions have been realized in Chengdu.

2. Resources and Marketplaces

Chengdu has a vast area of fertile land, with different characteristics in the east, west, north and south due to different geographical environment. According to Yang Xiong's "Ode to the Capital of Shu," there are two mountains in the east of Chengdu, Tongliang and Jintang, with

Tianfu Culture and the Modern Pursuit of Chengdu

fire wells and deep abysses, rich in jade, cinnabar, Qiong bamboos, Taozhi bamboos, stone swallows, stone crabs, strange snakes, etc. In the south of Chengdu, there are two counties, Qianwei County and Keke County, full of high mountains and rich in underground waters, and in its areas closer to Chengdu, there are precious stones, and farther away, there are silver, lead, tin, horses, rhinoceros, elephants, etc. In the west of Chengdu, there are copper and iron mines, salt wells, endless orange and shaddock trees, and between Lake Qionghai and Heishui, many auspicious beasts in myth or legends could be seen walking on the wetland. In the north of Chengdu, there is Minshan Mountain, where Baima Tibetans and Qiang people live, with many birds and animals, such as sheep, elk, cattle, musk deer, leopard and yellow bear. Thanks to its fertile land and humid climate, Chengdu provides a good environment for the reproduction of animals and plants. Therefore, there are many kinds of precious birds, animals, flowers and fruits in Chengdu. Chengdu is also known as the world's granary because of its abundant grain produce. Since the Qin, Han, Wei and Jin dynasties, Chengdu has been the most important food supplier region in China. With such an endowment of natural resources, Chengdu has gained the title of "Land of Abundance."

When the city of Chengdu was built in the Qin Dynasty, the market operation mechanism began to be established, such as the implementation of "Liesi" and "Shiji." "Liesi" refers to the establishment of several different trading areas in the market according to the nature and types of commodities; "Shiji" refers to a special household registration management system for merchants. In addition, Chengdu City was divided into Da Cheng (Larger City) in the east and Shao Cheng (Smaller City) in the west, the former being taken as the main administrative area, the latter as the main living and trade area. In Shao Cheng markets, there were all kinds of shops that attracted merchants around, and a dazzling array of goods was piled up like hills. Yang Xiong's "Ode to the Capital of Shu" also contains a vivid description of the bustling scene of Chengdu market in the middle and late Western Han Dynasty, especially the interesting scene where businessmen from all over the country found it hard to communicate and bargained in northern and southern dialects.

Chapter Four
Chengdu in the Literary Works of the Past Dynasties

3. Folkways and Customs

Ancient books record that Shu people are clever, brave, and fond of a leisurely life and delicious food. Yang Xiong mentioned in "Ode to the Capital of Shu" that Shu people enjoyed the custom of watching fish, meeting friends and having a feast. From the early spring to the late summer, both ordinary people and noble families in Chengdu were happy to watch fish by the river. The rich families made a feast with all kinds of delicacies in their mansions. Yang Xiong spared no efforts to give a thorough description of all the delicacies of the time: no other sea fish than abalone and mackerel from Jiangdong would catch their eyes, and only cattle and sheep from Longxi, pigs fed with rice, game from mountain hunting, young birds, the essence of mountain animal brains, the delicious abdominal fat of water animals, and so on could satisfy their taste. Then if you would encounter a famous chef like Yi Yin, who removed fishy smell with onion, leek, ginger, garlic, etc., you could simply get the best taste in the world so delicious beyond words. Nowadays, Sichuan cuisine is well known as one of the main cuisines in China, and this has a lot to do with its long history of catering culture.

Chengdu is rich in natural resources and beautiful in mountains and rivers. During the Sui and Tang dynasties, with the economic development, Chengdu's folkways and customs also kept pace with the times, such as visiting temples and worshiping Buddha on the first day of the first lunar month, going to the lantern show on Lantern Festival night, climbing mountains and chanting poems on Shangsi Festival. These customs were gradually formed with the historical progress of Chengdu.

Tianfu Culture and the Modern Pursuit of Chengdu

Chengdu in the Sui and Tang Poetry

During the Sui and Tang dynasties, Chengdu witnessed the second climax of economic and cultural development. When Emperors Xuanzong and Xizong entered the Shu region, they brought advanced technology and many cultural celebrities into it, injecting new elements into the development of Chengdu. With the time passing by, Chengdu became prosperous, and more standardized, orderly and international. Apart from its extant famous places of historic interest, many new cultural landscapes were formed with more scholars' entering the Shu region and their poetry chanted. The city not only respected Confucianism and adhered to ethics, but also saw the rapid development of Buddhism and Taoism, thus forming a cultural pattern of coexistence of three religions.

1. Urban Development

During the Sui and Tang dynasties, Chengdu formed a lively and regular market atmosphere like festivals. The prosperity of the market not only met the needs of commodity trade, but also brought about a kind of folk custom of amusement and enjoyment, such as the Lantern Market and Flower Market, which later evolved into folk festivals such as Lantern Fair and Temple Fair. The downtown area of Chengdu, represented by Wanli Bridge, was also gradually taking shape at that time. Zhang Ji's "Song of Chengdu," Liu Yuxi's "Zhuzhi Ci" and Li Bai's "Wild View" all describe the grand occasion of Wanli Bridge crossing Jinjiang River, with numerous restaurants

Chapter Four
Chengdu in the Literary Works of the Past Dynasties

and shops by the riversides and wonderful scenery and beautiful ladies. With many tourists and men of letters gathering here, chanting poems and drinking wine, Wanli Bridge became the liveliest place in Chengdu.

After entering the Shu region, Du Fu deeply felt the richness of this place. "Village by the River," written by him, describes Chengdu's happy and self-sufficient life: In the summer slack season of farming, clear water goes around fields; swallows and water gulls are at ease; people play chess, fish, and live a happy life. His "Cold Food" describes the riverside scenery on the Hanshi (Cold Food) Festival, with light smoke curling up beside the stream, green bamboo whirling in the sun, villages lying so close that chickens and dogs can be heard from one another. Chengdu looks like a paradise. "Rejoicing in Rain on a Spring Night" describes a drizzle on a spring night. All things are moistened. In the morning, thousands of flowers bloom in Jinguan City. These poems show the general situation of city life in Chengdu after the An-Shi Rebellion. The war did not directly affect the Shu region, and people there were still busy farming and living a delicate life, regardless of the impact of the war on silkworms.

2. Poetic Atmosphere

Emperor Xuanzong's entry into the Shu region not only brought skilled handicraftsmen, but also attracted a number of men of letters, who left behind many famous poems when they met and sent off friends and relatives, attended poetry occasions, or judged and commented on other people, such as "farewell poems." Although some of the poets might not be in Chengdu, the scenery and customs of Chengdu still weighed much in their poems, such as Luo Binwang's "Sending Wu Qi for the Shu," Si Kongsu's "Sending Liu Zhen Back to the Shu," Li Shangyin's "Sending Cui Jue to Xichuan," etc. In the Sui and Tang dynasties, many famous poets were born or lived in the Shu region. Although they were different in age and circumstances, they formed more or less the same feelings of hometown and brotherhood when they met each other in a world of disorder and separation, such as Gao Shi and Du Fu. The theme of these kinds of poems is the life of poets living in Chengdu. It is the inner reflection of most scholars in the Shu

Tianfu Culture and the Modern Pursuit of Chengdu

region, and it has become a historical part in the history of Chengdu poetry. There is another kind of admiring poetry, which mainly describes Xue Tao. Xue Tao, who was originally a singer in Chengdu, was good at calligraphy. She lived by the Huanhua River and planted acorus in the courtyard. At the same time, most of the officials and literati who came to the Shu region composed poems to reply to Xue Tao's. Xue Tao was also a poetess and had more than 90 works. She was good at writing short and exquisite poems. To write them, she also invented a kind of narrow letter paper, which is the famous "Xue Tao Paper."

3. Places of Interest

In "Ten Poems of the Emperor Visiting the Southern Capital," Li Bai praised the "Flower Scattering Tower" (Fig. 32) in Chengdu as beautiful as the royal garden "Shanglin Garden" in Chang'an. This tower was built in the reign of Yang Xiu, King of the Shu Prefecture in the Sui Dynasty. As Yang Xiu believed in Buddhism, he named it "Tian-nü-san-hua (the heavenly maids scatter blossoms)." This exquisite and beautiful building was built beside the famous Maha Pool at that time, located in the northeastern corner of Chengdu City, and became one of the landmark buildings in Chengdu. Standing on the bank of Jinjiang

Fig. 32 Flower Scattering Tower

Chapter Four
Chengdu in the Literary Works of the Past Dynasties

River, reflected in the shining water waves, and famous for the legend of "The heavenly maids scatter blossoms," it was one of the most popular scenic spots for literati.

Another equally famous building like the Flower Scattering Tower is Zhang Yi Tower, also known as Baitu Tower, which was originally the Xuanming Gate Tower at the Southern Gate of Chengdu in the Qin Dynasty. As it was very high, Zhang Yi Tower became the best place for people to get the whole view of Chengdu, thus attracting many men of letters to come for parties. Duan Wenchang, the governor of Xichuan in Jiannan Prefecture at that time, once led his friends to enjoy the scenery and write poems in Zhang Yi Tower, describing the appearance of Zhang Yi Tower – soaring up into the sky and surrounded by green water. As Zhang Yi Tower was in the western suburbs of the city and faced Xiling Snow Mountain (Fig. 33), according to Cen Shen's memory, one could enjoy a panoramic view of Chengdu City under the feet, and Xiling Snow Mountain in the distance. Such beautiful scenery is beyond one's knowledge.

Fig. 33 Xiling Snow Mountain

Tianfu Culture and the Modern Pursuit of Chengdu

In the Sui and Tang dynasties, the most famous garden and waterside pavilion in Chengdu was the Maha Pool, which was built in the period of Yang Xiu, King of the Shu Prefecture in the Sui Dynasty. The lake park was formed by digging earth for the expansion of the Shao Cheng (The Smaller City). Maha means large. The Maha Pool was a popular place for literati to go boating and have a feast. Du Fu's "Boating with Yan Zhenggong in the Maha Pool in Late Autumn," Chang Dang's "Banquet at the Maha Pool in the Western Shu" and Wu Yuanheng's "Feast at the Maha Pool" vividly portray the beautiful watery scenery of wind breezing green willow trees and water reflecting red flowers in the pool.

4. Temple Culture

During the Sui and Tang dynasties, Chengdu developed into the center of Buddhism in Western Sichuan, with 43 temples, large and small, and many famous monks. At that time, Buddhism in Chengdu reached its peak, and various temple cultures emerged, such as poems and paintings created after one's visit to the temple, Buddha statues and Buddhist festivals. (Fig. 34)

Fig. 34 Temple Culture — Wenshu Temple

Chapter Four
Chengdu in the Literary Works of the Past Dynasties

In ancient times, men of letters were fond of staying in temples and making friends with Buddhist monks, and it might become more elegant to visit temples at leisure time. For example, Du Fu's "Ascending the Bell Tower of Si'an Temple in Dust with Words to Pei Di," complained that Pei Di were busy writing poems and neglected friends; Zheng Gu's "Eight Lines for Pine Stream in Jingzhong Temple of Western Shu," described the quiet and elegant environment of Jingzhong Temple, through which streams were quietly flowing. Most of these Buddhist and Taoist temples, away from noisy downtowns, were built in beautiful places, like gardens with pavilions and towers set in a fairy land-like circumstance. In addition, the monks and Sanskrit sound added some mysterious color to the temples.

In general, the unified political situation of the Sui and Tang dynasties and the geographical advantages in Southwest China provided a guarantee for the development of Chengdu. The Shu people adhered to the core spirit of Tianfu Culture, such as "Optimism and Tolerance," worked hard and lived in peace and contentment in Chengdu. Because of its relatively stable and developed economy, it became the first choice of refuge for many literati and poets during the war. A large number of literati and Confucians lived in Chengdu, chanting poems, composing and replying poems, visiting the resorts in Sichuan, and left a large number of masterpieces, making Chengdu a "famous metropolis" with dual economic and cultural development.

Chengdu in the Poetry of the Song Dynasty

The prosperity of Chengdu in the Song Dynasty stepped onto a new stage on the basis of that in the Sui and Tang dynasties, and Chengdu made great contributions to the economic leadership of the Song Dynasty over other countries in the world.

1. Flourishing of "Twelve Months' Markets"

In the Song Dynasty, Chengdu took a leading role nationally in commodity economy, and the emerging of the "Twelve Months' Markets" and "Night Market" was undoubtedly an invention based on previous market development. Especially the "Twelve Months' Markets," the commodities sold there varied with the change of seasons, and this feature slowly developed into a conventional custom in Chengdu. This is a stroke with unique local characteristics in Chengdu's history, meanwhile reflecting the city's booming economy.

According to "Ancient and Modern Chengdu" by Zhao Yi of the Northern Song Dynasty, every month there were different markets in Chengdu, "Lantern Market in the first lunar month, Flower Market in the second, Silkworm Market in the third, Brocade Market in the fourth, Fan Market in the fifth, Incense Market in the sixth, Antiques Market in the seventh, Fragrans Market in the eighth, Medicine Market in the ninth, Wine Market in the tenth, Plum Market in the eleventh and Taofu Market in the twelfth." However, it was not so strict to hold the market of one kind just in the right month, and more kinds of commodities might be traded in the market every month. For instance, the Silkworm Market and Medicine Market were often open several times a year. "Wangjiangnan: Silkworm Market" by Zhang Zhongshu, and "Reply to Ziyou's 'Silkworm Market' " by Su Shi, are about the scene of busy transactions and surging crowds in the silkworm market; "Medicine Market on Double Ninth Festival" by Song Qi, describes the prosperity of the market with various kinds of rare medicines or herbs piled like hills and the whole street full of fragrance of medicine.

From the late Tang Dynasty, night markets sprang up in Chengdu, and become more common in the Song Dynasty. Like Twelve Months' Markets, night markets were also located in the most prosperous areas of Chengdu. Night markets were usually open until midnight in the Northern Song Dynasty, and over night in the Southern Song Dynasty. Tian Kuang's "Visiting the Night Market at Daci Temple Pavilion on the Night of July 6th" recorded the situation that the whole night market was brightly lit against the night sky, and women wanted to pray to the Vega on the Double Seventh Festival; Lu You's "A Poem from the Horse Saddle on July 8th" also depicted the bustling scene of the night markets around the Double Seventh Festival, when the lights were on and people's voices were in full swing.

2. The Prosperity of Shu Studies

This "Shu Studies" refers to the prefecture-run educational institutions in Chengdu and the academic culture. As the Song Dynasty carried out the policy of "respecting civil officials and restraining military officers" and only assigned civil officials as magistrates of prefectures and counties, this situation greatly promoted culture and education throughout the country. Especially in Chengdu, the school buildings expanded on a large scale, local officials were selected to teach students directly. Talents were put in important positions and the imperial examination was greatly valued. Therefore, there is a saying that "In terms of the education at the prefecture level, one can find it most prosperous in Chengdu."

In the fifth year of Qingli (1045), Wen Yanbo, the prefecture magistrate of Chengdu, presented a memorial requesting the court to order Long Changqi from Renshou County to lecture at the Chengdu prefecture-sponsored educational institutions. He was well versed in classics. When he set up a rural school, all the wise people around came to formally acknowledge him as master and studied with him. Later, after Tian Kuang was appointed the governor of Chengdu, he organized human resources to continue to inscribe and publish the "Shu Stone Classics." Then, when Song Qi was Governor of Chengdu, he started the reconstruction of Wen Weng's Stone Chamber School, built Wen Weng's statue inside, and painted the pictures of ten ancient sages such as Yan Zun, Wang Bao, Yang Xiong and Sima Xiangru, known as the "Picture Group of Ten Sages of Chengdu Prefecture-run Schools." Han Jiang, who was the governor of Chengdu after Song Qi, expanded the school buildings on a large scale, and the finished school was considered the largest one in China at that time. So far, the Chengdu prefecture-run schools in the Northern Song Dynasty had reached a considerable scale.

In the Southern Song Dynasty, Fan Zhongyi, a professor of Chengdu Prefecture-run School, wrote to Emperor Gaozong, asking for the plaque of "Hall of Dacheng," which later made Chengdu prefecture-run schools a tiger with wings added, developing with rapid speed. During the Shaoxing's Reign, Li Shi served as a professor of Chengdu Prefecture-run School. During his tenure, the school had a large number of students, with civil service learners and military learners totaling 1,200. Later, Chao Gongwu headed Chengdu Prefecture and proofread "Shu Stone Classics" by using the version of the year 932 (the third year of Changxing's Reign in the Later Tang Dynasty) of Confucian classics reprinted by Directorate of Imperial Academy. After Chao Gongwu, Fan Chengda, Governor of Chengdu, made large-scale repairs to the schools. Once again, the Chengdu schools seemed too small to accommodate any more students. In the 16th year of Chunxi's Reign (1189), Jingtang took office in Chengdu. He later expanded and rebuilt Chengdu's school buildings in an unprecedented scale and with dazzling exquisite design.

In the Song Dynasty, the development of Chengdu prefecture-run schools also promoted the academic culture of Chengdu, attracting many masters of Yi Xue (Study of Changes), historiography, and literature. According to statistics, there were more than 40 historians and 86 works in the Shu region in the Song Dynasty. In the Song Dynasty, there was a saying, "The Shu is rich in literati." Su Shi, Su Xun, Su Zhe, Zhang Yu, Fan Zhen and Yu Wenxu were all famous scholars at that time. Lu You and Fan Chengda, who came to Shu from other places, were all influential figures in the literary world at that time. At the same time, a large number of scholars of Neo-Confucianism emerged in the Shu region, represented by the three literati from the Su family in the early stage and Wei Liaoweng in the later stage, who laid the foundation for the development of Neo-Confucianism in Sichuan.

3. The Leisure Culture

"Chengdu people are fond of enjoying themselves." When Tian Kuang headed the Chengdu prefecture, he wrote 21 poems titled "Chengdu's Roaming for Fun," which recorded the scenes of people playing together on various festivals from the Lantern Festival to the Winter Solstice. On the Lantern Festival, the whole city of Chengdu was in the display of fireworks and the sea of lanterns, and thunder-like laughs and voices from the crowed people. They rushed to see the lanterns at Jinli, bustling all the way along, shoulder against shoulder, and following on others' heels. Still, the Southern Song Dynasty also saw this kind of bustle. In "Jiangdouchun: Lantern Festival," Jing Tang also described the joyful scene of Lantern Festival, when people's voices mixed with the sound of carts and horses, and the tune of jade flute echoed over the city, and the colorful lanterns were lit in Jinli like the stars in the sky (Fig. 35-1, Fig. 35-2).

After entering the Shu region, most of the literati and Confucian scholars were also fond of roaming, represented by Lu You. During his stay in Sichuan, he visited many places of historic interest and scenic beauty, and left a lot of poems directly related to the tour of Sichuan. For example, "Public Banquet of Chengdu Prefecture," which describes the scene of officials and people having fun and a feast together at the time; "Jisheng Pavilion," is about this pavilion, located on the Baozi mountain on the Bank of Minjiang River in southeast Xinjin, with a bird's eye-view of Minjiang River; in "Cuiping Pavilion in Xiyan," Lu You's feelings about life and official

Tianfu Culture and the Modern Pursuit of Chengdu

Fig. 35-1 One night in Jinli

career are all expressed in the mountains and rivers. These travel poems are records of the development of urban civilization.

The enjoyment of Chengdu in the Song Dynasty was also reflected in the pursuit of delicacy and the enjoyment of curiosities. During Lu You's stay in the Shu region, he wrote "Talking about Sichuan Food and Opera with Master Pu'an in Winter Night," "A Causal Piece on Foods," "Having Chestnut" and "A Post-Meal Impromptus Poem," praising the exquisite products in the Shu region. Apart from Lu You, Shu people were fond of enjoyment and particular about the taste as part of their folk custom. The monks of Xishu Temple also gave a vivid picture of the colorful and delicious temple dishes in "Steamed Pork." Even the temple dishes were aimed to be good in color and taste, let alone the city life there. Besides, enjoyment of curiosities was also a leisurely way of life in the Shu region, which is rich in natural resources and various kinds of excellent

Chapter Four
Chengdu in the Literary Works of the Past Dynasties

products, such as birds in Lu You's "Herb Pounding Birds," the peony in "Memories of Prosperous Peony in Tianpeng," the plum blossom in "The Quatrain of Plum Blossom," and the begonia in Wu Zhongfu's poem "Begonia." These poems not only show the prevalence of roaming and pleasure seeking, but also reflect the rich urban life in the Land of Abundance.

Fig. 35-2 One night in Jinli

Tianfu Culture and the Modern Pursuit of Chengdu

Chengdu in the Yuan and Ming Literary Works

At the end of the Song Dynasty, the Mongolian cavalry moved down to Southern China and Chengdu was severely damaged. Ruled by the Yuan Dynasty for nearly a hundred years, Chengdu failed to recover to its previous prosperity. At the end of the Yuan Dynasty, the peasant uprising broke out. Ming Yuzhen, Li Xixi, et al. captured Sichuan and established the Kingdom of Great Daxia. In the fourth year of Hongwu (1371), Zhu Yuanzhang, the emperor of the Ming Dynasty, decided to attack Sichuan, and finally incorporated Sichuan into the unified territory of the whole country. The Ming Dynasty ruled Chengdu for nearly three hundred years, and thus ensured the relative stability of Chengdu; as a result, the urban operation was gradually on the right track. After a long period of recuperation, at the end of Ming Dynasty, Chengdu's population, taxes and grain production were all in the leading position in the country, and finally the "Land of Abundance" reappeared.

1. Customs and Personages

Chengdu in the Yuan Dynasty was no longer as prosperous as it was in the Sui and Tang dynasties. "Records of Local Customs" by Fei Zhu from Huayang records his memories of Chengdu's prosperous social customs and urban life in the Song and Yuan dynasties. It was the custom to set banquets at certain times or occasions in Chengdu. Every time when banquets were held, men, women, old and young, dressed up meticulously, took their seats and gathered in the big courtyard to wait for a good performance. On New Year's Day, people went to Anfu Temple with colorful flags to pray, and the prefecture chief would hold the banquet in front of the Anfu Temple Tower; in the sixth lunar month, the prefecture chief would meet with officials in Jiangdu Temple every ten days, eating and wining at a banquet after boating in the pool; on the day before the Winter Solstice, the prefecture chief would lead people out of the Northern Gate to watch the Taoist ceremonies, and then to have dinner at Tianchang Temple; On the day of the Winter Solstice, he would hold a banquet in Daci Temple; on the next day, the morning and evening banquets would be held in Jinshen Temple and Daci Temple respectively. Around the popular temples in the city, various fairs were gradually formed. These busy banquets and yearly and monthly activities are just the portraits of the rapid development of urban culture and economy as well as the momentary customs.

Chengdu in the Yuan and Ming dynasties inherited the social customs developed since the Tang and Song dynasties. With the gradual recovery of social economy, Chengdu nurtured cultural celebrities in the new era with profound historical accumulation, who were either sentimentally attached to Chengdu when far away from home for a long time or born in Chengdu and familiar with the customs and human feelings of hometown. From their poems, we can see that Chengdu in the Yuan and Ming dynasties was claiming with confidence the style of "Land of Abundance."

2. Prince Shu's Residence of the Ming Dynasty

Zhu Chun was granted the title of King of the Shu State in the 11th year of Hongwu's Reign (1378), when he was only 7 years old. In the 23rd year of Hongwu's Reign (1390), Zhu Chun moved to Chengdu, Sichuan Province. He was the first archduke of the Shu State of the Ming Dynasty, reigning for 52 years in total, with his posthumous title of "Xian." In the Ming Dynasty, there were 13 archdukes and one prince in the Shu region. From King Xian to the last king Zhu Zhishu, the Ming Shu Regime ruled Chengdu for more than 260 years.

Prince Shu's Residence of the Ming Dynasty, built by Zhu Yuanzhang, the first emperor

Tianfu Culture and the Modern Pursuit of Chengdu

of the Ming Dynasty, was very magnificent. According to *Sichuan Chronicles: Prince Shu's Residence* during the Zhengde and Wanli reigns of the Ming Dynasty, the architecture was built in Da Cheng of Chengdu, surrounded by several walls inside and outside; it was not only magnificent, but also invested with great efforts in security measures. Shaoqi, a monk of Shijing Temple in Longquanyi, was once summoned by the king of Shu and had a chance to see the grandeur of the residence. He wrote a poem saying that the residence was like the Holy Land in the Sutra, with sweet flowers, green grass and jade-decorated buildings. During the Wanli period, after Cao Xuequan was invited to enjoy the peonies in the Prince Shu's Residence, he wrote in his poem that the complex was the most stunning in Chengdu, surrounded by green water, blooming flowers like pieces of brocade, and even said that such a palace would make people forget all the worries and bothers in the world.

As an old saying goes, something unexpected may happen at any time. The former emperors and generals may become today's defeated roving bandits. After Zhang Xianzhong conquered Chengdu, Zhu Zhishu, the last king of the Shu region, led his concubines to commit suicide in a well, and the once splendid residence was burnt to the ground, only with the broken bricks and tiles covered with moss and the swinging weeds unattended in the courtyard, telling the heavy and sad changes in current affairs.

**Chapter Four
Chengdu in the Literary Works
of the Past Dynasties**

Chengdu in the Poetry of the Qing Dynasty

At the end of the Ming Dynasty and the beginning of the Qing Dynasty, Chengdu experienced several catastrophes, such as Zhang Xianzhong's massacre in the Shu region and burning the Prince Shu's Residence, the wars between the Qing army and Zhang Xianzhong's rebelling force and between the army of the Ming Dynasty. Soon after Chengdu was taken into the map of the Qing Dynasty, it saw the "San Fan Rebellion" (Three Archdukes' Rebellion) in the recovery stage. Wu Sangui sent his troops to attack Sichuan twice, "bringing Sichuan great disasters for more than six years," when Chengdu was devastated and ruined everywhere. It was not until the rebellion of Wu's army was pacified in the 20th year of Emperor Kangxi's Reign (1681) that Chengdu really entered a relatively stable recovery period.

1. The Urban Reconstruction

Chengdu's urban reconstruction began in 1664, the third year of Emperor Kangxi in the Qing Dynasty, and lasted for more than 100 years. In the 57th year of Emperor Kangxi (1718), the Qing government ordered the construction of Da Cheng (the larger city) supported by official funds. In the 48th year of Emperor Qianlong (1783), Fu Kang'an, Governor of Sichuan Province, requested the court to allocate funds to rebuild Da Cheng. Later, when Li Shijie took charge of Chengdu, he ordered to "plant hibiscus, sandwiched with peach and willow trees everywhere" in the streets of Chengdu, resulting in neat and lush streets in Chengdu and the completion of an

Tianfu Culture and the Modern Pursuit of Chengdu

overall transformation of Da Cheng.

In addition to the construction of city walls and government office facilities, there are three important measures for the reconstruction of Chengdu City.

(1) Building the Manchu City

Since the early Qing Dynasty, there had been eight banners of Manchuria garrisoning in Chengdu. In the 57th year of Kangxi (1718), Nian Gengyao, the then governor of Sichuan Province, was ordered by the imperial court to build a new city within the west wall of Da Cheng of Chengdu, which was specially used to accommodate those officers and soldiers. The city was called the "Manchu City." The layout of houses in the city was like a centipede, with the General's Mansion as its head, the main street as the body, and alleys spreading on the left and right as the feet. "Zhuzhi Ci" in Chengdu in the Qing Dynasty vividly recorded the situation that the Manchu City, as a smaller city within a larger city, was blocked by the city wall and people could not go inside or outside it without special allowance. For example, Yangxie's "Zhuzhi Ci of the Brocade City" mentioned that "Half Bridge" built in Shaanxi Street. When the city was built, the bridge was divided into two parts, half in the Manchu's City and half in Da Cheng. After the outbreak of the 1911 Revolution, the Manchu's City lost its necessity of existence and went to the end. In 1913, the local government of Sichuan ordered the demolition, and the Manchu's City and Da Cheng merged into one.

(2) Building the Imperial Examination Hall

In the early Qing Dynasty, the government restored the imperial examination hall, which was located at today's Sichuan Provincial Science and Technology Museum in the Tianfu Square – the former site of the inner city of the Prince Shu's Residence in the Ming Dynasty, commonly known as the "imperial city." The first time to restore the examination hall was in the fourth year (1665) of Kangxi's Reign. "The Imperial Examination Hall" written by Yang Caiyi, a poet of the Qing Dynasty, depicts the scene of the numerous single rooms of imperial examination academies and the strict discipline of the examination hall. The rule of examination was that each examinee had a single room (i.e. room). Once entering the room, he couldn't leave it until all the subjects were completed, regardless of the three common emergencies of eating, drinking and defecating. The room was usually equipped with a charcoal fire and a candle for candidates to use. In the 31th year (1905) of Guangxu's Reign, the imperial examinations were abolished and schools were founded nationwide, and the imperial examination academies were transformed into various new schools.

(3) Building Cities in Counties and Prefectures

Chengdu's infrastructure was renovated and rebuilt in the Qing Dynasty. During the reign of Guangxu, Ding Baozhen, Governor of Sichuan Province, presided over the repair of Dujiangyan Irrigation System. He wrote "Memorial of Erwang Temple," in which he recalled that since Li Bing, the ancient governor of the Shu Prefecture, successfully controlled the water, there has been no flood or famine in Sichuan, and people in the Shu region built Erwang Temple to commemorate Li Bing and his son Erlang. Ding Baozhen lamented that although he was a governor and had the heart to work for the people's welfare, he could not do as well as Li Bing.

2. The Popularity of "Zhuzhi Ci"

"Zhuzhi Ci" is a poetry genre, evolving from the folk song style in the ancient Ba-Shu region, usually in the form of seven-character quatrains, and in plain and simple language. People usually take it to describe the folk customs, so it has strong local flavor and important historical value. In the Qing Dynasty, Chengdu was the creation base of "Zhuzhi Ci," which produced a large number of famous writers, such as Liu Yuan, or Zhitang, from Shuangliu County. He wrote 31 pieces of "New Year's Zhuzhi Ci in Sichuan" when he was 81 years old. Yang Xie, or Duishan, and nicknamed "Liu Dui Shan Ren," is the author of "Zhuzhi Ci of the Brocade City" (more than 100 poems). Wu Haoshan, born in Pengxian County, created "Zhuzhi Ci of Chengdu" (more than 90 poems). In addition, Wang Zaixian created "Chengdu Zhuzhi Ci" (12), Feng Hui's

"Jianglou Zhuzhi Ci" (12), Zhao Xi's "Zhuzhi Ci" (30), etc.

"Zhuzhi Ci" contains profound realistic meanings because it is often composed based on in-time affairs and events. We could therefore learn about the social customs and urban life in Chengdu during a particular Qin period. Yang Xie wrote more than 100 pieces of "Zhuzhi Ci of the Brocade City," recording all aspects of Chengdu, writing the history of "Yang Yi Yi Er" (Chengdu is the most prosperous city only next to Yangzhou all over the country), writing the actors or actresses in Chengdu in Qing Dynasty, or writing the Imperial Examination Hall in Chengdu in Qing Dynasty. Through the "Zhuzhi Ci," we can understand the urban layout, street planning and the development of economy and culture in Chengdu in the Qing Dynasty.

In a simple and straightforward language, "Zhuzhi Ci" describes the life, urban construction, customs and folklores of Chengdu in the Qing Dynasty. It shows us that with the recovery of economy and the completion of urban infrastructure, Chengdu's culture and education, literary creation, academic research, etc. developed rapidly in the Qing Dynasty.

3. Immigration Culture

After the turmoil of the late Ming Dynasty and the early Qing Dynasty, the population of Chengdu decreased dramatically, and the Qing government put forward the policy of letting people from the northern and southern provinces immigrate into Sichuan. In the 20th year (1681) of Kangxi's Reign, the court began to appease the Sichuan refugees to return home; in the 29th year (1690) of Kangxi's Reign, memorials were issued to offer preferential treatment of immigrants from other provinces; in the 31st year (1692) of Kangxi's Reign, large-scale immigrants began to open up wasteland for farming in Sichuan. At that time, immigrants mainly came from Hunan and Guangdong (Caton). During the Qianlong's Reign, Sichuan's population gradually returned to stability, and its economy and culture also developed steadily.

The earliest guildhall was established in the second year (1663) of Kangxi's Reign by the Shaanxi people who moved to Sichuan. Subsequently, a large number of guildhalls appeared successively, such as Jiangnan Guildhall, Guizhou Guildhall, Huguang Guildhall, Shanxi

Chapter Four
Chengdu in the Literary Works of the Past Dynasties

Guildhall, etc., and many guildhalls were established around Chengdu, such as Guangdong Guildhall, Huguang Guildhall, Jiangxi Guildhall, etc. In general, the construction of guildhalls was often led by the fellow townspeople who were enthusiastic about public welfare and had strong financial resources, and completed by the common donation of the fellow townspeople. The meeting hall was used to offer sacrifices to the sages, discuss major events, meet relatives and feast friends, and even provide lodging for participants of the imperial examination.

(1) The Prosperity of the Guildhall and Chengdu "Quyi"

When meeting in each guildhall, there would be entertainment activities of singing and drama performances, which promoted the development of Chengdu drama in the Qing Dynasty. According to Yangxie's "Zhuzhi Ci of the Brocade City," most dramas played on the stage of guildhalls were completely moved from the original provinces and towns of immigrants. At first, there was no time limit for operas in Chengdu. However, after the Shaanxi immigrants entered Sichuan, they set up a rule in the Shaanxi guildhall that the three explosions of firecrackers would be taken as the time node. If the curtains were still not opened after the third explosion, the opera group would not be invited to perform in their guildhall the next time. This is the influence of immigration culture on the opera art of Chengdu from the perspective of performance rules. Moreover, from the aspect of scripts and music, the effect of "Outside the Box" was more outstanding. Yan Qiaosou's "Chengdu Zhuzhi Ci" was about Shanxi opera, Canton Opera, Chaozhou Drama, etc., which were on various stages in Chengdu by taking the opportunities of gathering and banquets in various guildhalls. Among the foreign scripts, "Kunqu Opera" became the favorite aria of the upper class in Chengdu at that time and became the main item of "Music Party" of literati and scholars.

(2) Immigration and Social Life in Chengdu

Immigration to Sichuan had a wide impact on local urban life in Chengdu. For example, Yang Xie's "Zhuzhi Ci of the Brocade City" wrote about immigration impacts on food. It is said

Tianfu Culture and the Modern Pursuit of Chengdu

that when officials in Chengdu treated guests and kitchen workers carelessly damaged the appearance of a dish, they quickly mixed lotus flowers and tofu with it, and called it "Lotus tofu soup." However, officials thought it delicious, so they turned to chanting and praised the dish to others. This incidence soon was on everyone's lips in town for a while. The influence of immigrants on Chengdu's social life was visible on custom. Yan Qiaosou's "Chengdu Zhuzhi Ci" wrote dragon dances on the Lantern Festival. There were different patterns of dragon dances and lion dances from different places in Chengdu. In the Qing Dynasty, the dragon dance team from Huangzhou Guildhall in Chengdu was the most lively and lasting.

With the immigrants moving into Sichuan, there was an urgent need for the reconstruction of Chengdu City after the war. Of course, there were other reasons. According to Wu Haoshan's "Chengdu Zhuzhi Ci," Chengdu had a relatively stable political ecology, coupled with the excellent natural environments, so many immigrants from other provinces entered Sichuan. In history, Chengdu had experienced many immigration tides since the Qin Dynasty. Immigrants brought hometown culture into Chengdu, which had a certain impact on Chengdu's cultural characteristics, such as the optimism, inclusiveness, kindness and public welfare.

4. Reform in the Late Qing Dynasty

In the late Qing Dynasty, a number of famous figures emerged in Sichuan, such as Liao Ping, Song Yuren, Yang Rui, and Liu Guangdi. The first three figures were all from Zunjing Academy (Academy of Respect Statue). Yang Rui and Liu Guangdi were also "Six Gentlemen of 1898." Scholars and persons of ideals and integrity played an important role in the reform of the late Qing Dynasty.

Liao Ping, or Jiping, was born in Jingyan County. In 1874, he took the exam of Zunjing Academy and was appreciated by Zhang Zhidong. In 1876, he was selected as the student of the first batch of Zunjing Academy. Liao Ping did scholarly research of *Spring and Autumn Annals: Commentary of Gongyang* and *Spring and Autumn Annals: Commentary of Guliang* in order to serve the society with his historical knowledge. In the course of his later studies, he constantly innovated the old and created new works, such as *Modern and Ancient Confucian*

Chapter Four
Chengdu in the Literary Works of the Past Dynasties

Classics, Knowledge of Confucius, On Liu Xin's Fake Classics, etc. Scholars believe that there are "six changes" before and after Liao Ping's study. Although the six changes failed to break out of the traditional pattern of modern and ancient Confucian Classics, they eventually reflected the positive factors of seeking new, change and reform.

Song Yuren was a native of Fushun County. In the first year (1875) of Guangxu's Reign, he passed the test of the county-level imperial examinations and won title of "Xiucai," and later, he entered the Zunjing Academy to study. In the 12th year (1886) of Guangxu's Reign, he went to Beijing and passed the highest imperial examination. Song Yuren wrote tens of thousands of words on "Discussions of Current Affairs," arguing that China must improve. After returning to Sichuan from a European trip in 1896, he actively organized people of lofty ideals from Chengdu and Chongqing to participate in the Chengdu Society of Shu Studies, founded the *Journal of Shu Studies*, taught together with Liao Ping, advocating reform, and effectively promoted the reform movement.

Yang Rui, or Shuqiao, was from Mianzhu. During his study in Zunjing Academy, he was the youngest and the best in his schoolmates, and thus called the first of the "five teenagers of Zunjing." In the 15th year (1889) of Guangxu's Reign, he was awarded the Secretary of the cabinet, and then joined Zhang Zhidong as staff.

Liu Guangdi, a native of Fushun County, passed the highest imperial examination in the ninth year (1883) of Guangxu's Reign. When the First Sino-Japanese War of 1894–1895 broke out, Liu Guang submitted a written statement named "My Statement on the War," boldly and forthrightly requesting reform. Unfortunately, this statement did not reach the emperor, but four measures of reform in the memorial were accepted by most of the reformers. In 1898, Yang Rui and Liu Guangdi established the "Shu Study Society" in Beijing, discussing the national affairs and "Western learning" together.

The reform movement went on like a raging fire, varying from time to time. We can see that scholars and men of lofty ideas of Sichuan origin were pushing forward the reform process in terms of theoretical knowledge and practical measures. Finally, they chose "to die for a righteous cause if not succeeding," showing firmness and fearlessness from the land of the Shu.

Tianfu Culture and the Modern Pursuit of Chengdu

Chengdu in Modern and Contemporary Literature and *Quyi*[1]

In 1911, Wuchang Uprising broke out, and Chongqing and Chengdu established military governments respectively, declaring their independence. In January 1912, the Republic of China was established, and the military governments of Chongqing and Chengdu merged. In 1937, "Lugou Bridge Incident" triggered the War of Resistance against Japanese Aggression. As an important military strategic base and war rear area, Chengdu was only second to Chongqing's military and political center and became the cultural and educational center at that time, also the great granary after the war. Although it went through difficulties during this period, Chengdu kept pace with the times and maintained development in economy, culture and education, urban construction, social customs, etc. In a large number of literary works, we can see the features of Chengdu in modern times.

1. Chengdu in Novels

During the period of the Republic of China, many writers and scholars in Chengdu created times novels with Chengdu or its surrounding towns as the story scenes. For example, Professor. Li Jieren's *Ripples in the Stagnant Water* is called the modern *Chronicles of Huayang*, which is a valuable material to understand the social life, political culture, and folk customs

---

1 *Quyi*: Chinese folk-art forms, including ballad singing, storytelling, comic dialogues, clapper talks, cross talks, etc.

Chapter Four
Chengdu in the Literary Works of the Past Dynasties

of Chengdu at that time. For more examples, Ba Jin's *Torrent Trilogy* takes Gao Mansion in Chengdu as a clue to reproduce the conflict between the old feudal family and the new culture. Ai Wu's *Journey to the South* describes the folk customs and scenery in the Western Sichuan frontier. These literary works vividly represent the life of Chengdu at that time.

(1) Commercial Streets and Urban Markets

According to the record of *Ripples in the Stagnant Water*, we can see the general situation of the East Street among many streets and lanes of Chengdu. Dongda Street (the East Street) has been the most prosperous and bustling block in Chengdu since the end of the Qing Dynasty. At this time, Dongda Street has become the most eye-catching business circle in Chengdu. The most beautiful are the Middle East Street and the Upper East Street, where all shops are tall and tidy, with signs in black lacquer and golden characters; the streets here are equipped with kinds of fireproof facilities and covered with red sandstone slabs, wide and flat, full of traffic in the daytime and brilliant lights at night, so much so that alcohol is ready on dinner tables for busy social life. This fashionable business street makes foreigners from afar admire it.

In *Ripples in the Stagnant Water*, the writer wrote about his going to a fair in Tianhui Township, which reflects the market consumption in the surrounding towns of Chengdu: in the big and small fairs of Tianhui Township, all kinds of crops, livestock and handicrafts are arranged and laid in order, and people from the countryside flock to the market from the fields, paths and roads. The ears are full of voices of all kinds of peddling and bargaining mixed with talking, shouting and livestock shouting.

(2) "Paoge" and Its Social Influence

"Paoge" was the most influential civil organization in Sichuan from the Qing Dynasty to the Republic of China. The "Paoge" Gang was good at fighting injustice and upholding brotherhood so that it attracted many people. It was very influential in the local area since it could do things that even the local government was unable to. "During the period of the Republic of China,

Tianfu Culture and the Modern Pursuit of Chengdu

the power of Paoge in Chengdu was at its peak, and the influence and energy of all kinds of Paoge organizations were very large. From coolie to government officials, as well as soldiers and police, they all took Paoge membership as a talisman." In *Ripples in the Stagnant Water*, it is written that a Paoge, Luo Waizui, is in charge of the situation of Tianhui Township. For example, the casino in Tianhui Township requests Luo Waizui to solve the problem because the staff is not competent, and the revenue is very low. Moreover, when Gu Tiancheng wants to get an official position by donating a remarkable amount of silver, he also comes to Luo Waizui for help. Chengdu Paoge gang had its multi-level organization structures, such as the "benevolence branch for celebrities, righteousness branch for wealth persons, etiquette branch for craftsmen." When their power grew, they infiltrated into the army and political situation. At the end of the War of Resistance against Japanese Aggression, Paoge's organization expanded and overflew, and there were more and more bullies and bandits robbing houses in Hunshui Paoge ("bastard/bad Paoges").

(3) Conflict Between New and Old Cultures

Before and after the May 4th New Culture Movement, Chengdu was actively absorbing the fruits of the new culture movement. At that time, the new cultural movement of pursuing democracy and freedom had a fierce conflict with the traditional culture of defending the old interpersonal relations of social hierarchy, and the three cardinal principles and five constant virtues as specified in the feudal ethical code. Ba Jin's representative work *The Family* (originally known as *Torrent*) is the epitome of social and cultural change, reflecting the important influence on the growth of new youth caused by the confrontation between two forces of old and new culture at that time.

The three young masters in *The Family* represent the characters and fates of three different sorts of people in the conflict between the old and the new cultures. The eldest young master Juexin, the eldest grandson, is given the life path from the moment of birth; the second young master Juemin and the third young master Juehui, greatly inspired by the new culture movement, want to break through the traditional ethics and get rid of the shackles of the feudal culture; the senior old master of Gao Mansion is naturally the representative of the feudal parents and the feudal forces, and he strongly opposes the new culture, with tyrannical, cold and inhumane attitudes.

In the novels of these times, the writers have vividly portrayed the urban development, social features and figures of Chengdu in the late Qing Dynasty, the Republic of China and the War of Resistance against Japanese Aggression. In addition to the above mentioned, there were also teahouses, popular gambling, all kinds of opium houses, brothels, and beggars everywhere in Chengdu. All these were part of the rich and cultural Tianfu Chengdu in Southwest China in the transition period of the new and old cultural changes.

2. Chengdu in Dramas and Films

During the period from the late Qing Dynasty to the early Republic of China to the War of Resistance against Japanese Aggression, Sichuan Opera and movies in Chengdu were widely developed, which became a way of entertainment for citizens to actively participate in and enjoy after dinner, and also a vivid expression of Chengdu's social atmosphere and uran culture.

In 1912, famous Sichuan Opera artists, such as Kang Zilin, Yang Sulan, Xiao Kaichen, Li Jiasheng, and more than 100 actors, Qinshi (music players) and drummers from eight theatrical troupes, formed the first Sichuan Opera artists' autonomous organization "Three Celebrations," which made Sichuan opera performance more refined; in 1913, Chengdu established "Education Society," which is dedicated to the innovation of Sichuan Opera. At that time, the new drama with specific current affairs as its content was called "current affairs drama," and its representative plays were *Recovered Map*, *Bloody Sichuan Road*, *Recover Wuchang*, *Kill Duanfang*, *Kill Zhao Erfeng*, etc. These dramas, which take real historical events and characters as the creation objects, have strong flavor of the times and local color, and can often produce strong social sensation in the aspect of communication.

In addition to the "current affairs drama," there was also the "fashion drama" focusing on

Tianfu Culture and the Modern Pursuit of Chengdu

the social phenomena and social atmosphere of Chengdu at that time. The representative of fashion drama, such as *The Great Black View*, *The Smoker's Mirror*, *The True Colors of the Smoker*, *The Phenomenon of Opium Banning*, etc., told the stories of opium smoking leading to the destruction of the family, criticizing the harm of opium to people; *The Mistress's Gun, Sad Calls*, *The Chivalrous Girl in the Boudoir*, *Who Harmed Her*, etc., accused the abuse of women by warlords and bullies; *Sorrow in the Midnight*, *Love and Ethics*, *Business Marriage*, *A Heartbroken Letter*, etc, reflected the fettered marriage between men and women. Although this kind of "fashion drama" does not necessarily refer to Chengdu every time, nor criticize a real person in every play, it is epitome of common social phenomena in the period when the new culture was going to replace the old one and feudal society, turning to the end.

Another kind of "revolution-themed modern drama" mainly reflects the heroes and revolutionary events in Chengdu and other areas during the War of Resistance against Japanese Aggression and the Chinese People's War of Liberation. Influential plays are *Red Crag (Hong Yan)*, *Sister Jiang*, *Xu Yunfeng*, *Yibing's White-Haired Girl*, *Huang Jiguang*, *Ba River Ferry*, etc. From current affairs drama, fashion drama to revolution-themed modern drama, Sichuan Opera itself is constantly absorbing new performance elements, and closely following current hot events and key figures in theme selection and script writing. It is a valuable material for us to understand various social phenomena and the state of urban life in Chengdu in popular literature at that time.

Chengdu in modern times was a developing city swaying in the midst of raging storms, a city that adhered to the traditional values while integrated into the world by absorbing in the Western progressive thoughts, and a city that was the rear area during the wartime, where people called for democracy, freedom and science, meanwhile lighting opium, drinking tea and listening to reviews. At anytime, there are fresh and spicy Sichuan dishes, and there are also straightforward and courageous citizens hotter than the Sichuan dishes. Tianfu Chengdu in the thousands of years of historical changes has always been a metropolis favored by people all over the world with relatively stable political environment, abundant resources, profound cultural heritage and convenient land and water transportation.

Chapter Five
Historical and Cultural Relics of Chengdu

    Chengdu's historical and cultural relics come in large quantities and varieties, including residential addresses, castles, roads, bridges, water conservancy projects, etc., existing in form of ruins and remains either underground or on the ground. They are the specific carriers of Chengdu's civilization history of thousands of years, containing profound regional cultural connotations and characteristics of Chengdu, and with high historical, scientific and artistic value.

Tianfu Culture and the Modern Pursuit of Chengdu

Historic City Sites of Chengdu

During the 1990s, it was very exciting to the archaeological circle that the discovery of Baodun Ancient City Site opened a series of excavations of historic city sites on the Chengdu Plain. In less than ten years, archaeologists discovered seven more ancient city sites of the late Neolithic Age on the Chengdu Plain, consisting of the oldest (about 4,500–4,000 years ago) and the largest and most densely distributed historic city site group in Southwest China, including the Baodun Ancient City in Xinjin, Yufu Ancient City in Wenjiang, the Ancient City Site in Pixian, Mangcheng Ancient City in Dujiangyan, Shuanghe and Zizhu Ancient Cities in Chongzhou, and Yandian and Gaoshan Ancient Cities in Dayi. The eight ancient cities, having witnessed the history and to enlighten the future, are not only the products of the vicissitudes of life on the Chengdu Plain, but also the precious treasures of Chinese culture.

1. Baodun Ancient City Site

Baodun Ancient City Site is located in Baodun Village, Longma Township, five kilometers north of Xinjin County at the southwestern edge of the Chengdu Plain. The ancient city is rectangular in shape circled by broken earthen walls, the northern and eastern parts of which are well preserved; the western, incomplete; the southern, destroyed. The eastern earthen wall is the highest, about five meters. According to local people, it was the "Meng Huo City," where Zhuge Liang captured and released Meng Huo seven times. However, the excavation in 1995

Chapter Five
Historical and Cultural Relics of Chengdu

and 1996 proved that the architectural age of the Baodun Site is not only far earlier than the Three Kingdoms Period, but also even earlier than the Spring and Autumn Period, and can be traced back to 4,500 years ago. Of all the invaluable relics buried in the site, many production tools such as stone axes, utensils and pottery pieces were unearthed, all testifying that Baodun Culture is the earliest source of ancient Shu civilization.

2. Yufu Ancient City Site

Yufu Ancient City Site, one of the historic city sites on the Chengdu Plain, is the remains of the late Neolithic Age, located in Wanchun Township, Wenjiang District, spanning three villages – Yufu, Zhishu, and Bao'en, and about 20 kilometers from the city proper of Chengdu (Fig. 36). According to historical records, the ancient Shu Kingdom experienced five reigns of kings, including Cancong, Baiguan, Yufu, Du Yu and Bieling. Yufu was the third king of the Shu Kingdom. He came from the upper reaches of Minjiang River to the Chengdu Plain and

Fig. 36 Yufu Culture reliecs in Wenjiang

Tianfu Culture and the Modern Pursuit of Chengdu

established his capital in Wanchun Township of Wenjiang. Dozens of pottery wares, and more than 100 elaborately polished small-sized stone implements were unearthed in 1996. The discovery confirmed that Yufu Ancient City dates back to approximately 4,000 years ago to the Neolithic Age.

3. The Historic City Site in Pixian County

Pixian Ancient City Site is located in Gucheng Village of Sandaoyan Township, Pixian County (now Pidu District) of Chengdu City (Fig. 37). Local people said it was the "horse raising city," where Zhuge Liang, Prime Minister of the Shu Kingdom of the Three Kingdoms Period, raised horses. However, the post-excavation and research shows that the city wall of the ancient city was built twice, the first time in the third phase of the Baodun culture, and the second time in the late period of the fourth phase of the Baodun culture. Not until the fourth phase of the Baodun culture, did the ancient city begin to decline. Therefore, it belongs to the remains of the late Neolithic Age of approximately 4,000 years ago, and is one of the historic city sites on the Chengdu Plain.

Fig. 37 The Historic City Site in Pixian County

4. Mangcheng Ancient City Site

Located in Mangcheng Village, Qingcheng Township, Dujiangyan City, Mangcheng Ancient City Site is commonly known as "Mang Cheng Zi" to local people. It is said that it is also called "Busy City," because Zhang Xianzhong built it in a hurry at the end of the Ming Dynasty. In fact, Mangcheng Site is a small site among the historic cities of the Chengdu Plain, which was built about 4,300–4,500 years ago in the late Neolithic Age. After the large-scale excavation and research, it is believed that Mangcheng Ancient City resembled Baodun Ancient City in the cultural styles and features. There are five cultural layers in the site deposit, including those of the Neolithic Age and the Song Dynasty, mainly the Neolithic cultural layer. There are ash pits, ash ditches, house foundations and other relics in the site. One of the house foundations is well preserved, rectangular in shape, with a double suite and the mud wall reinforced with bamboo and wood as the frame, covering an area of about 50 square meters. The discovery of the housing bases is of great significance to the study of human social process.

5. Other Ancient City Sites

Apart from the above-mentioned ancient city sites, the historic city sites also include Shuanghe Ancient City Site, or the Site at Shuanghe Village, Zizhu Ancient City Site, Yandian Ancient City Site, and Gaoshan Ancient City Site. Shuanghe Ancient City, locally called "Lower Mangcheng," is situated in Shuanghe Fair, Mangcheng Village, Shangyuan Township, Chongzhou City. As the late Neolithic remains, this site is more than 4,000 years old, and it is also one of the central settlement sites of the Baodun culture. Zizhu Ancient City Site, located in Zizhu Village, Liaoyuan Township, Chongzhou City, falls into the category of the late Neolithic remains. It is a typical historic city site of Chengdu Plain with a single cultural nature and distinct cultural characteristics. Yandian Ancient City Site is located in Group 6 of Yandian Village, 3 km southwest of Dayi County. From December 2002 to March 2003, it was explored and excavated by Chengdu Municipal Cultural Relics and Archaeology Reseach Institute and Dayi County Institute of Cultural Relics Management. They preliminarily determined that it is the remains from about 4,300 years ago in the late Neolithic Age, and the seventh historic city site discovered in Chengdu. Gaoshan Ancient City Site is located in Gucheng Village, Gaoshan Township, Dayi County. In 2003, archaeologists from Chengdu Municipal Cultural Relics and Archaeology Research Institute and Dayi County Institute of Cultural Relics and Management found it during the environmental investigation on the site of Yandian Ancient City. The excavation recovered 10 ash pits and six burials, from which pottery wares, stone implements and animal bones were unearthed. The types and decors of the pottery wares hinted that their dates would be Phase I of the Baodun culture. It is the eighth historic city site discovered in Chengdu.

**Chapter Five
Historical and Cultural Relics
of Chengdu**

The Splendid Sanxingdui Site

As for the former capital of the Shu Kingdom, there are few materials handed down from Cancong and Baiguan. In the 1980s, with the survey and tentative excavation of Sanxingdui Site, a large number of cultural relics were unearthed; a large quantity of historical vestiges, excavated; especially the ancient city walls, discovered. All these evidences have confirmed that Sanxingdui City Site was the former capital of the Shu Kingdom from the late Xia Dynasty to the Shang Dynasty. Therefore, a legendary capital of the ancient kings of Shu Kingdom was really displayed in front of us, marking a rapid progress of scholars' efforts in exploration of the former capital of the Shu Kingdom for decades.

Sanxingdui Site, located on the Yazi riverbank of Nanxing Township in the west of Guanghan City in the north of Chengdu Plain, is a huge site group composed of many ancient cultural relics scattering here and there. Sanxingdui Site group belongs to the remains from the late Neolithic Age to the late Shang and early Zhou dynasties. Archaeologists divide the cultural relics of the site group into four periods. The first stage is the early accumulation, which belongs to the late Neolithic culture, and the second to the fourth stages belong to the Bronze culture. The site group dates from the late Neolithic Age to the turn between the Shang and Zhou dynasties. (Fig. 38)

Tianfu Culture and the Modern Pursuit of Chengdu

Fig. 38 Sanxingdui Museum

The Sanxingdui site group is of large scale and wide range. Most of the ancient cultural relics are distributed on the tableland of the northern and southern sides of Mamu River on the southern bank of Yazi River. It takes the shape of an irregular trapezoid broader in the south and narrower in the north, 5-6 kilometers long from east to west and 2-3 kilometers wide from the south to the north, and covers a total area of about 12 square kilometers. This site group was the most important archaeological discovery in China in the 20th century, and is also the site of the ancient Shu culture that has been ascertained of the widest scope, relatively early formation and longest lasting time, and the richest cultural connotation.

The culture of Sanxingdui Site has distinct regional characteristics. Its various unearthed cultural relics are significantly different from those of the Central Plains, but very similar to those discovered from Chengdu Jinsha Site later, and this feature shows that the Sanxingdui Site is not only a typical representative of the ancient Shu culture, but also an ancient civilization hub in the upper reaches of the Yangtze River. The discovery of Sanxingdui Site reveals the

Chapter Five
Historical and Cultural Relics of Chengdu

early formation and development of the ancient Shu civilization, and provides important and conclusive authentic materials for the study of the origin of Chinese civilization.

When Baodun Culture developed to the fourth phase, the ancient Sanxingdui city was born during the development of the Sanxingdui Site from the first phase to the second one. With its strong attraction of the splendid civilization, the Sanxingdui city eventually replaced the Baodun and other ancient cities, and became the center of the ancient Chengdu Plain. And with the gradual decline of the Baodun culture, the new era of civilization started with the coming of the Sanxingdui civilization.

Tianfu Culture and the Modern Pursuit of Chengdu

The Shi'erqiao Cultural Sites

There were three peaks in the development and change of Chengdu City in the Pre-Qin Dynasty, the second of which was marked by the rise of the Shi'erqiao culture.

1. The Shi'erqiao Site

Located at Shi'erqiao Road, Shudu Avenue, Chengdu, the Shi'erqiao Site is distributed along the Pi River and its tributaries. It is the central settlement ruins of the Shi'erqiao culture, and the remains of the Shang and Zhou dynasties. From 1985 to 1986, a large-scale wood structure complex of the late Shang Dynasty was excavated at the site, with a total area of more than 15,000 square meters, and the vestiges of the veranda of large-scale wooden palace building were found. Around the main building, there was a dense array of small stilt style architectures, functioning as the ancillary buildings of the large-scale wooden palace building. The large-scale main building and the small-scale auxiliary buildings were connected to each other, arranged in an orderly way and integrated into a large-scale building group. The Archaeological Department has ascertained that the site of the Shi'erqiao Site was an important dwelling ruin for the ancestors of ancient Shu from the Shang Dynasty to the Western Zhou Dynasty.

**Chapter Five
Historical and Cultural Relics
of Chengdu**

2. Yangzishan Earthen Platform Site

Located to the north of the Shi'erqiao Site in Chengdu, this earthen platform is square in shape and of three layers with an earthen step between, and the walls are made of adobe bricks, and the inside is compacted with soil. With the flat stretch of the Chengdu Plain, the earthen platform of more than 10 meters high stands even loftier. It is supposed that the upper limit of the initial building age of the earthen platform is in the late Shang Dynasty or at the turn of the Shang Dynasty to Zhou Dynasty. The five polished stone implements found in the lower part of the foundation site are the earliest cultural relics in Chengdu, with a history of more than 10,000 years.

3. Jinsha Site

Jinsha Site, located at the Jinsha Site Road, Chengdu, is the remains of the Shang and Zhou dynasties. There are four major localities of Jinsha Site, namely Huangzhong Village, the northeastern area of Meiyuan, the northeastern area of Lanyuan and Tiyu Gongyuan. According to the excavation results, the whole Jinsha Site is composed of four parts: palace area, sacrifice area, living area, and burial area, with the sacrifice area as the core and in massive distribution. It is an open-styled capital city of the ancient Shu Kingdom with obvious functional characteristics and a clear layout. The palace buildings of Jinsha and the large etiquette platform of Yangzishan to the north of Jinsha echo each other at a distance. It has become the most obvious sign of the early urban architecture pattern. There are more than 200 pieces of gold wares unearthed in Jinsha Site, ranking the most either in quantity or type of gold wares unearthed in sites of the Pre-Qin period in China. The gold assemblage mainly consists of gold leafs, usually packed or pasted on the surface of other artifacts as an accessory, with the Gold Belt, the Gold Leaf Image of Sunbirds and gold masks as the most representative ones (Fig. 39-1, Fig. 39-2).

Tianfu Culture and the Modern Pursuit of Chengdu

Fig. 39-1 Jinsha Site

Fig. 39-2 Jinsha Site

**Chapter Five
Historical and Cultural Relics
of Chengdu**

Buddhist and Taoist Cultural Relics

There are many famous religious buildings in Chengdu, such as Baoguang Temple, Shijing Temple, Wenshu Temple, Zhaojue Temple, Daci Temple, Qingyang Palace, Taoist temples in Qingcheng Mountain, Ping'anqiao Catholic Church, Pengzhou Annunciation Convent, etc. In Chengdu, a particularly open and inclusive city, Buddhism, Confucianism and Taoism spread side by side, and the coexistence of the three doctrines has not only built the spiritual home for the officials and the common people of all ages to develop their peaceful and positive mental states, but also cultivated the humanity and religious feelings of the people of Chengdu, such as compassion, kindness and equality, towards their compatriots.

1. Baoguang Temple

Located in Xindu County, north of Chengdu City, Sichuan Province, Baoguang Temple (Fig. 40), with a long history, a large scale, a complete structure and a quiet environment, is the only Buddhist Zen temple in China that follows a typical layout of the early Chinese Buddhist temple – a temple integrated with and centered on a pagoda. Therefore, it is also called "Baoguang Zen Temple." The pedigree of Baoguang Temple originated from the 56th generation of Linji School of Zen in the late Tang Dynasty. As one of the famous Zen Buddhist temples in China, Baoguang Temple has a high reputation at home and abroad. Over thousands of years, Baoguang Temple was destroyed in the chaos of war several times. For instance, the temple's halls and monks'

Tianfu Culture and the Modern Pursuit of Chengdu

Fig. 40 Baoguang Temple

residence areas were almost razed to the ground in the end of the Ming Dynasty and the beginning of the Qing Dynasty. However, destroyed, and then rebuilt again, numerous times of Nirvana rebirth finally made it one of the most famous temples in China – founded in the Tang Dynasty, popular in the Song Dynasty and rejuvenated in the Qing Dynasty. Thanks to the perseverance and efforts of generations of eminent monks, Baoguang Temple became larger and more prosperous with its growing reputation and by spreading Buddhism and academic knowledge at the same time. In the end of the Qing Dynasty, Baoguang Temple, together with Wenshu Temple in Chengdu, Jinshan Temple in Zhenjiang and Gaomin Temple in Yangzhou, became the famous "Four Temples" of Zen in the Yangtze River Basin. There is a saying popular among modern Buddhist monks and laymen, "to sit in meditation, why not go to Baoguang."

Chapter Five
Historical and Cultural Relics of Chengdu

2. Wenshu Temple

Located at No. 15, Wenshuyuan Street, Chengdu, Wenshu Temple is the best-preserved Buddhist temple in downtown of this city. It is one of the four major Buddhist temples in China, with its grand scale, elegant and simple architecture, strict layout, compact and complete structure, and solemn atmosphere. Originally, it was called "Miaoyuan Pagoda Yard," when built in the Southern Qi Dynasty. Because Emperor Wuzong of the Tang Dynasty (814–846) suppressed Buddhism, the temple was destroyed. During Xuanzong's (810–859) Reign, it was rebuilt and named "Xinxiang Temple." In 1691, Zen Master Cidu (years of birth and death unknown) rebuilt the temple again. He first named it "Xinxiang Wenshu Temple." In front of the gate of Wenshu Temple, there is a screen wall, on which the three characters of "Wen Shu Temple" by Cidu are inlaid with porcelain chips. In 1697, it was renamed Wenshu Temple. In 1701, Emperor Kangxi (1654–1722) granted it the plaque of "Infinite Temple" inscribed by himself. During the period from Emperor Jiaqing to Emperor Daoguang, Wenshu Temple was rebuilt and expanded again. (Fig. 41)

Fig. 41 Wenshu Temple

3. Temples in Qingcheng Mountain

Qingcheng Mountain, stretching to the east of the Chengdu Plain and backed with the snow peaks of Minshan Mountain, has been famous for "the most secluded Qingcheng Mountain in the world" since ancient times. Many poets in the Tang and Song dynasties left famous poems here, praising the beautiful scenery of Qingcheng Mountain. Qingcheng Mountain is also one of the famous Taoist mountains and one of the birthplaces of Taoism in China. Taoism calls it "The Fifth Cave." It is said that at the end of the Eastern Han Dynasty, Zhang Daoling (34-156), formerly known as Zhang Ling, one of the great masters of Taoist School, came there and created Wu Dou Mi Dao – the earliest sect of Taoism, and after this he was known as the father of Taoism. After the Jin Dynasty, Taoism gradually flourished in Qingcheng Mountain. At its peak, there were more than 70 Taoist temples and 108 Taoist scenic spots. Therefore, Qingcheng Mountain is famous for its Taoist culture and unique architectural culture in Chinese history, together with its traditions of Qingcheng Dongjing ancient music, Qingcheng martial arts, Qingcheng Yi studies, Qingcheng alchemy, etc. In Qingcheng Mountain are many scattered Taoist temples, most of which are well preserved, including Changdao Temple (the core), Jianfu Palace, Shangqing Palace, Zushi Hall, Yuanming Temple, Laojun Pavilion (Fig. 42), Yuqing Temple, Chaoyang Cave, etc. To this day, people can still feel the heavy touch of Taoist culture and the legends here and there in Qingcheng Mountain.

Fig. 42 Temple in Qingcheng Mountain – Laojun Pavilion

4. Qingyang Palace

Qingyang Palace is the largest and oldest Taoist temple in Chengdu. It is called the first Taoist temple in Western Sichuan. It is said that the house was first built in Zhou Dynasty, and was named "Qingyang Fair." At the beginning of the Three Kingdoms Period, it was renamed "Qingyang Palace." In the Tang Dynasty, it was renamed "Xuanzhong Temple." When Emperor Xizong came to Chengdu, it was used as his temporary palace. At that time, when a Taoist priest held a ceremony to pray for blessings in Xuanzhong Temple, he suddenly saw a ray of red light across the southeastern bamboo groves like a bullet. Emperor Xizong ordered people to dig out the place and got a jade brick with some characters written on it. He believed it was the epiphany of Lord Lao Zi (Fig. 43) to bless the Tang Dynasty, so he rebuilt Xuanzhong Temple,

Fig. 43 Qingyang Palace

rebuilt the palace and gave it the name "Qingyang Palace." The rebuilt Qingyang Palace became the most famous and influential in Sichuan at that time. In the Five Dynasties, "Qingyang Palace" was renamed "Qingyang Temple," and in the Song Dynasty it was renamed "Qingyang Palace" again, and since then its name has remained unchanged. In recent years, Qingyang Palace has become one of the most important open Taoist temples in China. With the bells and drums ringing and the smoke of incense winding, Qingyang Palace is not only the place where Taoists practice in meditation, but also a tourist attraction.

Chapter Five
Historical and Cultural Relics of Chengdu

Varied Ancient Bridges and Ancient Towns

Bridges is one of the cultural symbols of a city. With water, a city has vitality; with bridges, a city is full of poetry and culture. Chengdu has a long history, and countless bridges have been built since ancient times, such as Jiuyan Bridge on the water of Jinjiang River, Anshun Covered Bridge of ancient flavor, Mozi Bridge still reminding people of the smell of grinding beans, and other old bridges with full memories, including Jiang Bridge, Wanli Bridge, Ximian Bridge, Sima Bridge, Wanfu Bridge, Sandong Bridge, Qingshi Bridge… Some of them can be traced back to the distant past, some with many beautiful stories, some with a graceful look, and some with a poetic flavor. Water has nourished the bridge culture of Chengdu, and the bridge, as the carrier of civilization of thousands of years, has bred and highlighted the bridge culture created by the inventive mind of Chengdu people. The bridges in Chengdu are full of stories; the bridge culture of Chengdu is rich and colorful, through which Chengdu has been on the way to a city of international fame.

1. Wanli Bridge

Wanli Bridge, also known as "Changxing Bridge," is one of the "Seven Star Bridges" in Chengdu, including Jiang Bridge, Wanli Bridge, Yi Bridge, Shi Bridge, Chongli Bridge, Changsheng Bridge and Yongping Bridge. During the Three Kingdoms Period, "Changxing Bridge" was the ferry terminal and transportation juncture at the Southern Gate of Chengdu,

Tianfu Culture and the Modern Pursuit of Chengdu

where people gathered to take boats eastward. At that time, when Fei Yi (?-253), a famous official of the Shu-Han Regime, was sent as the emissary to the Wu Kingdom, Zhuge Liang saw him off. Fei Yi sighed here, "The journey of ten thousand *li* begins here!" The story full of emotion, scene and dialogue is very vivid. Since then, the name of "Wanli Bridge" (ten thousand *li*-long bridge) has been spread. However, eroded by wind and rain, Wanli Bridge was damaged several times. Fortunately, from the Qin Dynasty to the Qing Dynasty, the repair of "Wanli Bridge" never stopped. During the Kangxi reign of the Qing Dynasty, Zhang Dedi, the new governor of Sichuan Province, led the officials to donate money to get Wanli Bridge repaired, set up a stone tablet of "Wanli Bridge" beside the bridge, and hung a plaque of "Wuhou Seeing Fei Yi Off Here." During the reign of Emperor Guangxu, Wanli Bridge was restored again. But with the development of urbanization, the millennium old bridge was demolished in 1995. The new bridge is a single-aperture cement structure with a much wider deck. On the southern bank of the bridge, "Wanli Hotel," a giant ocean ship-shaped modern landmark building was built.

2. Anlan Cable Bridge

A cable bridge is one of the forms of suspended bridge built by ancient Chinese with local bamboo and wood resources, and it is also a model of bridge construction in the world. Anlan Cable Bridge, 313 meters long and located on the Yuzui diversion dike of Dujiangyan Irrigation System, Minjiang River, Chengdu, Sichuan Province, is one of the five famous ancient bridges in China. At first, people called it the Rope Bridge or Bamboo-vine Bridge. The legend has that in 1803, the Minjiang ferry sank, killing more than 100 people. Shocked by such tragic news, Mr. and Mrs. He Xiande (dates of birth and death unknown) proposed to build the bamboo-vine bridge. They made the survey of the terrain, looked up the historical materials of bridge construction, consulted local boatmen and carpenters, reported it to the government for approval, lobbied everywhere to raise funds, and finally led the people to start the construction of the bridge. At the beginning, the bridge had no guardrails, and its whole body of about 500 meters long was suspended in the air cross both the inner and outer flows of the Minjiang River.

Chapter Five
Historical and Cultural Relics of Chengdu

The bridge body was paved with wood and bamboo boards, and every step would make a "click" sound. Later, with the guardrails added, pedestrians would feel much safer while walking along the bridge. That's why people called it "Anlan Bridge" (a bridge that makes people free from dangerous waves). In order to commemorate the He Family, the people also call this bridge the "Couple Bridge," "Mr. He and Mrs. He Bridge," etc. (Fig. 44)

Fig. 44 Anlan Cable Bridge

3. Jiuyan Bridge

The ancient Jiuyan Bridge is a nine-aperture stone arch bridge, also known as Hongji Bridge. Located at the southeastern corner of Chengdu City, connecting Hongji Road in the north and South Taiping Street in the south, and crossing the Fuhe River, it is one of the famous ancient bridges in Chengdu City and known as the "the Beautiful Scene in Southeast Chengdu."

Tianfu Culture and the Modern Pursuit of Chengdu

Once upon a time, on both sides of this river section were distribution centers for loading and unloading, transfer and storage of shipping cargos, and pedestrians and vehicles crossed the river by boat. At the end of the Qing Dynasty, there were still busy wharfs with piles of freight in this area. Until the early 1950s, people could also take a boat to Leshan, Chongqing and other places from the wharfs of the ancient Jiuyan Bridge. The cultural connotation of the ancient Jiuyan Bridge is different from that of the ancient Wanli Bridge and Anshun Cable Bridge in Chengdu, neither special in its structure nor gorgeous in its exterior decoration. It is only an ancient bridge with a long history and mainly of traffic function as the main arteries of the Eastern Gate of Chengdu. After the new and modern Jiuyan Bridge was built and put into use, the old bridge was abandoned and then demolished in 1992. It lasted for more than 400 years from its construction to demolishment. In 1999, the Chengdu Municipal Government rebuilt the antique Jiuyan Bridge on the Fuhe River at the southeast end of Wangjianglou Park. (Fig. 45)

Fig. 45 Jiuyan Bridge

Chapter Five
**Historical and Cultural Relics
of Chengdu**

In addition, Chengdu ancient towns are very much worthy of mentioning. The town group on the Chengdu Plain is one of the five largest town groups in China, characterized with its large scale, dense population, balanced distribution and distinct features. By the end of 1991, there had been 366 cities and towns in Chengdu's Jurisdiction, including many ancient towns distributed around Chengdu. With the increasing pace of urbanization, the spatial patterns of many ancient towns in Chengdu have changed with the evolution of history; some towns have even disappeared in the long history, but there are still some historic towns that have experienced severe tests of time with strong vitality, by retaining the old streets and buildings, keeping the simple folkways and profound customs, adhering to the rich cultural connotations and distinct lifestyles of Western Sichuan, so as to show the characteristics and charm of Chengdu ancient town culture. Especially since the 1990s, Chengdu has strengthened the protection of ancient towns. Each town has formulated protection plans, defined protection areas, and paid attention to the excavation of its own cultural connotation and historical value, so as to achieve the comprehensive development with remarkable results by implementing a well-balanced policy between protection and development. By 2005, many ancient towns in Chengdu, such as Anren, Pingle, Huanglongxi, Luodai and Xinchang, had been among the famous historical and cultural towns at the national or provincial level. These ancient towns preserved in the time-beaten history have become another showcase through which people can understand the city and cultural development of Chengdu.

Chapter Six

Chengdu in the Map of World Civilization

Tianfu Culture and the Modern Pursuit of Chengdu

Chengdu and the Silk Road

In the history of the "Silk Road," in addition to the land passage from Chang'an to Eurasian countries Zhang Qian used to take to the West Asian regions, there are other channels to the outside world, one of which is called the "Southern Silk Road." The "Southern Silk Road" starts from Chengdu, stretches southward, and then is divided into the Eastern and Western Lines. The Eastern Line is the "Butou Road" and "Jinsang Road" from Chengdu to Vietnam, and the Western Line is the "Shushendu Road" from Chengdu to India. The Southern Silk Road, developed as early as in the Shang and Zhou dynasties, has always been an important transportation route for Chengdu to communicate with East Asia, West Asia and other countries.

1. Introduction of Foreign Cultures

In Sanxingdui Site, archaeologists found a large number of ivory and seashells from the Indian Ocean, and similar discoveries were made in other areas of Sichuan and Yunnan. According to the excavation site and related documents, scholars determined that these seashells and ivory were introduced into Chengdu from ancient India through the Southern Silk Road. Dr. Duan Yu believes that "elephants are not the original animals of the Chengdu Plain," and the ivory found in Sanxingdui and Jinsha Site should be foreign. At the same time, a large number of seashells scattering around the bronze wares at the bottom of the sacrificial pit, such as tiger scallops and gold-ringer cowries, were unearthed at Sanxingdui Site. The large number

Chapter Six
Chengdu in the Map of World Civilization

of seashells and ivory unearthed would undoubtedly be the clue of commodity trade between ancient Indian merchants and ancient Shu people when we sketched the Shang and Zhou dynasties. In the case of different languages and different writings, the ancient Indian merchants went all the way to today's Guanghan and Chengdu urban areas through the Southern Silk Road we developed.

The recent discoveries of a sizable number of Buddhist statues along the main road between Yunnan and Sichuan have proved that Buddhism should be introduced from India to Sichuan through Yunnan in the Eastern Han Dynasty. In addition to Buddhism, we can also capture the influence of foreign culture from those unearthed bronze statues and masks. Among the cultural relics unearthed in Sanxingdui Site, the bronze standing figures are tall and exquisite, with broad eyebrows and big eyes, high bridge of nose, flat mouth and perforated earlobes. These features have not been found on bronze figures unearthed from other areas of ancient China. Scholars believe that "they are very similar to the civilization of the Near East, and they are later than the civilization of the Near East and the Indus Valley Civilization in South Asia." That is to say, the emergence of bronze statues should be the result of the influence from the Indus Valley Civilization in South Asia, which integrated the civilization of the Near East. To reach the ancient Shu region, the Indus Valley Civilization in South Asia had no other choice but the Southern Silk Road then.

2. Export of Ba-Shu Culture

When Zhang Qian went to the western regions, he found the Qiong bamboo stick and Shu cloth of ancient Shu region in the Daxia Kingdom (Afghanistan). This shows that before his time, the Southern Silk Road had become the main route of trade between ancient India and ancient Shu region. Chengdu is rich in products, and there are many famous foreign trade products, such as Shu brocade and Shu cloth. According to Duan Yu's research, the Sanskrit name of "Shu cloth" is cinapatta, originating from the Assam language and then widely accepted in India, for Sichuan silk is likely to come into Assam at first, then to other parts of India. Now it is a fixed

Tianfu Culture and the Modern Pursuit of Chengdu

word for "Sichuan cloth" in Sanskrit. It can be seen that the introduction of Shu cloth to India, East Asia, South Asia and other places has an impact on the development of local languages.

The emergence of the Southern Silk Road is an expression of the innovative spirit of the ancestors. With boundless courage and limited human and material resources, the Ba-Shu ancestors opened up the road to the East Asia and the Near East and made the famous products of ancient Shu region the first Chinese commodity on the international stage. At the same time, Tianfu Chengdu integrated foreign cultures with self-confidence and inclusiveness.

Chapter Six
Chengdu in the Map of World Civilization

The Spread of Buddhism in Chengdu

1. The Development of Buddhism with the Boom of More Eminent Monks

Buddhism was introduced into China in the Eastern Han Dynasty and developed in Chengdu in the Southern and Northern Dynasties. At that time, because there were frequent wars in the Central Plains, and Chengdu was located in the southwest, where the political environment was relatively stable, many eminent monks from the Central Plains fled to the Shu region, and Chengdu became one of the centers of Buddhist communication in China. Because of the social disturbance in the end of Sui Dynasty, many great masters of Buddhist doctrine researches gathered in Chengdu, thus promoting Chengdu to be the center of Buddhist doctrine researches in China.

By the middle of the Northern Song Dynasty, the Zen and Pure Land School of Buddhism had developed in full swing in the Central Plains. At that time, the Buddhist doctrine researches centered on Daci Temple still occupied a prominent position in Chengdu. Duan Yuming pointed out, "It was due to the eminent monk named Weisheng that the influence of Zen began to expand in the central area of Chengdu and gradually replaced the position of Yixue (studies of Buddhist doctrines)." Weisheng, whose common surname called Luo, was from Zhongjiang, Sichuan Province. At the age of 15, he became a monk. As he had profound knowledge of Buddhist doctrines, when he taught scriptures, everyone was convinced. He achieved his satori from

Master Huinan in Huanglong Temple successively, and then he settled in Jintang to propagate Dharma on Yunding Mountain. At that time, Zen School of Buddhism was not accepted by the majority of monks in Chengdu. When Weisheng was invited to propagate the essence of Zen in Zhaojue Temple, Chengdu, the audience regretted not to have known him before, and some even wept at the loss of joy. His lectures changed the situation that Zen was not advocated in the central area of Chengdu. Later, the eminent monk Keqin stayed in Zhaojue Temple twice and set up an altar to advocate Zen, whose influence then came to its peak in the central area of Chengdu. Keqin, whose common surname was Luo, was from Tangchang Town, Pidu District. After he took the tonsure, he first studied the Buddhist classics under the guidance of Masters Wenzhao and Minxing in Chengdu, and then turned to Weisheng to learn Zen. Through the activities of propagating Dharma by eminent monks such as Weisheng and Keqin, the Zen thought, taking Zhaojue Temple (Fig. 46) as the center, gradually developed into the core of the Zen School of the Southern Song

Fig. 46 Temple Culture – Zhaojue Temple

Dynasty. The development trend of Buddhism in Chengdu showed the characteristics of equal emphasis on the studies of Buddhist doctrines and the Zen thoughts.

In the Ming and Qing dynasties, the monks in Chengdu were generally more enthusiastic about the secularization of Buddhism instead of the study of Buddhist doctrines. At that time, two major Zen schools were formed with a great influence in Chengdu, taking Shaoqi and Tongzui as their representatives respectively. Shaoqi, a native of Chongzhou, Sichuan Province, at first presided over Lingyin Temple in Dongshan for 10 years, then went touring, and finally stayed in Tiancheng Temple of Chengdu, where he wrote *Quotations of Zen Master Shaoqi*. Shaoqi's Zen thought mainly includes advocating the unity of mind and matter, the unity of Confucianism, Taoism and Buddhism, the integration of the Chan Sect and the Pure Land School, and understanding Buddhism through threads of discourse. With Shaoqi as the core figure and Tiancheng Temple as the center of propagating and lecturing, the Zen School of Chushan was established. The Zen School of Zhangxue, with Tongzui as the core figure, mainly took Zhaojue Temple as the propagating center. Tongzui, with his common surname Li and his ancestral home in Macheng, Xiaogan, Hubei Province, moved to Neijiang, Sichuan Province in the Ming Dynasty. He became a monk at the age of five, and successively studied under several Zen monks. As there were frequent wars at the end of the Ming Dynasty, Tongzui went by way of Yelang and Zunyi to Yumen Temple on the Bank of the Le'an River, where he obtained disciples and propagated the Buddhist doctrines. In the second year of Kangxi's Reign, he returned to Chengdu and began to revive Zhaojue Temple. It took him 24 years to restore Zhaojue Temple to its old look. In the 32nd year of Kangxi, Tongzui passed away. His works include *Quotations of Zen Master Xuezui of Zhaojue Temple*, *Zen Temples in Chengdu*, etc. Tongzui maintained the integration of the Chan Sect, Pure Land School, doctrines and precepts, and identified Buddha nature as the origin of all things in the world, which is not only the basis of social governance, but also the foundation of consciousness of all living beings. There were many disciples in Tongzui's life. Some scholars mentioned that Tongzui was not only the restorer of Ba-Shu Buddhism in the early Qing Dynasty, but also the pioneer of Buddhism in the surrounding areas of the Ba-Shu region.

2. Buddhist Culture and Famous Temples

With the development of Buddhism in Chengdu, more and more Buddhist temples were springing up in Chengdu, adding a different style to the city construction and the life of the citizens. During the Northern and Southern dynasties, there were ten temples in Chengdu and its surrounding areas, such as Duobao Temple, Jingde Temple, Dacheng Temple, Kangxing Temple, Fadeng Temple, etc. In the Tang and Song dynasties, the number of temples doubled. Among the new-built temples, Daci Temple and Zhaojue Temple were the famous ones and have remained till today.

Zhaojue Temple, located outside the northern Chengdu, is one of the famous local Buddhist temples built in the Tang and Song dynasties. It is said that the temple was the former residence of Dong Chang, a disciple of Wang Tong, built in about the Zhenguan period of Emperor Taizong of the Tang Dynasty. At the end of Tang Dynasty, when Zen Master Xiumeng presided over the temple, Cui An, Governor of Jiannan Prefecture, sent his memorial requesting the change of the temple's name. Emperor Xuanzong gave it the title of "Zhaojue Temple" and Xiumeng a purple suit. Later, when Emperor Xizong entered the Shu region and Wang Jian served as Governor of the Eastern and Western Sichuan, they showed more respect to Xiumeng. When Xiumeng presided over Zhaojue Temple, he built the temple in a big way; for example, Sun Wei, Zhang Xun and other famous painters were invited to draw murals in the temple. At the beginning of the Song Dynasty, Zhaojue Temple was very magnificent in scale with hundreds of halls and houses, some of which were destroyed in the war at the end of the Ming Dynasty. During the period between the Northern and Southern Song dynasties, Zen Master Weisheng gave his lecture in Zhaojue Temple and Keqin presided over this temple twice, and these events made Zhaojue Temple the communication center of the Zen of the Southern Song Dynasty. Zhaojue Temple has played an important role in the process of Buddhism exchange between Chengdu and South Asia, and Tibetan Buddhism.

Wenshu Temple, formerly known as Xinxiang Temple, was built in the period of Daye in the Sui Dynasty. The temple was destroyed when Wuzong of the Tang Dynasty ordered to destroy

Chapter Six
Chengdu in the Map of World Civilization

Buddhism, and reconstructed during the period of Emperor Xuanzong. There was a stone stele inscribed with "Records of Gao Pian in City Construction," written by Wang Hui from the Imperial Academy in the fourth year of the Zhonghe's Reign of Emperor Xizong. According to this, the reconstruction might have occured before the fourth year of the Zhonghe's Reign. Therefore, it was also called Zhonghe Xinxiang Temple. Wenshu Temple is famous for the presidency of Master Cidu. Cidu Chaocun, with his common surname Liu, was from Chengdu. When he was a child, he became a monk under Master Jingqu at Xingxiang Temple. At the age of 19, he finished precepts from Tongzui of Zhaojue Temple, and then achieved his satori from Zen Master Deyu of Huayan Temple in Yuzhou. In the 20th year of Emperor Kangxi, when Cidu settled at the abandoned site of Xinxiang Temple, monks and the mundane people often saw the firelight at the site and suspected that Manjusri Bodhisattva appeared. Therefore, Xinxiang Temple was rebuilt and renamed as Xinxiang Wenshu Temple. In the 41st year of Kangxi's Reign, the emperor granted the plaque of "Infinite Temple," the *Vajracchedika's Sutra and the Bhaisajyaguru Sutra*. For nearly 30 years, Master Cidu had been the chair of Wenshu Temple, making the greatest contribution to the re-prosperity of the temple in the Qing Dynasty. Wenshu Temple has thus become one of the most influential temples in Chengdu.

In the process of Buddhism dissemination, in addition to the major temples, there are many mountains famous for Buddhist activities, such as Wuzhong Mountain, located in the Wushan Township in the north of Dayi County. During its peak in the Ming Dynasty, there were 48 nunneries and 180 temples headed by Kaihua Temple, with thousands of monks, and this phenomenon was a highlight of Buddhism in Chengdu in the Ming Dynasty. Sanxue Mountain, located in today's Jintang County, with the so-called holy lamp, Bodhisattvas and plaque of "Sanxue," obtained fame and became one of the famous Buddhist mountains in Chengdu. Tiantai Mountain, located in the Qionglai Mountains in the southwest of Qionglai County, bears the well-known remark of "Tiantai, Tiantai, the platform to the sky" because of its three-level terraces from the foot to the top. Tiantai Mountain used to be the place where Buddhism and Taoism competed. In the Song Dynasty, there were more than 100 religious buildings in the mountain.

In the Yuan Dynasty, its religious influence gradually declined. Other famous mountains include Yunding Mountain and Jiulong Mountain.

3. Buddhist Influences and Popular Lives

Buddhism has penetrated into Chengdu people's life in many ways. It was originally the lifestyle of believers to listen to scriptures and practice Zen in temples; however, in the Tang and Song dynasties, it evolved into a social tradition to visit temples and burn incenses and entertain in festivals. Famous Buddhist temples in Chengdu, such as Daci Temple, Zhaojue Temple and Wenshu Temple, all of garden style buildings, with winding paths, watery pavilions, beautiful buildings, surrounded by Sanskrit sound, evening drums and morning bells, became the best places for scholars and common people to visit. Around the major temples in the city, commercial streets were gradually formed. In the Song Dynasty, there were large-scale fairs every month in Chengdu, such as the Lantern Market in Daci Temple and Zhaojue Temple in the first lunar month, the Flower Market in Qingyang Palace in the second lunar month, and the Silkworm Market in Shengshou Temple, Daci Temple, and Baoli Temple in the third lunar month. Today, these traditions have still remained unchanged in Chengdu. The business circle centered on Daci Temple is also the most fashionable and prosperous consumption place in Chengdu.

Buddhism in Chengdu played an important role in social development, urban construction, and ideological and cultural communication. The co-existence and development of Confucianism, Buddhism and Taoism was also the regional feature of Buddhism's own development in Chengdu. Buddhism in Chengdu not only widely absorbed the achievements of the Buddhism of the Central Plains and foreign countries, but also actively exchanged with East Asia and South Asia. In history, Prince Wuxiang of the Xinluo Kingdom founded "Zen of Jingzhong" in Daci Temple, and now "Wuxiang Zen Tea" is still popular in South Korea and other places; Keqin, who resided in Zhaojue Temple two times, wrote *Biyan Lu* and *Yuanwu Xinyao*, which are listed in Japan's *Taisho Tripitaka*. At present, many Buddhist temples in Japan and Southeast Asia regard Zhaojue Temple as their ancestral hall. Lanxi Daolong, at the age of 13,

**Chapter Six
Chengdu in the Map of
World Civilization**

became a monk in Daci Temple. Upon finishing studies, he led his disciples to travel eastward propagating Buddhism in Japan. Emperor Uda of Japan granted him the title of "Zen Master of Dajue," which was first time to grant such a title of "Zen Master." In the context of the East Asia and South Asia cultural circles, Buddhism in Chengdu has strengthened the exchange between local and foreign cultures, and in turn, promoted the widespread and innovative development of Buddhist culture.

The Three Kingdoms Culture and Chengdu

The Three Kingdoms Period is the most commented period in the Chinese history of thousands of years, whose culture has permeated all kinds of literature and art forms and is popular all over the world. The Three Kingdoms, together with Confucius and *The Analects of Confucius*, are the hot keywords when foreigners are mentioning about the traditional Chinese culture and Chinese history.

1. The Shu-Han Regime

At the end of the Eastern Han Dynasty, with the warlords fighting, the Three Kingdoms of Wei, Shu and Wu were successively established in the history of China, confronting with each other while being likely to get a double-pronged attack. Thus, "Three Kingdoms stand like the three legs of a tripod." In the 26th year of Jian'an (221), Liu Bei took the throne in the south of Wudan Mountain, Chengdu, the capital of Shu-Han Regime, and changed the year name to Zhangwu. Zhuge Liang was appointed as Prime Minister, Xu Jing as Minister of Education, Zhang Fei as General and Inspector. They built the regime, appointed officials and constructed imperial ancestors' temples. Since then, Chengdu had been under the rule of the Shu-Han Regime for nearly 50 years (from Liu Zhang's surrender in 214 to the fall of the regime in 263).

After Liu Bei ascended the throne in April, he led his troops to attack Wu in July, and try to recapture Jingzhou. In June of Zhangwu's second year, Lu Yi broke Liu Bei's army in Yiting.

Chapter Six
Chengdu in the Map of World Civilization

In August, Liu Bei withdrew the army to Mount Wu. In April of Zhangwu's third year, Liu Bei died of illness in Yongan Palace, entrusting an orphan to Zhuge Liang. In May, the coffin was carried back to Chengdu from Yong'an. He was buried in the Hui Mausoleum in August with his posthumous title "Emperor Zhaolie." From his accession to the throne to his death, Liu Bei had little time to govern the affairs of state in Chengdu. After the establishment of the Shu-Han Regime, Liu Bei mainly led troops to conquer outside regions, and Zhuge Liang actually dealt with various internal affairs of the Shu-Han Regime.

During his stay in Chengdu, Zhuge Liang expanded the Shu Palace, built Jiuli Dike in the northern suburbs, and built the Hui Mausoleum and the new Ancestral Temple in the southern suburbs. The expanded Shu Palace was likely to be built in the south of the Wudan Mountain in accordance with the standard of the Han imperial palace, backed with the mountain and overlooking the river, doors to doors and courts upon courts, and having an imposing appearance. Located in the northern suburbs of Chengdu, the Shu Palace was linked with Da Cheng and Shao Cheng in the south of Chengdu. The Jiuli Dike at today's Dongzikou, Jinniu District, was first built by Li Bing, Prefect of the Qin Dynasty, and rebuilt by Zhuge Liang. When Zhuge Liang implemented Liu Bei's order to station in the northern and southern suburbs of Chengdu, he selected talents and handled daily affairs. During Liu Chan's Reign, Zhuge Liang sent troops for the Northern Expedition five times successively. Although it was only a partial victory, his dedication to serving the first lord and being loyal to the later lord has been sung from the ancient to modern times.

Liu Chan, the later lord, lived in Chengdu for about 50 years. He had been in Chengdu for 41 years since he ascended the throne in 223. Liu Chan is known as "a lame duck," but he was not so weak in his character and governance of the state affairs. Zhuge Liang once affirmed Liu Chan's "profound knowledge," "talent and benevolence." After Liu Chan ascended the throne, he said that he was willing to "do things according to Zhuge Liang just as a son does for his father," and left almost everything big or small up to the prime minister. Although there were different opinions on this matter, Liu Chan's forbearance was obvious. After Zhuge Liang's death and

Tianfu Culture and the Modern Pursuit of Chengdu

Jiang Wan and Fei Yu were in power, most of the actual political power was still in the hands of Liu Chan. It was not until Jiang Wei came on stage that Liu Chan's power was out of control, that the Shu-Han Regime was finally put to an end.

2. The Temple of Marquis Wu in Chengdu

The Temple of Marquis Wu[1] is located in today's Wuhou Street at the Southern Gate of Chengdu. At that time, the Temple of Marquis Wu was outside the main city, surrounded by cypresses and dense forest. Today, the area around the Temple of Marquis Wu has long been bustling commercial streets in Chengdu. In the second year of the Zhangwu's Reign, when Prime Minister Zhuge Liang followed the order to "station in the northern and southern suburbs in Chengdu," he himself presided over the Southern Suburb Project of construction of the Hui Mausoleum and the new Ancestral Temple, located at the present Temple of Marquis Wu.

The Hui Mausoleum is a mausoleum built before Liu Bei's death. According to the ritual system of the Han Dynasty, the second year after the emperor's accession to the throne, the pre-built mausoleum was to be built by the prime minister, who would be in charge of the construction. From site selection, planning, design, supervision to the final check before acceptance, Zhuge Liang did it all himself. The location at the southern suburbs was also out of respect for the traditional etiquette system. According to the tradition of the Han Dynasty, the imperial mausoleum should be near the capital city. The location of the Hui Mausoleum in the south of Shu Palace (from Beijiaochang Street to Babao Street today), was just on the North-South connecting line with Wudan Mountain, where Liu Bei took the throne. Since ancient times, the south has been regarded as the most prestigious place in the Shu region. Located in the southern suburbs and planted with pines and cypresses, this arrangement meant prayers for the Shu-Han Regime. According to the system of the Han Dynasty, as long as the imperial mausoleum was built, a temple should be built beside it; therefore, the "Zhaolie Temple of the Han Dynasty" was built altogether. It was so named because his reign fell in the Han Dynasty,

---

1 The Temple of Marquis Wu refers to the one dedicated to Zhuge Liang.

Chapter Six
Chengdu in the Map of World Civilization

and Liu Bei's posthumous title was "Emperor Zhaolie." It was a new ancestral temple.

The Temple of Marquis Wu was built in the Eastern Jin Dynasty, initially in the western part of Chengdu. Forty or fifty years after the collapse of the Shu-Han Regime, Li Xiong, then the king, presided over the construction. Later, Heng Wen invading the Shu region resulted in the destruction of many buildings and temples, but the Temple of Marquis Wu was preserved. During the Southern and Northern dynasties, the Temple of Marquis Wu was moved from the western part to where the Hui Mausoleum lay in the southern suburbs, reflecting the Confucian idea of the monarch and his minister being of one heart and one mind. In the Song Dynasty, with the concept of "the king accompanied by his ministers" going popular, the Song people built Guan Hou Temple and Zhang Fei Temple along each side of the Hui Mausoleum. In the Hongwu Period of Ming Dynasty, King Xian of the Shu State ordered the renovation of the Temple of Marquis Wu. In this merging of temples, the Zhuge Liang's statue was moved to the east of the Liu Bei's statue, and the Guan Yu and the Zhang Fei's statues were moved to the west of the Liu Bei's statue. As a result, the Hui Mausoleum, the Zhaolie Temple of Han Dynasty and the Temple of Marquis Wu became all in one, forming the "Temple of Marquis Wu" in a broader sense. It is the only one in China that houses the statues of both the king and ministers. In the Qing Dynasty, the Temple of Marquis Wu underwent several repairs and renovations, with sculptural figures added and discarded and halls expanded. However, in any case, the pattern of worshiping the monarch and his ministers at one time in the same place has remained unchanged in the Temple of Marquis Wu.

3. The Global Craze of Three Kingdoms Culture

In recent years, with the development of video games, in addition to other countries in Asia, many countries in Europe and America have also known and loved the culture of Three Kingdoms through various games and movies.

The Three Kingdoms Period is a relatively short period in Chinese history. Then why is the culture of the Three Kingdoms so popular? Luo Kaiyu mentioned that the theme of the Three

Tianfu Culture and the Modern Pursuit of Chengdu

Kingdoms culture is the product of the high combination of Confucian culture and strategist culture. Kindness, favor, leniency and severity can be told in the scheming and deceits, and loyalty, righteousness, benevolence and filial piety can be seen from the shadow of swords and knives. The states of Wei, Shu, and Wu and many other military groups fought one another to death. The culture of the Three Kingdoms that presents the military, economic and cultural features of that chaotic war era is rich and colorful, breathtaking and adventurous. Moreover, the understanding and research of the Three Kingdoms in the past dynasties, including the derivative works such as films and television works and computer games on the themes of the Three Kingdoms, constitute a more abundant and powerful subcultural phenomenon of the Three Kingdoms. This is the reason why the culture of the Three Kingdoms continues to attract more and more people around the world. Its charm lies not only in fighting and killing, or in the deep loyalty to one's lord, but also explaining in many ways the reflection on human nature, ambition and impermanence of the world in Confucian philosophy. Although the culture of the Three Kingdoms may be selectively accepted and transformed when it spreads to other cultural circles outside the country, its concern for human nature as core values has remained unchanged, so have the key ideas regardless the form, language and region of communication.

Today, as a famous historical and cultural city with a profound Three Kingdoms culture, Chengdu has built the Temple of Marquis Wu and Jinli Street Cultural Tour Circle of much ancient charm. Jingchuan Hotel with the Three Kingdoms culture as its theme also strives to recreate the past scenery. Sichuan specialty Zhang Fei beef has become the favorite commodity of friends from other places. These are a very vivid presentation of the Three Kingdoms Culture in Chengdu. With the innovation of art forms and the emergence of various new performance skills, there will be more brilliant ways to spread the culture of Three Kingdoms, which will lay a profound cultural foundation and provide more opportunities for Chengdu to develop into a world-famous cultural city and a national central city embodying new ideas of innovative development.

Chapter Seven
Tianfu Chengdu Towards a New Era

The previous chapters have given us an overall review of the history of Chengdu. Since Zhang Yi's conducting the city construction, Chengdu City has gone through development for more than 2,300 years; since the ninth emperor of the Kaiming Dynasty moved his capital to Chengdu, Chengdu City has boasted a history of over 2,600 years; based on the Jinsha Site, the history of Chengdu City can be traced back to 3,200 years ago. In the long history of around 3,000 years, Chengdu once was the center of the ancient Shu Kingdom, a state annexed by the Qin State, one of the five metropolises during the Eastern and Western Han dynasties, the Southern Capital in the prosperous Tang Dynasty, a place of strategic importance in stabilizing Southwest China in the Ming and Qing dynasties, and a solid rear of the War of Resistance against Japanese Aggression. In different historical periods, Chengdu has always kept the pace with the times. Since the 1980s, with the tide of globalization, China has experienced the unprecedented reform. Along with the rapid change of internal and external environment, Chengdu has begun its new journey towards a new era.

Tianfu Culture and the Modern Pursuit of Chengdu

Modernization of the City

Modernization is the common trend of development for cities around the world. He Mingyi, a contemporary famous urban-research expert indicates, "The modernized city is a giant composite career based on highly developed economy, armed by the most advanced science and technology and composed of good buildings, beautiful environment and highly perfect infrastructure." According to this standard, well-developed economy, advanced science and technology, beautiful buildings, healthy environment and highly perfect infrastructure are the basic characteristic of a modernized city. Looking back the developing history of Chengdu in line with this definition, we can see its track of modernization clearly.

1. Transformation of Industrial Structure

The Chengdu Plain spreads over a wide and fruitful land crisscrossed with irrigation canals and ditches. Such unique abundant land and water resources have given birth to the oldest agricultural civilization of China, made the area free from floods or draughts, and the local people from starvation. Over thousands of years, agriculture has always been the pillar industry of Chengdu. However, after the founding of the People's Republic of China, Chengdu became the key area of the "Three Lines" Construction and saw many major enterprises move to it. In 1953, 8 out of the 156 national key projects aided by the Soviet Union were settled in Chengdu, and piles of large enterprises started their construction in its eastern suburbs. After Sichuan

Chapter Seven
Tianfu Chengdu
Towards a New Era

Province and Xikang Province merged into one in 1955, Chengdu as the provincial capital had a new historical orientation, that is, the city of precision instrument, machine manufacturing and light industry. Through large-scale construction of China's 1st and 2nd Five-Year Plans, Chengdu improved its supporting industries step by step, and the industries such as electronics, medicine, machinery, metallurgy, chemical engineering, textiles, light industry, building materials, food, etc. began to take shape. Up to 1965, there had already been 2,700 industrial enterprises with the annual GDP of 1.052 billion *yuan* in total, 10 times that of 1949. More than 100 modern industrial products took the lead in the country, such as seamless steel tube, automobiles, mechanical equipment, cutting tools, chemical fertilizer, chemical raw materials, antibiotics, etc. Till 1977, there were altogether 4,010 enterprises at township or higher level; the annual GDP reached 3.653 billion *yuan*. So far, Chengdu generally formed the industrial structure dominated by industries, and basically realized the industrialization goal.

Since China's reform and opening-up policy, Chengdu's industrial structure has been adjusted again. From 1978 to 1986, the primary industry in Chengdu kept on shrinking, while the secondary and tertiary industries slightly improved. From 1986 to 2000, Chengdu's tertiary industry took off and become the core force of the economy, while the proportion of primary and secondary industries dropped. Since 2000, Chengdu's industry has launched again. The proportion of secondary industry has remained around 45% all the year round, that of primary industry has decreased to 3.9%, and that of the tertiary industry has remained at a relatively high level of about 50%. As a result, there has been a "321" pattern of the industrial structure (the tertiary industry, secondary industry and the primary industry in order) reaching the optimal state of modern industrial development.

2. Reconstruction of the City's Environment

Before 1949, with the city wall as its boundary, Chengdu achieved the basic spatial segmentation of the city with the Imperial City within Da Cheng (the Larger One), Da Cheng in the east connecting Shao Cheng (the Smaller One) in the west, the Fu River and the Southern

Tianfu Culture and the Modern Pursuit of Chengdu

River surrounding it distinctively. After the founding of the P.R.C., Chengdu carried out some transformation, while reserving the old layout of the city surrounded by two rivers and with the coincidence of three cities. With the city space breaking through the limit of old-age city wall and new buildings springing up, the city's environment was revitalized. These changes have laid a beneficial foundation for the modernization of the city's environment.

(1) Spatial Arrangement

In the 1980s, the city scale of Chengdu increased day by day, the flat space extended further, and then formed the rather distinctive mono-centered circle-radial urban layout, which took the four streets – Dongchenggen Street, Hongxing Road, Xinhua Road, and Binjiang Road as its center, formed the circle network with the Inner Loop Road, the First Ring Road, the Second Ring Road, the Third Ring Road, and the Outer Express Ring Road, and constituted the radiating arteries with several traffic roads to and from the city. This layout took full advantages of the spatial supremacy of the Chengdu Plain. It not only broke up the traditional Chinese rectangle and fixed pattern of city layout, but also kept its regular and rigorous basic structure. As a result, it became the world-recognized paragon of ring-radial urban layout.

In the 1990s, along with the extension of the city size, some weaknesses of ring-radial urban layout were exposed. Regional advantages of the central area were so obvious as to cause the large concentration of population and the increasing pressure upon the central area. On that account, Chengdu promulgated the Overall Plan of Chengdu City (1995–2020) in 1994, proposing to transform the extension mode of the city from the ring-radial urban layout to the axially vane-shaped one. Then two axes to the east and north were established respectively, between which the city's functional layout was refined further on the fan-shaped surface. The area inside the First Ring Road was the central area with relatively centralized public facilities; the area between the First Ring Road and the Third Ring Road was the main urban area; the area between the Third Ring Road and the Outer Express Ring Road was the around-city area dotted with relatively independent small towns, industrial parks, and biological green lands. This layout paid more attention to urban-rural integration and sustainable development. It was conducive to the further development of Chengdu.

Coming to the 21st century, the urbanization process of Chengdu has been accelerated. In order to adjust to the new form and realize the integral and coordinative development, Chengdu proposed the "All-for-One" idea in the country firstly. The "All-for-One Chengdu" is meant to actively accelerate the construction of satellite cities and towns to serve the central urban area, so as to achieve the all-for-one coverage of the city planning, the all-for-one convenience of traffic, and the all-for-one balance of public service. Then, Chengdu's urban spatial layout evolved into "one city, two belts and six corridors." "One city" refers to the central city, the "two belts" are Longquan Mountain Range and Longmen Mountain Range, and the "six corridors" include the urban development axes extending in six directions from the central city to Longquanyi, to Huayang and Zhengxing, to Shuangliu, Xinjin and Pujiang; to Wenjiang and Qionglai; to Pidu District and Dujiangyan, and to Xindu, Qingbaijiang and Jintang. This new layout reoriented Chengdu's urban layout, and was conducive to the free flow of population and materials and the realization of overall development.

In 2017, in the context of constructing the national central city, Chengdu adjusted the overall planning of city development and designed the brand new city layout called "One Mountain + Two Wings." This plan would turn Chengdu's original layout of one central urban area with Longquan Mountain and Longmen Mountain subsidiary to it to that taking Longquan Mountain as the center with the western central urban area and eastern new urban area as two wings. So far, Chengdu has developed from the old city of only 18 square kilometers around 1949 to the modernized new city of several hundred square kilometers. Now Chengdu has basically completed the space layout of balanced urban and rural development, with the small cities as the bond, the small towns as the base.

Tianfu Culture and the Modern Pursuit of Chengdu

(2) Transformation of the Old City

Chengdu was transforming the old city while optimizing the space layout and extending the urban area. In 2002, there were still dangerous old houses of more than five million square meters remaining in the central urban area. Lots of low and shabby buildings were sandwiched by high-rise buildings in different regions in the urban areas, and exerted negative influence on the city image and its development potential. From May 2002, Chengdu invested more than 18 billion *yuan* in 244 demolition and renovation projects of dilapidated houses, covering an area of nearly 8.35 million square meters. It demolished and resettled 113,600 residential and non-residential houses, and demolished various sorts of dilapidated houses of 5.714 million square meters in total. These endeavors basically eliminated the old shanty areas within the Second Ring Road, obviously improved the housing conditions of about 370 thousand residents from over 100 thousand families, and greatly improved the image of the old urban area. In 2012, Chengdu launched the Northern Chengdu Transformation Project, aiming at the unified transformation of the northern urban area under the jurisdiction of Jinniu District, Chenghua District and Xindu District. This project had its planning area of 195 square kilometers, investment of about RMB 330 billion *yuan* in total, and more than 900 transformation projects involved. This project would implement a comprehensive transformation of the planned area, and build it into the modern urban area that is livable, business friendly and offered high-quality employment and a pleasant ecological environment. After five years of the implementation of the project, the image of the northern urban area has been thoroughly changed. The modern new city integrated with dwelling, commerce, culture, recreation and tourism is coming into shape.

(3) Optimization of Ecological Environment

The optimization of ecological environment has always been the key content of urban environment transformation of Chengdu. As early as at the beginning of reform and opening-up, Chengdu citizens already paid attention to ecological environment, and turned their sights on the mother river of the city – the Fu River and the Nan River. At that time, there were five problems

Chapter Seven
Tianfu Chengdu Towards a New Era

about the Fu River and Nan River: weak flood control capacity because of the insufficient flood discharging capacity, serious water pollution with the worsened ecological environment, narrow roads with incomplete pipe networks, the shabby old houses along the river banks obstructing the city image, and the serious lack of afforest and planning management. In 1993, the Funan River Comprehensive Improvement Project was fully launched. During the four years, 2.7 billion *yuan* was invested into this project, and four major projects were completed, including the river regulating, sewage treatment, pipe network construction, and shabby houses dismantling with resettling the residents. When the whole project was completed in 1997, the width of the river channel was expanded from the original 30-80 meters to 40-120 meters, and the flood control capacity was improved from the flood level greater than 10 years to that of 200 years. The sewage closure project cleared up over 650 sewage outlets, intercepting the sewage of 250 thousand cubic meters every day and purifying urban water area of 85 million square meters. The construction of 41-kilometers-long riverside roads greatly improved the traffic condition. Over 20 new constructed residential districts were built, more than 10 million residents alongside the river removed, with new public greenbelt of 25 thousand square meters. After this project, the Funan River has been revitalized, and the ecological environment of Chengdu urban areas improved strikingly. Thanks to this project, Chengdu has won five international awards: "Habitat Scroll of Honour Award," "Local Government Innovation Award," "Best Model of Residential Environment Improvement Award," "Regional Environment Design Award," and "Excellence on Waterfront Award."

In 2016, Chengdu Municipal Government has published Ecological Civilization Construction Program of Chengdu until 2025, put forward 37 indicators for Ecological Civilization Construction, with 18 key indicators such as total water consumption, forest coverage rate, and annual average concentration of PM 2.5. The Program also worked out 238 major projects and planned to invest RMB 561.9 billion *yuan* to support the implementation of the mission and the achievement of the aims. In April 2017, the 13th Party Congress of Chengdu further put forward that the most rigorous industry access rules and environment protection policies must be implemented. The smog problem, traffic congestion, water pollution and lack of afforest must be treated and regulated in a serious and scientific manner to reproduce the prosperity of Chengdu with plenty of afforest, flowers, and purified water resource, to make the citizens "slow down, calm down, close to nature, and pleased with life" and to make Chengdu the pilot city of Beautiful China. In order to implement the spirit of the congress of Party representatives and respond the citizens yearning for a better life with beautiful ecological environment, in June 2017, the Chengdu Municipal Government published the working schemes of "Ten Measures" in four aspects – Ten Measures to Reduce Smog, Ten Measures to Reduce Water Pollution, Ten Measures to Reduce Traffic Congestion, and Ten Measures to Improve Greenery, together with the 47 detailed methods. Naturally, the ecological environment optimization work has been advanced to a new stage.

3. Construction of Transportation Facilities

Transportation facilities are an important guarantee for the quality of city life. Since the 1980s, Chengdu has launched a series of traffic facilities construction in order to improve the city form and optimize the city function.

(1) Reconstruction of Roads and Bridges

In 1949, Chengdu had only 497.3 kilometers of roads and 118 bridges with a total length of 3,329.8 meters, of low technical grade, poor in disaster resistance and relatively backward in mileage and quality. Up to the initial stage of reform and opening-up after nearly 30 years of construction, the total mileage of roads in Chengdu increased to 2,457.5 kilometers, but four-fifths of them were four-grade roads and substandard roads, with almost no high-grade roads, let alone expressways. Since the reform and opening-up, Chengdu has increased its investment in road and bridge construction, and the urban road traffic has changed accordingly.

In 1979, the section from Liangjia Lane to Tianhui Township along the Sichuan-Shaanxi Road – Chengdu's main northbound road out of town, was widened and renovated, with a

Chapter Seven
Tianfu Chengdu Towards a New Era

mileage of 9.2 kilometers. This was the first Grade A highway built in the whole province at that time, and greatly relieved the traffic congestion at the area around the Northern Gate of Chengdu. From 1980 to 1990, Chengdu rebuilt 298 roads of 2,581.4 kilometers, 23,566 bridges and culverts with a total length of 156,300 meters. Road and bridge construction standards were also greatly improved, and high-grade highways sprang up in large numbers. In 1986, Chengdu completed the expansion project of the First Ring Road on the basis of the original urban streets. The reconstructed First Ring Road, with a total length of 19.38 kilometers and two-way four lanes (later converted into two-way six lanes), spans Jinniu District, Qingyang District, Wuhou District, High-tech Zone, Jinjiang District and Chenghua District and becomes the main artery of urban traffic. In 1993, the 28.327 kilometers-long Second Ring Road was completed and opened to traffic. The road section was initially designed as a two-way four-lane road, connecting with the main roads in and out of the city through six overpasses (gradually increasing to more than 10 after), and a circular radial traffic network began taking shape. The Third Express Ring Road of Chengdu, with the investment is 6.6 billion *yuan* and a total length of 50.89 kilometers, was officially opened to traffic on October 28, 2002. In 2001, Chengdu Ring Expressway (later renamed Chengdu Fourth Express Ring Road) was completed and opened to traffic, 85 kilometers long and with two-way and six lanes. It is an important part of Chengdu's circular radiation traffic network. In 2013, Chengdu Second Ring Road Elevated Road was completed. The project is a 28.3 km high-rise urban expressway built on the original Second Ring Road, with no traffic lights on the main line and multiple flyovers and ramps for traffic conversion. A total of four bus rapid transit lines have been set up on the Second Ring Elevated Road, expanding urban public transport from flat to three-dimensional space, which is the first of its kind in the country. At the end of 2015, Chengdu's Second Ring Expressway (later renamed Chengdu Sixth Express Ring Road) was fully opened to traffic. This section of road is located more than 10 kilometers outside the Forth Express Ring Road, with a total length of 223 kilometers and a design speed of 100 kilometers per hour. It connects 12 districts (cities) and counties such as Qingbaijiang District, Jintang County, Longquanyi District, Shuangliu District,

Tianfu Culture and the Modern Pursuit of Chengdu

Xinjin County, Chongzhou City, Wenjiang District, Pidu District, Xindu District, Pengzhou City, Guanghan City and Jianyang City, thus forming the "Chengdu One-Hour Economic Circle." While continuing to expand the circular radiation traffic network, it is also conducive to guiding and optimizing the layout of Chengdu's industry, logistics and market.

(2) Rail Transit

The perfection and development degree of rail transit is one of the important indicators of a modernized city at home and abroad. Chengdu's rail transit system mainly includes three parts: metro, tram and city railway.

Chengdu Metro was conceived as early as in 1985. In August 2005, the National Development and Reform Commission officially approved the construction plans of Chengdu Metro Lines 1 and 2. At the end of 2005, Chengdu Metro Line 1 broke ground. The line is the main line in the north-south direction, running through the central urban areas such as the North Railway Station, Tianfu Square, Luomashi and South Railway Station. The first phase of the 18.5-kilometer construction, with 17 designed stations, is the first metro in Chengdu, Sichuan Province and even the entire Western China. In September 2010, the first phase of Line 1 was completed and opened to traffic, making Chengdu the 10th city with rail transit in the Chinses Mainland. From 2010 to 2017, Line 2, Line 3, Line 4, Line 10 and Line 7 were opened successively, with 140 kilometers of operation mileage, more than 100 stations, the volume of passenger traffic of more than 500 million per year, and the top 10 of passenger flow intensity in the country. In 2018, there are still 10 metro lines under construction in Chengdu, 46 lines in pipeline with a design mileage of more than 2,370 kilometers.

The tramcar is another important component of Chengdu rail transit, mainly laid on the ground or via ducts. Compared with the metro, it has the advantages of low investment and low cost; compared with other road traffic, it is more environment friendly, convenient, safer and of a larger traffic volume. The Chengdu tram project was officially launched in 2015. Currently, lines of Rong 1, Rong 2, Xinjin R1 and Dujiangyan M-TR are already under construction (due to the construction of Tianfu Avenue and Jiannan Avenue, the construction of Line Rong 1 has been

Chapter Seven
Tianfu Chengdu
Towards a New Era

suspended). Five other lines are under planning with a total planned mileage of more than 160 kilometers. These tramlines can not only operate independently, but also seamlessly connect with the metro network and the road public transportation network, making it convenient for people to transfer, thus becoming an important supplement to the Chengdu rail transportation network.

Chengdu regional railway is a long-distance, high-speed and large-capacity public transportation within the scope of Chengdu city, which connects the central urban areas with the surrounding cities. As its size and shape are between the national railway and the urban rail, it has the characteristics of high speed, low investment and fast approval. Furthermore, it can also realize the interconnection with the national railway trunk lines and enhance the city's external radiation capability. Chengdu's first regional railway Chengguan Express started construction in 2008 and opened in 2010. Its main line is 67 kilometers long (94.2 kilometers long plus the Lidui branch line and Pengzhou branch line), and it can transfer passengers at a speed of nearly 100 kilometers per hour from the central urban area to the peripheral clustered cities within one hour.

On the basis of these lines, a crisscrossing and convenient rail transit network covering the main urban areas and surrounding counties and cities has taken shape.

(3) International Airports

Sichuan is an inland province in Western China, while Chengdu is China's nearest national central city to Europe and a national pan-European and pan-Asian open gateway city, with frequent international exchanges. In the process of modernization, Chengdu pays special attention to the construction of air transportation.

The Shuangliu International Airport is the first international airport owned by Chengdu. Its predecessor was Chengdu Shuangguisi Military Airport built in 1939. In 1956, with the airport assigned to the civil aviation administration, it was renamed as "Chengdu Shuangliu Airport" and opened many air routes to Beijing, Taiyuan, Xi'an, Chongqing, Kunming, Guiyang, Nanchong and other cities. In the 1990s, with the accelerated pace of Chengdu's modernization process and the surging demand for foreign air transportation, Chengdu Shuangliu Airport was approved

as an international airport, officially renamed Chengdu Shuangliu International Airport, and a series of expansion projects including the international terminal area and the second runway were started. In December 2009, the second runway of the airport was officially put into use, and Chengdu Shuangliu International Airport became the fourth civil airport with two runways in the Chinese Mainland. At present, Chengdu Shuangliu International Airport has 178 parking spaces in 3 parking areas with a total area of 1 million square meters, two passenger terminals with a waiting area of 500,000 square meters and an annual throughput of 50 million passengers, three air freight terminals with an annual cargo and mail throughput of over 600,000 tons. With 270 routes to 209 cities at home and abroad, it is one of China's eight regional airline hubs.

In 2011, the site selection of Chengdu's new airport began. After more than two years of investigation, comparison and demonstration, the National Civil Aviation Administration finally approved Lujia Township, Jianyang as the airport site. In 2015, the State Council and the Central Military Commission issued a document approving the establishment of Chengdu's new airport. In the same year, the Civil Aviation Administration approved the designation of the airport as Chengdu Tianfu International Airport. In May 2016, the construction of Chengdu Tianfu International Airport was officially started. The first phase of the project, with a total investment of 71.86 billion *yuan*, has three planned runways, 670,000 square meters of terminal area and 202 flight parking spaces, with a designed annual passenger throughput of 40 million and a cargo and mail throughput of 700,000 tons. According to its long-term plan, there will be six runways, the terminal area of 1.26 million square meters in total with an annual passenger throughput of 90 million. With the start of construction of the airport, Chengdu has become the third city with two top-grade civil international airports in the Chinese Mainland after Shanghai and Beijing. With a developed, efficient, environment friendly and economical transportation system as the guarantee, Chengdu will also move towards the world and modernization with a more open and inclusive attitude.

**Chapter Seven
Tianfu Chengdu
Towards a New Era**

The Regional Central City

Chengdu has been the political, economic and cultural center of Southwest China since ancient times. Since the 1980s, Chengdu's position as a "center" has been continuously strengthened. Entering the 21st century, Chengdu has undertaken more and more important missions in the national strategies of "Western Development," the "Belt and Road Initiative" and the "*Yangtze* River Economic Belt" and has realized the transformation from a regional central city to a national central city.

1. The Center of City Clusters in Western Sichuan

Chengdu is not an isolated city standing alone on the plain; instead, it belongs to city clusters of different scopes and scales with its surrounding cities and towns. In these clusters, Chengdu has always played a leading and driving role.

From the minimum scope, there is a smaller-scaled city cluster that takes Chengdu's main urban area as the core, covering all the areas of Shuangliu, Xindu, Pidu, Wenjiang and Longquanyi, as well as part of Qingbaijiang, Xinjin, Chongzhou, Pengzhou, Dujiangyan and Jianyang within a radius of 30 to 50 kilometers. This city cluster is a typical center-satellite city structure with high spatial accessibility. Each satellite city is within a 30 minutes' drive from the main urban area of Chengdu. Since all the regions are within the jurisdiction of Chengdu, with very close economic and social ties, this cluster shows a trend of high integration. Chengdu's downtown area plays a strong leading role.

If the above-mentioned smaller-scaled urban cluster is regarded as a whole, Chengdu and the surrounding small and medium-sized cities together form a medium-scaled urban cluster with a radius of about 50-150 kilometers, including Chengdu, Deyang, Mianyang, Ya'an, Leshan, Meishan, Ziyang and other cities. Cities in the cluster are connected to Chengdu by railways, expressways and high-grade highways within less than one and a half hours' drive. Chengdu, as the first city, has the most outstanding advantages in terms of capital, talents, technology reserves, urban construction, cultural accumulation and development potential among other neighboring cities.

Further, in Sichuan Province, Chengdu is still in a central position of various surrounding city clusters. The distance between Neijiang, Zigong, Yibin, Luzhou, Nanchong, Guang'an, Dazhou, Guangyuan etc. and Chengdu varies from 150 to 300 kilometers, even more than 300 kilometers. As far as spatial accessibility and development potential are concerned, Chengdu has, in fact, much weaker influence on them. However, in terms of the trend of people, materials, funds and information, these cities are still taking Chengdu as their center.

2. One of the Dual-Core Engines of Chengdu-Chongqing Urban Agglomeration

In 2016, the State Council issued the "Official Reply on the Development Plan of Chengdu-Chongqing Urban Agglomeration," which approved the "Development Plan of Chengdu-Chongqing Urban Agglomeration" formulated by the National Development and Reform Commission, the Ministry of Housing and Urban-Rural Development and other departments, provided guidance for the urbanization development of Chengdu and Chongqing and established the aim to build Chengdu-Chongqing Urban Agglomeration into a National Urban Agglomeration by 2020. This decision has clearly defined the important task of the two major metropolises – Chengdu and Chongqing, as the double core engines, to jointly build the center of population, industry, information, science and technology, and culture in the western region,

Chapter Seven
Tianfu Chengdu
Towards a New Era

and to co-construct a city agglomeration with vibrant economy, good quality of life, and beautiful ecological environment, so that Chengdu's development goal has exceeded the boundaries of a single provincial administrative region. So far, as one of the twin cores of Chengdu-Chongqing region, Chengdu has put the construction plan of "Chengdu Urban Agglomeration" on the agenda to coordinate with the neighboring cities for common development.

As far as Chengdu Urban Agglomeration is concerned, it covers Chengdu, Mianyang, Deyang, Suining, Meishan, Ya'an, Ziyang and most part of Leshan. This city cluster, located in the central place connecting the southwestern and northwestern regions of Southwestern China, is the core area where population, industry and towns are highly concentrated in the Chengdu-Chongqing Urban Agglomeration. Among them, Chengdu, as the "first city," with a long history and culture, strong economic strength, obvious advantages in science and education, and a high level of openness, is the core "engine" to promote the development of Chengdu Urban Agglomeration and even the entire Chengdu-Chongqing Urban Agglomeration as well as Chengdu-Chongqing Economic Development Zone. Such a central positioning is bound to put forward higher requirements for Chengdu's development.

First, Chengdu's own industrial transformation and upgrading will become the driving force for industrial innovation in urban agglomerations. It has successfully explored an innovation-driven development path with Chengdu characteristics through industrial transformation promoted by high-tech, which will promote the transformation of the industrial upgrading path to the technological innovation-driven strategy within the framework of the urban agglomeration. Secondly, Chengdu's open development will become a showcase for the city cluster to strengthen foreign exchanges and build a multi-level cooperation platform, which is conducive to promoting the open development of Chengdu Urban Agglomeration. Third, Chengdu, as the "first city," will play a coordinating role in promoting the integrated development of the urban agglomeration.

As far as the Chengdu-Chongqing Urban Agglomeration is concerned, Chengdu also plays an important role in the contact, interaction and coordinated development between Sichuan and Chongqing. In this agglomeration, the development momentum of Chengdu Urban

Agglomeration is extremely strong, and is the engine to promote the regional economic takeoff. Taking 2016 as an example, Chengdu-Chongqing Economic Zone achieved a total regional GDP of 459.303 billion *yuan*, consisting of 306.842 billion *yuan* from Sichuan and 153.461 billion *yuan* from Chongqing. Among them, Chengdu alone reached 1,217.023 billion *yuan*, accounting for 26.5% of the total GDP. The Chengdu Urban Agglomeration, including Chengdu, achieved 207.739 billion *yuan*, accounting for 45.2% of the total GDP. The Chengdu Urban Agglomeration contributed nearly half of the total economic volume to that of the whole economic zone. Considering the existing economic foundation and future development goals, Chengdu and Chongqing have already formed a certain division of functions within the framework of Chengdu-Chongqing Economic Zone and their Urban Agglomeration, but the problem of convergence of urban functions and positioning still exists. As one of the two cores, it will be its major mission under the strategic orientation of the new era that Chengdu, while shouldering the important task of being a regional center, will coordinate its development relationship with Chongqing and strive to build "a system revolving around two gravitations."

Chapter Seven
Tianfu Chengdu
Towards a New Era

A Central City in the National Strategy

1. The Junction of the "Belt and Road Initiative" and the "Yangtze River Economic Belt"

If we are looking at Chengdu's urban positioning from a larger scope across multiple regions, instead of only on the basis of the regional central city, it is also the intersection of several national top-level strategies such as the "Belt and Road Initiative" and the "Yangtze River Economic Belt."

The so-called the "Belt and Road Initiative" refers to the "Silk Road Economic Belt" and the "21st Century Maritime Silk Road." It is not only trans-regional, but also trans-national, with a huge volume. The "Belt and Road Initiative" represents a new round of China's major strategy of opening up to the outside world, and indicates that China's opening-up focus will extend from the coastal areas to the vast inland areas in the central and western regions. In particular, the Silk Road Economic Belt, taking land as a link, has solved the problem of access to the outside world, providing an unprecedented opportunity for the western regions to narrow the development gap with the eastern coast regions. Relying on this, strengthening ties with cities along the "Belt and Road Initiative" and building an international cooperation platform will provide more historical opportunities for Chengdu.

First of all, the "Belt and Road Initiative" will strengthen the position of the "first city" and "core city" of Chengdu in the western urban agglomerations. Chengdu is the starting point of the Southern Silk Road in history and is in the forefront of the country's geopolitical strategy of opening to the west and south. Taking the "Belt and Road Initiative" as an opportunity to drive the surrounding and southwest inland areas to open to the outside world as a whole can further consolidate Chengdu's position as a regional center. Secondly, the "Belt and Road Initiative" will strongly promote the development of Chengdu's high-tech industry. The "Belt and Road Initiative" is a new type of regional cooperation strategy based on mutual connectivity and exchanges, characterized by multiple-cooperation system and aimed at building a community of shared future for mankind. With research and talent reserve universities represented by Southwest Jiaotong University, design units represented by China Railway No. 2 Institute, the construction units represented by China Railway No. 2 Engineering Group Co., Ltd. and China Railway No. 8 Engineering Group Co., Ltd., and the rolling stock manufacturers represented by CSR Chengdu Rolling Stock Co., Ltd., Chengdu possesses extremely strong competitiveness because of its complete rail transit industry chain from scientific and technological innovation to personnel training, planning and design, construction and manufacturing. Finally, the "Belt and Road Initiative" will also help Chengdu to expand its cultural influence in the world. The "Belt and Road Initiative" is a "going out" strategy, and the cultural ties among countries, regions and cities along the route will also become very close. With this major artery of cultural exchange, Chengdu will fully display its cultural charm on the world stage.

2. A National Central City

The national central city is the core city that plays a leading and driving role in the political, economic, social and cultural fields of the country. In the national strategic layout, the national central city is the spatial fulcrum to coordinate regional development and the important gateway to represent the country in international competition and cooperation. In April 2016, the State Council approved the "Chengdu-Chongqing Urban Agglomeration Development Plan," explicitly demanding that Chengdu should take the construction of a national central city as its goal and enhance the functions of the important economic center, science and technology center,

Chapter Seven
Tianfu Chengdu
Towards a New Era

culture and creation center, foreign exchange center and comprehensive transportation hub in the western region. This marks Chengdu as the 6th national central city after Beijing, Tianjin, Shanghai, Guangzhou and Chongqing. In September 2016, the Seventh Plenary Session of the 12th Chengdu Municipal Committee proposed that "Chengdu's current and future development goal is to build a national central city," further defining Chengdu's development direction with the goal of a national central city. (Fig. 47-1, Fig. 47-2)

For Chengdu, the conditions for building a national central city are already in place. First, Chengdu is at the core of the strategic concept of "Chengdu, Chongqing, Xi'an and Kunming Diamond Economic Circle," which, with Chengdu, Chongqing, Xi'an and Kunming as the four supporting points, is surrounded by the "Yangtze River Economic Belt," the "Southern Silk Road," the "Northern Silk Road" and the "21st Century Maritime Silk Road." Chengdu, as the polar nucleus of its development, has in fact taken on the strategic task of coordinating regional development, optimizing the allocation of resources and improving the urban functions. Second, after a long period of accumulation, Chengdu has become a city with the highest level of economic development in the western region, with good industrial foundation, business service function and innovation and entrepreneurship potential. Third, through the early stage of construction, Chengdu has become a comprehensive transportation hub in the western region, and played an important role in connecting every part of the country, and exchanging with other countries. Chengdu is one of the eight major railway hubs in the country, and is the gateway city to Central Asia and Europe via railway lines in Western China. Superior traffic conditions and a good foundation for overseas cooperation are conducive to Chengdu's implementation of the requirements that the country's central city should strengthen the opening-up.

Tianfu Culture and the Modern Pursuit of Chengdu

Fig. 47-1 Chengdu Global Center

Chapter Seven
Tianfu Chengdu
Towards a New Era

Tianfu Culture and the Modern Pursuit of Chengdu

Fig. 47-2 Tianfu Square

Chapter Seven
Tianfu Chengdu
Towards a New Era

A World Famous Cultural City

From history to modernity and from an isolated area to a major character on the stage of the whole country, Chengdu's past has proven that it is a city that has never stopped growing, has the courage to climb higher, dares to pursue any new and keeps practicing. Today, standing at the height of the new era, Chengdu has put forward new goals and started a new journey of building it into a world-famous cultural city.

The key word of a world-famous cultural city is culture. General Secretary Xi Jinping pointed out in the "19th Congress" report, "Cultural confidence is a more basic, deeper and more lasting force in the development of a country and a nation." From a strategic perspective, it has planned how China, an ancient civilization, deals with the relationship between tradition and modernity, history and future, inheritance and development at the cultural level.

Specifically to Chengdu, on April 25th, 2017, at the 13th CPC Chengdu Congress, Party Secretary Fan Ruiping formally put forward the vision of city development on behalf of the Party Committee: "Inherit the Ba-Shu civilization, develop Tianfu Culture, and strive to build a world famous cultural city." In detail, this historic work also includes the following four aspects. First, to conserve Tianfu Culture and make a show of the city's charm. Through in-depth exploration of regional cultural characteristics and extraction of nutrition from citizens' rich and colorful production and living practices, efforts will be made to promote the creative transformation and innovative development of Tianfu Culture, and make an exciting cultural scene in Chengdu.

Tianfu Culture and the Modern Pursuit of Chengdu

Fig. 48-1 Jinli near the Temple of Marquis Wu

Second, to inherit the historical context and consolidate the root of the city. That is to say, Chengdu's unique charm as one of the ten ancient capitals and famous historical and cultural cities in the country should be deeply explored, and the brand building and marketing of Tianfu Culture should be strengthened to highlight the era style of Tianfu Culture and make Chengdu famous in the world. Third, to stimulate cultural innovation and improve the city's grade. Extract the essence of Tianfu Culture to integrate creativeness, innovativeness and wisdom into one, and make Chengdu a pioneer of the times. Fourth, to build a spiritual home together and cast the soul of the city. Adhere to the socialist core values as the guide, vigorously carry forward the the spirit of the nation and the times, lead the direction of cultural construction, enlighten people with culture and nourish the city with virtue, and make Chengdu brilliant with truth. (Fig. 48-1 to Fig. 48-10)

**Chapter Seven
Tianfu Chengdu
Towards a New Era**

Fig. 48-2 Bar street near Jiuyan Bridge

Fig. 48-3 Chengdu Museum

Fig. 48-4 Chunxi Road seen from viaduct, Chengdu

Fig. 48-5 Fang Suo Commune

Chapter Seven
Tianfu Chengdu
Towards a New Era

Fig. 48-6 Sichuan Library

Tianfu Culture and the Modern Pursuit of Chengdu

Fig. 48-7 Taikoo Li, integration of traditional and modern culture

Chapter Seven
Tianfu Chengdu
Towards a New Era

Fig. 48-8 Taikoo Li, integration of traditional and modern culture

Fig. 48-9 Taikoo Li, integration of traditional and modern culture

Tianfu Culture and the Modern Pursuit of Chengdu

Fig. 48-10 Teahouse in downtown Chengdu

It can be seen from this that the construction of a world famous cultural city that takes the "Humanistic Chengdu" as the core is to enhance the soft power and cultural competitiveness of the city by well dealing with the relationship between tradition and modernity, history and future, inheritance and development at the cultural level so as to push Chengdu to the world, expand its international influence, and push Chengdu's urban development to a new level. Under this vision, the core element is "Tianfu Culture" that has been developing throughout the whole history.

Seen from the height of the times, it is Chengdu's completely new development task to build a world-famous cultural city with Tianfu Culture as its core in the context of modernization. Relying on Tianfu Culture to build a world-famous cultural city requires rooting in history, facing the future, cultivating the humanistic spirit of Tianfu Culture, stimulating the vitality of Tianfu

Chapter Seven
Tianfu Chengdu Towards a New Era

Culture, inheriting the historical context of Tianfu Culture, and shaping the style of Tianfu Culture, so as to expand Chengdu's international popularity and recognition, enhancing its international radiation and influence, and further building Chengdu into an internationalized and modernized metropolis on the basis of its current statuses of a modern city, regional central city and national strategic central city.

Copyright Notice for Photos

All figures in this book have been authorized and licensed by relevant copyright owners. Among them, Figures 2, 9 and 12 in Chapter 1, Figure 27 in Chapter 2, Figure 28 in Chapter 3, Figures 32, 34, 34, 35 and 36 of the fourth chapter, Figure 40, 44 and 46 in Chapter 5 and all figures except Teahouse in Chapter 7 were taken by Tan Junfeng, the translator of this book. Figure 8 in Chapter 1 was taken by Xu Yiyang; All other figures are from Huitu.com and obtained the authorization of the website and the photographers.